Raised Up Down Yonder

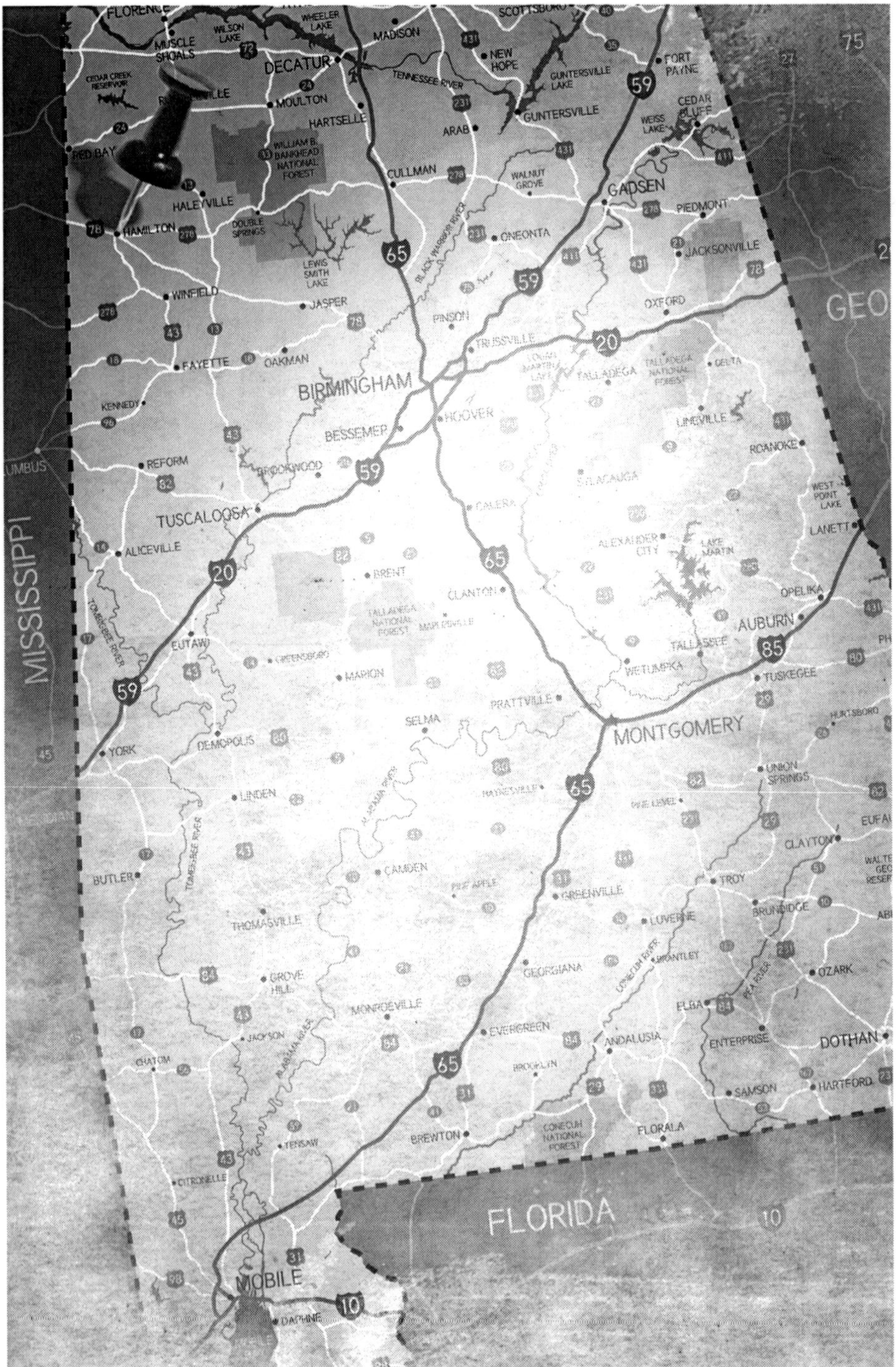
MISSISSIPPI
FLORIDA
FLORENCE
MUSCLE SHOALS
DECATUR
MADISON
SCOTTSBORO
NEW HOPE
FORT PAYNE
GUNTERSVILLE LAKE
GUNTERSVILLE
TENNESSEE RIVER
MOULTON
HARTSELLE
ARAB
CEDAR BLUFF
WEISS LAKE
RED BAY
WILLIAM B. BANKHEAD NATIONAL FOREST
CULLMAN
WALNUT GROVE
GADSEN
PIEDMONT
HALEYVILLE
HAMILTON
DOUBLE SPRINGS
ONEONTA
JACKSONVILLE
LEWIS SMITH LAKE
WINFIELD
JASPER
PINSON
OXFORD
TRUSSVILLE
FAYETTE
OAKMAN
BIRMINGHAM
TALLADEGA
KENNEDY
HOOVER
LINEVILLE
BESSEMER
ROANOKE
REFORM
BROOKWOOD
SYLACAUGA
TUSCALOOSA
CALERA
WEST POINT LAKE
LANETT
ALICEVILLE
ALEXANDER CITY
LAKE MARTIN
BRENT
CLANTON
OPELIKA
AUBURN
EUTAW
GREENSBORO
TALLASSEE
MARION
WETUMPKA
TUSKEGEE
PRATTVILLE
SELMA
MONTGOMERY
YORK
DEMOPOLIS
UNION SPRINGS
LINDEN
CLAYTON
BUTLER
CAMDEN
TROY
GREENVILLE
THOMASVILLE
BRUNDIDGE
LUVERNE
GEORGIANA
OZARK
GROVE HILL
MONROEVILLE
ELBA
ENTERPRISE
DOTHAN
EVERGREEN
ANDALUSIA
JACKSON
CHATOM
SAMSON
HARTFORD
BREWTON
FLORALA
CONECUH NATIONAL FOREST
TENSAW
CITRONELLE
MOBILE
DAPHNE

Raised Up Down Yonder

Growing Up Black in Rural Alabama

Angela McMillan Howell

University Press of Mississippi   Jackson

Margaret Walker Alexander Series in African American Studies

www.upress.state.ms.us

The University Press of Mississippi is a member
of the Association of American University Presses.

First printing 2013

Library of Congress Cataloging-in-Publication Data

Howell, Angela McMillan.
 Raised up down yonder : growing up black in rural Alabama / Angela McMillan Howell.
   pages cm — (Margaret Walker Alexander series in African American studies)
 Includes bibliographical references and index.
 ISBN 978-1-61703-881-5 (cloth : alk. paper) — ISBN 978-1-61703-882-2 (ebook) 1. African American youth—
Alabama—Hamilton—Social conditions. 2. African American youth—Education—Alabama—Hamilton. 3.
Hamilton (Ala.)—Social conditions. 4. Hamilton (Ala.)—Rural conditions. 5. Hamilton (Ala.)—Race relations.
I. Title.
 E185.93.A3.H69 2013
 305.8009761—dc23   2013015105

British Library Cataloging-in-Publication Data available

For Ricardo and Lily

Contents

Acknowledgments

For many years, this project resided in academic purgatory. I felt ambivalent about my inability to choose one theoretical frame that would neatly house the experiences of my ethnographic subjects, rural African America youth who live in Black Belt Alabama. Yet, each time I taught the graduate class, "Race, Education, and Social Inequality," I was struck by the lack of current resources available on African American youth in the rural South. If one were to perform an academic search for African Americans—and, heaven forbid, add youth, adolescents, or teens to that description—95 percent of the data one will find will center on urban or suburban youth; 75 percent will have "hip-hop" in the title; and 85 percent will analyze the social problems of black young people (why they keep having babies; why they can't learn; why their families, schools, and communities are crumbling). If one were to perform an academic search to obtain information about African Americans in the rural South, one will primarily conjure up history, fiction, and memoirs. The terms antebellum and Jim Crow might dominate the results.

After years of expounding to my graduate students that African American youth are more than social problems and telling my own field stories in cases where no published stories exist, I decided to rescue, revive, and refresh this ethnography. It theoretically pales in comparison to some of my favorite books, such as Annette Lareau's *Unequal Childhoods* or Paul Willis's *Learning to Labor*. I hope that another scholar will be motivated by my simplistic ethnographic portrayal to take up the cause of making rural African American youth visible *and* develop a seamless theory to house their experiences. For now, *Raised Up Down Yonder* will have to suffice. What I present in this study is the sincerest form of what I observed. It is not bent to any one theoretical position. To deny that inequality is actively shaping the future lives of my subjects would be dishonest. Yet, to reduce their stories and the meaning of their everyday lives to how they did or did not push back against the system would likewise be disingenuous. Therefore, this story rests somewhere in the middle of these perspectives.

During my very first graduate class at Brown University, one of my professors posed a simple question to me and three of my colleagues: Should the goal of anthropology be to analyze structures and social inequality or are we just storytellers? Having just graduated from my sociology undergraduate program, I was eager to give "the right answer." Of course, as anthropologists we should use our power to critically analyze structures and make changes . . . "truth to power" for everyone! All these years later, I humbly consider myself to be a storyteller . . . and I have the youth of Hamilton, Alabama, to thank for my conversion.[1]

I owe an enormous debt of gratitude to God, my family, friends, colleagues, students, research informants, and mentors for the completion of this work. I am grateful to my current colleagues at Morgan State University who were once my undergraduate instructors and mentors: Dr. Maurice St. Pierre and Dr. Stella Hargett. Their long-term commitment to the improvement of the conditions of black folk through their research and in real time is inspiring. Although he has retired, Dr. Stefan Goodwin's energy still occupies the hall where my office now resides. As the very first anthropologist whom I ever met, he ultimately has exerted a huge impact on the course of my life. As I stated above, my students have now become central to how I view my work, and my desire to have this work published. I am grateful to be on the other side of this student/teacher relationship now.

Dr. Karl Alexander, Dr. Alford A. Young Jr., and Dr. Frances K. Goldscheider have been academic mentors for me over the years, welcoming me into their laboratories, offices, and homes and providing me with all sorts of insight about the life of the mind. My commitment to interdisciplinary teaching and work stems largely from how highly I value their research and my experiences with them. I must also acknowledge the programs that introduced me to such wonderful mentors: the Howard Hughes Research Fellowship, the Committee on Institutional Cooperation Summer Research Opportunity Program, and the Leadership Alliance Early Identification Program.

From my extended Brown University family, I would like to thank Dr. Lina Fruzzetti, whose support and guidance have been immeasurable. I continue to admire her constant professionalism, scholarship, work ethic, commitment to students of color, and commitment to loving people of all kinds. I would also like to thank Dr. Nicholas Townsend for his guidance on this ethnography. The breadth of his wisdom is matched only by the size of his heart. Further, over the years I have come to appreciate Dr. Matthew Gutmann's always-needed succinct words of instruction, advice, and encouragement. Finally, I owe a debt of gratitude to Dr. William Beeman, Dr. Wanni Anderson, and Dr. Oka Obono for reading and commenting on early forms of the ideas presented here, as well as to Mrs. Katherine Grimaldi and Mrs. Matilde

Andrade, the anchors in the Department of Anthropology at Brown University, during the time that I was a student there.

For various forms of support, I would like to gratefully acknowledge Dr. John L. Jackson Jr., who has been a constant source of academic discourse and a wealth of information; Clem Harris and the Africana Studies Writer's Group at the University of Pennsylvania; Dr. Walter Earl Fluker and the Leadership Center at Morehouse College; Dr. Steve Lubar and the John Nicholas Brown Center at Brown University; Dr. Stephanie Larrieux and the Women of Color Writer's Group; Dr. Elizabeth Glater and the Wonderful Outstanding Women Writing Group; Professor Elmo Terry-Morgan and Dr. Paget Henry and the Africana Studies Department at Brown University; Dr. Ted Hamaan; Dr. Michael Plater; Ms. Barbara Kahn; Dr. Terrence Johnson; Mr. Peter Agree; Mrs. Virginia Norman; Mrs. Nettye Andrews; Mr. Frazier Lewis; Dr. Natasha Pratt-Harris; Dr. Carlene Turner; Dr. Cynthia Bragg; Ms. Patrice Jones; Dr. Jelani Favors; Mrs. Knachelle Favors; Ms. Francella Ochillo, Esq., Dr. Rory Goodwin and Mrs. Andrea Goodwin; Mr. and Mrs. Sylvester and Nadine Timmons; Mr. and Mrs. Dan and Nicole Turner; Dr. Elgin Klugh; Dr. Deborah Johnson-Simon; Dr. Ira Harrison; Mr. and Mrs. Edwin and Pamela Howell; Mr. Quentin Guy and Mrs. Sally Guy, Esq.; Mr. and Mrs. David and Jennifer McMillan; the Honorable Kweisi Mfume and Dr. Tiffany Mfume; Deborah Upton; and Dr. Marcia Chatelain, to whom I lovingly refer as my academic coach. She also introduced me to Mr. Walter Biggins, my editor at the University Press of Mississippi. It has been a joy to work with him; his unwavering support has been central to this project coming to fruition.

This ethnography would not have existed without the kindness of the people of Hamilton, Alabama, who opened their doors and hearts to me. I remain thankful for all of the valuable lessons that they taught me. I will never forget the generosity, laughter, and all of those home-cooked meals from cousin "Tiffany" and her family. Her Chrysler 300 is on back order. "Kelly," "Missy," "Sabrina," "Mrs. Smith," and "James" added more than their share to the insight and humanity in this book, and for that I am grateful.

Before I ever knew what anthropology entailed, my family taught me how to be a true anthropologist. I would like to thank my parents, Mr. and Mrs. Betha and Lois McMillan, for exposing me to diverse cultural experiences, while equally showing me the beauty in my own culture. I am grateful for their examples of loving God and others and valuing education. I am also indebted to them for entertaining my sweet, precious Lily while I put in the long hours on this book. I also appreciate my mom's long hours of proofreading this manuscript with the eye of an editor that has been honed through years of college teaching.

To the love of my life, Ricardo Orlando Howell, I thought I was going to Brown just to earn a Ph.D., but most significantly, I found you—my husband, my colleague, and my best friend. Thank you for managing my sources, solving my incessant technological crises, pulling the household load during the last stretch, and inspiring me to write! And thank you for giving me the greatest gift of all, Lily Isabella Howell, born September 28, 2010.

Raised Up Down Yonder

Introduction

In 2003, a few months before I began the research for this ethnography, reporters from a major national newspaper wrote a feature story about a small kindergarten through twelfth grade school from the perspective of the United States national No Child Left Behind (NCLB) policy. Articles like this one were commonplace during that time period. The 2004 presidential election was just about one year away, and newspapers capitalized on opportunities to highlight issues that would polarize "red" and "blue" states and invoke fear, wonder, and pity in the hearts and minds of its loyal readers. Of all the schools the newspaper could have featured for "project pity," it chose the very school where I was conducting my research, in a previously un-noteworthy community in Attala County, Alabama.[1]

Hamilton, Alabama, and the neighboring town of Carlyle provide the backdrop for this project. Hamilton is a small community of about 1,500 residents, 49 percent of whom are black, in western Alabama. The neighboring city of Carlyle includes about 7,500 residents, 51 percent of whom are black.[2] The overwhelming majority of the residents' families have lived in these locations for generations, and many of the black youth that grow up in Hamilton, and some from Carlyle, attend Jay Ellis School, the K–12 school that is featured in this newspaper article.

Why did this national newspaper choose to traverse major highways, bypass Birmingham, Montgomery, Selma, and all of the other small towns in between to arrive at this particular Alabama community in order to write an article about U.S. national education policy? According to the article, Jay Ellis School is the quintessential "poor," "rural" school. It argues that at schools like Jay Ellis, NCLB is unrealistic and unfruitful. In order to prove its point, the article emphasizes the dearth of resources at the school—and by extension, the limited resources in the community. The newspaper calls its library "a trip back in time" and points out that the school is "unable to attract a qualified music teacher or pay for instruments."

I could not fully comprehend the title of the article, which labeled the school as poor and rural. I certainly would not have argued that the Hamilton community was urban. In fact, investigating the behaviors, motivations, and lifestyles of twenty-first-century rural African American adolescents—and the mysteries therein—was what brought me to the field; in that way, I was not any different from the newspaper reporter. But something about seeing rural *and* poor in the headlines, in relation to "my" community, caused me to question what poor and rural really signify. Further, I wondered if the young people in this community, which was becoming less isolated to me each day, would describe themselves as markedly poor or rural.

Since the reporters had just left several months before I arrived in Hamilton, when I initially came to the field, the story was fresh in people's minds. The Jay Ellis High School English teacher, Mr. Edwards, was the first person to give me a copy of the article. He wanted to make sure that I did not fall into the same trap as the newspaper reporters, whom he felt failed to adequately place Jay Ellis into the correct historical context. According to Mr. Edwards, he was unsure of the reporter's "total motive" for the interview, but he was disappointed that the article did not highlight "what we have been able to achieve in spite of the things that may or may not be available to us."

After the article was published, saving Jay Ellis School became a cause célèbre among readers of this newspaper. Informants reported that money was sent to the school, and over a six-month period one national organization, Reading Incorporated, shipped a "mountain of books"—as they describe them in their newsletter—to Jay Ellis. The Reading Incorporated president begins this newsletter by writing, "This month I'd like to tell you about one of the *poor rural* schools we help in Alabama." Once again, the adjectives poor and rural appear, and their presence seems suited to justify the members' selfless donations of time and money. By the time I read this newsletter, Hamilton's inhabitants were many things to me: generous, hilarious, hard working, frustrated, creative, duplicitous, engaging, and "messy," certainly not just poor or rural.

One might expect journalists, academics, and philanthropists to appropriate the terms poor and rural, but I was surprised to discover that "insiders" use them, as well. In a thank-you letter to Reading Incorporated, the principal of Jay Ellis School during that time period detailed why she considered poverty and rurality to be significant. According to Ms. Moore, the tangible donation of books was disproportionately beneficial to these "poor" students because they are at an economic disadvantage, they are isolated, and they don't even know they are poor. She writes:

> We have 264 African American students. Most of them are poor. They don't know it though. I guess that's OK, but I hate it. I love my job though, it keeps me humble, and I learn a lot. The children seem to be happy,

most of the time. Still, I'd like to bus them all up and take them to a city school in Tuscaloosa, so they can see what a real library is really supposed to be.

Ms. Moore's comments led me to ponder if the donation of books would still be considered special if the students weren't actually "poor." What if Reading Incorporated knew, as I discovered, that many of the students had traveled out of state and weren't necessarily "stuck" in their rurality? And how do we read Ms. Moore's comments after unearthing the boxes of books that were never delivered to Jay Ellis's students, but remained in trailers and were eventually hauled away?

Raised Up Down Yonder is a story about what it's like for black youth to grow up in the twenty-first-century rural South. Despite my unease with the above article's use of the terms "poor, black, and rural," I applaud it for even featuring the story. Rural black youth and really the majority of young people in general from rural areas are invisible in our society. Because moral panics about the problems of black youth dominate popular discourse, rural children are usually left out of the discussion.[3] And since we know so little about them, people fall back on simplistic stereotypes and dichotomies: urban youth are equated with teenage pregnancy, hip-hop culture, the prison industrial complex, drug addiction, poor crumbling schools, and female-headed households; rural youth are equated with poverty, ignorance, shrinking industry, and religious fundamentalism.

My central goal in *Raised Up Down Yonder* is to help reorient society's approach to young African American subjects. First, I fill a void in their collective characterization by shifting focus away from urban centers and suburbs to an environment where African American youth have rarely been situated in the recent literature: the rural South.[4] The youth in Hamilton, Alabama, are thoroughly southern and rural, and they see themselves that way. By examining the character of their everyday lives, and the historical routes through which the current environment has been created, I call attention to what defines the twenty-first-century rural South. The young people in this ethnography go to a school that educates three hundred children from kindergarten through the twelfth grade and many of them live on dirt roads. Yet, they draw from diverse sources to form their identities. They have traveled to Michigan, Rhode Island, Tennessee, New York, and other destinations, and their CD players are filled with everything from pop chanteuse Christina Aguilera, to soft rock singer Michael McDonald, to gospel crooners the Blind Boys of Alabama, to popular rappers Pastor Troy, Lloyd Banks, and TI. They learn to grow food at home and learn to cook by watching Emeril Lagasse on the Food Network. Hamilton, Alabama, is not the stereotypically isolated rural area that is like "a trip back in time." It is a dynamic place that is fostering creative negotiations among its youth.

Yet, the old racial binaries and hierarchies of the South still undergird much of what the young people experience and do. The political economy of the school system privileges families with money and white children, and those categories usually overlap. Jay Ellis School, Hamilton's K–12 school, is vilified in the local press, and the superintendent feels that the community should be happy that Jay Ellis even is open and has a football team. In nearby Carlyle, Alabama, the parents still sponsor a "white" prom, despite the school's efforts to move beyond the entrenched history of southern racism. While in the field I was able to see the young people's frustrations expressed in the way they spoke and what they did. Indeed, forms of resistance that matched the character of their everyday lives—playful and subtle—were present. Young people and adults constantly sifted through who and what was "messy" or "up to no good." Furthermore, one young lady, Missy, in addition to intentionally missing class when she wasn't receiving proper instruction, found an avenue of expression through spirituality, as she began attending church one hour away from home. Most important, throughout *Raised Up Down Yonder*, it is the young people, themselves, who forcefully express what they wrestle against.

I attempt to reorient our approach to African Americans not only by shining a light on the rural South, but by also allowing the youth Down Yonder to speak for themselves. As I stated above, the stereotypes that define how the public has come to view African American teens are negative and have been partly created by researchers who, for presumably noble reasons, have sought to understand and help to combat any number of social problems. In doing so, however, they have inadvertently contributed to a view of these youths as problems to be solved, "a population to be controlled and contained."[5] In *The Souls of Black Folks*, W. E. B. Du Bois posed the classic and disturbing question: "How does it feel to be a problem?" Sadly, this question, which Du Bois described as part of the hidden transcript of race relations, has become part of the overt transcript of many research agendas. In fact, I have had difficulty when teaching my courses at Morgan State University to find books about the everyday lives of young African Americans that do not reduce them to categories such as "high school dropouts," "middle class kids that are academically mediocre," or "teenage parents." The young people in these texts often play second fiddle to larger topics, such as "the impact of hip-hop culture on youth." Even when qualitative research focuses on resistance, the meaningful aspects of their lives are reduced to how they resist class, gender, or racial oppression.[6] Furthermore, because of the hyper-political context into which research on black people enters, some scholars would rather not address behavior or meaning at all, preferring to focus on structural inequality. As the Distinguished Professor of African American Studies Cornel West succinctly describes, focusing on "structural constraints" to the exclusion of "behavior," and vice versa, has nearly suffocated academic discourse on African Americans—in this case, young African Americans.[7]

Raised Up Down Yonder, then, sheds light on the meaningful aspects of young people's everyday lives. Some of these aspects relate to race, class, and gender oppression, but many do not. Personal accomplishments, bitter divorces, physical injuries, loss of friends and mentors, birthday celebrations, and inside jokes are things that "poor," "rural," "black," "youth" experience in the same manner that other people do. In chapter 4, in my examination of a local metaphor and its reproductive quality, I intentionally replace the concept of "oppression" with "misfortune," which might seem on its surface to be a conceptual lightweight. However, misfortune allows me to imbue oppression with a degree of humanity and subjectivity that is important when thinking about *how* people experience and make sense of undesirable events. The use of the concept "spirituality" in chapter 5 helps me to accomplish the same goal.

In general, *Raised Up Down Yonder* brings subjectivities such as emotion, humor, and distrust to the forefront rather than relegating them to the margins. At times, I use literary devices such as irony to punctuate particular moods; at other times, I select direct quotations that are humorous or even contradictory. As a result of these strategies, in this ethnography the insider/outsider distinction is blurred, and my own voice, including implicit judgments and assumptions, is often presented with those of the other subjects.[8] To appropriate cultural anthropologist John Jackson's theoretical paradigm, this ethnography presents "sincere" subject-subject interaction rather than "authentic" subject-object interaction.[9] In the final analysis, I hope to engender empathy with these subjects rather than distant sympathy for academic objects.

Finally, from a theoretical standpoint, as one case study of modern practice theory, this book examines the interplay of rules/structures/systems and agency/practice/process. On the broadest level, Hamilton is one small spoke in the wheel of modern American capitalism. One can see how the school system helps to foster the inequality, which is required to produce the particular blend of occupations necessary to sustain this small community. In that vein, racism is bent to the service of broader socioeconomic structures. Further, football culture is thoroughly American, and similar to the analysis of football culture in Douglas E. Foley's influential book *Learning Capitalist Culture*,[10] chapter 4 presents a year-long drama involving the football team and its role in reproducing inequality. How the young people react, interact, and process what is happening sheds light on the process of reproducing inequality.

History is an essential tool in understanding the processes that define the young people's everyday lives. A historical look at education in Hamilton links it to the history of black schools in the United States. It shines a light on an often forgotten truth: that education for African Americans historically has been driven and funded by the black communities themselves. Yet, in Hamilton, ignoring or forgetting this history and instead perpetuating stereotypes about Jay Ellis help to maintain the political economic status quo. To add further complexity to the picture, lively, dynamic families and widespread homeownership create lifestyles comfortable enough that protest or social movements seem unlikely to erupt in Hamilton. Ironically, these same large, rooted, family structures contribute to young people's desire to stay nearby after graduating from high school, which, in turn, delimits their future career options. These juxtapositions connect Hamilton to small communities that are undergoing similar processes all over the country.

Finally, in this ethnography, biography is an additional critical level of analysis, rounding out a theory of the practice of everyday life. Not only do the biographies of several young people in Hamilton add to the subjective portrayals of African American youth that are so desperately lacking, but also they reveal complex negotiations, contradictory ideals, and acute cognitive awareness. Young people like Kelly love their big families and their small school, but are greatly impacted by divorce and remarriage and find interactions in these contexts to be awkward and sometimes painful. Missy's biography reveals that resistance, often viewed in public spaces, overshadows other important related domains of action and meaning such as spirituality, which is creative, generative, and largely invisible. Finally, James calls attention to how young people's popular culture practices and preferences intersect with their local experiences. Far from being dupes of a media machine, young people similar to James can powerfully integrate a strong rural identity, a masculine gender identity, an intense love of his family, an appreciation for *Saved by the Bell*, and an avowed loyalty to hard, "crunk" hip-hop. In the final analysis, *Raised Up Down Yonder* integrates analyses of structure, culture, history, agency, and subjective experience.[11]

Jay Ellis School senior Sabrina is one of the young people whose perspectives will illuminate the experience of growing up in the rural South. At the end of our interview, when I asked her if there was anything else she wanted the readers to know about growing up in Hamilton, she said:

> That we're not what people think we are, what city people think we are. We're not all country, can't talk, cannot pronounce words and you know talk like "down yonder" [said with drawl]. Some of us are educated people.

Sabrina's use of the phrase "down yonder" indicates her awareness that rural places and people are often objectified and viewed as distant, exotic, and sometimes backwards. Thus, the title of this book, *Raised Up Down Yonder*, signals an attempt to uncloak "down yonder" and the young people who grow up there. Sabrina's contribution to the title connotes the collaborative nature of the project, which was initiated and penned by me, but built by many subjects, who were glad that their lived experiences, and not just their supposed poverty or rurality, were found to be noteworthy.

Raised Up Down Yonder also refers to the intersections of local and translocal cultural elements in Hamilton and in the lives of young people there. "Down yonder" is someplace in particular, and this project attempts to highlight the persistence of the local in structuring young people's worldviews and charting their life courses. At the same time, it is hard to deny the influence that translocal forces, images, and ideas have on young people everywhere. In that sense, *Raised Up Down Yonder* could be read as a question—*Raised Up "Down Yonder?"*—one that this book attempts to answer. In other words, considering the twenty-first-century context, how "down yonder" really is this place and, by extension, the people who live there?

Finally, *Raised Up Down Yonder* is on par with the irony and humor sprinkled throughout the rest of the project. Sabrina's southern accent is thick. I only detected that she exaggerated her accent when she said "down yonder," because, after one year in the field, my ears had become finely tuned to the dialect of Hamilton. Sabrina's insistence that "we're not all country," while speaking in her finest southern accent, ironically and humorously nods to an almost Saussurian conceptualization of the deep relationship between symbols and their referents.

Some Conceptual Notes

As I have just stated, the primary purpose of this book is to illuminate the everyday lives of the young people in Hamilton. Because this is my goal, and the young people themselves are my primary units of analysis, I have resisted the temptation, urge, and in some cases urging to make the totality of this work a larger analysis of neocolonialism, class reproduction, or hybridity. Rather, the theory in this ethnography is bent to the service of understanding young people and the place that sustains them. In this way, they remain in "the subjective center." Bearing that general orientation in mind, however, I will clarify the meaning of several concepts that I use throughout *Raised Up Down Yonder*. Structure, culture, class, and identity have been so (over) used by scholars in various disciplines as well as by laypeople that it seems nearly impossible to pinpoint their conceptual targets. Culture, especially, has come to mean everything and nothing at the same time. Unfortunately, despite their convoluted origins and intentions, it is difficult to write without using these terms because they are so enmeshed in our folk understandings of everyday life.

Structure and Culture

Structure and culture are used liberally throughout *Raised Up Down Yonder*. However, I do not intend to conjure a structural functionalist analytical frame. Rather, in using such terms, I follow in the footsteps of the "practice theorists" who began writing in the 1970s. This broad category, "Practice theory," lumps together scholars of many different orientations. Sherry Ortner's influential article, "Theory in Anthropology since the Sixties," provides an excellent summary of the then emerging theoretical trend and its origins.[12] What all of these practice theorists share in common is a desire to understand how everyday actions are formed by and help to form the history, structure, and culture of a place, an institution, or a moment. It takes structure and culture from their comfortable and isolated places and throws them into an ongoing dialogue in which behavior becomes the mediator, reproducing, resisting, and radically changing social conditions.

This dialectical relationship among structure, culture, and behavior can be seen throughout the book. For example, chapter 1, "Rooted in Kin," shows how the family structure changes daily and continues to change as young people like Kelly interpret what they see in their own families and in others' and act based on those interpretations. Next, chapter 2, "Descendants of a First Choice School," brings a decidedly historical perspective to bear. By analyzing the history of Jay Ellis School, I highlight the vital role that history plays in the creation of current everyday social conditions. The claiming of history as a legitimate terrain within anthropology has underscored a dynamic view of both culture and structure.[13] Culture is history because when we write we are looking at only a snapshot of a moving target. The brief epilogue aims, once again, to call attention to the snapshot nature of ethnography. Since I left the field in 2004, the young people have continued to "grow up" and make a place for themselves in the world, and traces of change in the structure of the school and in the town have been left in their path.

Class, Culture, and Education

In the 2010 edition of Douglas Foley's *Learning Capitalist Culture*, he includes a newly updated chapter entitled "Constructing a Class Theory of Schooling."[14] In it, he elegantly reconstructs the history of class and culture theories, tracing the various examinations of class back to a distinction between Marxist and Weberian views of social class. In the traditional Marxist framework, social class is defined by the one's relation to the means of production, with the two largest, most well known groups being the bourgeoisie or the owning class and the proletariat or the working class. Additionally, there are a number of other intermediate groups, including the lumpenproletariat, or what W. J. Wilson might call the "truly disadvantaged," and the petty bourgeois, or middle managers. Their significance derives from where they fit in the capitalist system. Marx and his descendants remain critical of capitalist culture, in which everything is for sale and assigned a value in the marketplace, including material resources, freedom, ideas, and images. For Marx and his descendants, then, understanding how class functions is synonymous with understanding a struggle over owning financial capital and all the other elements of society that are at its service.

Weber's legacy, according to Foley, lay in wresting class from the great struggle between the two major social classes and instead focusing on "the market forces of consumption" rather than on who owns the means of production. This led Weber to categorize many social classes based on people's consumption or lifestyle choices. Weber's depoliticized version of social class has taken root in America's popular folk understanding of class, which we generally believe to be based on income, education, and various types of consumption.[15] In fact, this belief has led to a condition in which the material base of the middle class is rapidly shrinking but the overwhelming majority of Americans still consider themselves to be "middle class."

Foley's chapter further links the theoretical history of class and culture with ideology, identity, and schooling, especially as influenced by the marrying of ethnography and education in the mid-twentieth century. He outlines what many scholars take for granted: how we arrived at the notion that school is a highly contested space that produces systemic and structured inequality on many levels. He explicates that at one point in anthropological, sociological, educational, and other literature, school was seen from a primarily functionalist point of view; that is, scholars worked from the assumption that the primary purpose of school was to educate children. Disruptions to that process were generally viewed as dysfunctional and analyzed from there.

This new line of inquiry that has predominated the literature since the 1970s has examined education as a reproductive mechanism that helps perpetuate all of the inequalities in the global capitalist super-machine. According to one adage, "the devil is in the details," and for many of us who desire to understand this system, whether in order to critique, improve, or even revolt against it, understanding exactly how it works (that is how inequality gets passed on) has been critical. A number of truly influential scholars, such as Michael Apple, Henry Giroux, Peter McLaren, and Stanley Aronowitz, among many others, have dramatically changed the way educators understand educational institutions and their role in perpetuating class inequality.[16]

Much of this work can be linked to the descendants of Marx. One of the most influential of these descendants is French sociologist Pierre Bourdieu. First gaining widespread popularity in the 1970s, Bourdieu fostered a critical link between how class gets reproduced within institutions such as schools. He argued that individuals possess a certain "habitus," which can be defined as the attitudes, tastes, ways of dress, behaviors, and so forth, that allude to their class level. Certain kinds of habituses are privileged in "fields" such as schools, while other "habituses" are not.[17] The amassing of financial capital, then, can only partly explain the reproduction of social inequality. Other kinds of capital—for example, social capital (networks) and cultural capital (know-how)—are just as important to understanding how inequality is created and maintained. Bourdieu is classified as a "practice theorist," and the beauty in Bourdieu lies in the agility of his theory. His theoretical lens leads to a certain methodological stance that helps researchers to bridge the divide between everyday observable behavior and larger processes such as social class. By observing the structures and everyday behaviors of actors within those structures, one can document the small ways that the overarching order is creatively resisted, reproduced, or recreated by social actors.

How do these various understandings of social class relate to *Raised Up Down Yonder*? Well, class serves as the backdrop to my analysis of Jay Ellis School. Chapter 3, "Educated at the Last Chance School," explicitly uses a Marxist-based definition of class to critique the school system and show how it stands to benefit the privileged at the expense of Hamilton's youth. In addition, while this book is not a "school ethnography," per se, many of the theoretical and ethnographic contributions of these scholars inform my analyses in chapter 4, "Reproducing Misfortune through Mess," and chapter 5, "Resistance and Spirituality." In both of these chapters, I observe and consider the agency of the young people and the other social actors alongside them. I aim to demonstrate not just the existence of the social order but how it is created and resisted by social actors. Additionally, in chapter 4 I follow in the path set by Peter McLaren in applying Victor Turner's theories of metaphor, ritual, and symbol to highlight the reproductive quality of mess. While McLaren focuses primarily on reproduction and "ritual" in a Catholic school in Canada, I focus on reproduction and "social drama," as seen through the football team, the county board of education, and the community.

Identity, Youth, and Popular Culture

Throughout *Raised Up Down Yonder* I use the term *identity* to investigate the social categories to which young people belong that are meaningful in their everyday lives and in their conceptions of themselves. Crude Marxism views social class as one's only true identity, while the rest of the identities that might come to mind—for example, gender, racial, sexual, regional—are only considered to be significant in as much as they are used to create a false consciousness that perpetuates the economic status quo. While I do not deny the existence of a false consciousness, like the many critics of this viewpoint, I argue that all human experience cannot be reduced to our reactions to inequality.

In particular, because I am writing about the experience of these young people "growing up," I should emphasize that I do not mean identity in the traditional psychosocial sense, that is, "identity achieved" as the goal of a developmental stage that takes place during adolescence.[18] Rather, I treat identity as something that is developed socially, in response to social stimuli. In his influential book, *Ethnic Groups and Boundaries: The Social Organization of Culture Difference*, Fredrik Barth theorized that the development of a collective ethnic identity was the result of the presentation of a series of contrasts. He argues that "people's categories are for acting, and are significantly affected by interaction rather than contemplation."[19] In showing "the connection between ethnic labels and the maintenance of social boundaries of cultural diversity," he shows how categorization (whether it be ethnic group or other collective identities) can be both altered and reinforced by experience.[20]

Eric Hobsbawm and Terrence Ranger coined the much-quoted phrase "the invention of tradition" to highlight the role that myths, stories, and histories play in creating and sustaining group identities.[21] In his discussion of the creation of Greek and Hawaiian national identities, Jonathan Friedman confirms the importance of myth and history when he writes, "The discourse of history as well as of myth is simultaneously a discourse of identity; it consists of attributing a meaningful past to a structured present."[22] He argues that in the Greek case, a national identity was formed out of Europe's imagination of its own past, while Hawaiian history arose out of real experiences of Euro-American domination.[23]

Following the theoretical framework of Barth, Hobsbawm, and Ranger, I examine identity as something born of social reaction, whether a reaction to actual interaction or to collective or individual memory.[24] Therefore, in chapter 6, "Not Just Down Yonder," I treat rural identities as categories of meaning that have been derived from active comparisons. Many of the young people formulated a strong sense of a rural identity by traveling outside of their hometowns to cities and communities in the North that, by contrast, produced a strong sense of a rural identity. They then continued to perform these identities through behaviors such as walking around outside without shoes on.[25]

Additionally, however, I acknowledge that people have senses of selves that manage these various social forces, from culture, to interaction, to historical and collective memory, and so on. In *Identity and Agency in Cultural Worlds*, Dorothy Holland and her coauthors argue that these senses of self that comprise the inner private world of identity, do not just respond to social stimuli in rote fashion. Rather, they are critical in the filtering process, as they operate through an intimate terrain. In other words, they argue that behavior is mediated by senses of self or identities. This perspective is vital to my analyses in so much as they, once again, focus on the soft side of identity: categories of meaning like hurt and disappointment, found in chapters 1 and 5, and excitement, found in chapter 6.

One reader of an early version of this manuscript asked, "Where are the white people?" But the young people who attended Jay Ellis really did not interact much with people of other races or ethnicities, except for a handful of teachers—not at church or school and rarely on weekends. Therefore, race and racism were certainly omnipresent, and once again chapter 3 addresses these topics. But racial identities were taken for granted and were not in the forefront of many of the young people's minds.[26] Therefore, racial identity theorizing is not at the forefront of my analysis despite the fact that my subjects are all black.[27]

Finally, popular culture has been one of the most studied areas of youth identity in recent years. Two of the most influential generators of popular culture studies are the Frankfurt Schoolof Critical Sociology, which has studied the mass media's culture industry and the Birmingham Centre for Contemporary Cultural Studies. The Frankfurt School views the mass media as much darker and more powerful in its ability to manipulate the masses and maintain the economic supremacy of the ruling class through mindless entertainment and strategic use of images. The Birmingham school emphasizes how people repurpose these images and messages to their own end, resisting hegemony, and wrestling with not just class identity, but racial, gender, youth, and other identities as well.[28] Popular culture was ever present in Hamilton, and my brief foray into popular culture in chapter 6 highlights the ability of young people to creatively deploy media in the making of their identities.

"Down Yonder": The Place

As written at the outset of this introduction, Hamilton, Alabama, and the neighboring town of Carlyle provide the backdrop for this project. Hamilton is a small community of approximately 1,500 residents located in western Alabama. The neighboring city of Carlyle includes about 7,500 residents. The overwhelming majority of Hamilton's families have lived there for generations, and many of the black youth that grow up in Hamilton, and some from Carlyle, attend Jay Ellis High School, the K–12 school that is described in the introduction.

According to the 2000 U.S. Census, both Hamilton and Carlyle have approximately 50 percent white residents, 50 percent black residents, and less than 1 percent of all other ethnic groups. Thus, young people live in a racially dichotomized environment that is very much "separate" and "unequal." In 1999, whites' per capita income was over double that of blacks: $19,614 compared to $8,389. Even more alarming, the median household income for whites in Hamilton was nearly triple that of blacks: $46,583 in white households compared to just $16,250 in black households. Indeed, inequality, masked with a creed of opportunity for those who apply themselves, underpins daily life.[29]

The largest sector of the local economy comes from small- to medium-sized plants, such as one paper mill that employs approximately 544 people, and a clothing factory, which employs approximately 330 people. Residents of Hamilton also work in nursing, retail, education, and in churches and are self-employed as local repairmen, electricians, auto mechanics, caretakers, and cattle raisers.[30] In Hamilton, especially, the informal economy is vital to daily life, and people survive not only from income, but also from a system of reciprocity.

Hamilton is not actually recognized by the census as a "place," but its space is marked. It includes four community churches, two white and two black; two community centers, one black and one white; a small country store, and a historic post office. The land is speckled with large former plantation mansions, medium-sized brick homes, and small trailers. Formerly, Hamilton was dominated by profitable farmland. Now, residents plant crops, such as watermelon, okra, various kinds of greens, and tomatoes, primarily as supplements to feed their families and for recreation.

According to the distinguished economist Emery Castle, because of the decrease in profitable farming and the development of small nonmetropolitan urban areas throughout the traditional rural landscape, the definition of rural no longer means complete isolation.[31] This is certainly the case with Hamilton. Carlyle lies just ten minutes away, and going there is considered going to "town." The public library, Carlyle Hospital, Walmart, Attala Theatre (which plays one movie per week), restaurants, and shops are "in town." A great deal of time is spent crossing back and forth between "town" and "country" for various reasons. In addition, Hamilton and Carlyle lie between Meridian, Mississippi, and Tuscaloosa, Alabama, and people frequently travel to these areas to shop, attend doctor's appointments, or visit friends and family.

The Hamilton school, Jay Ellis School, is located just on the border between Carlyle and Hamilton. Before the integration of public schools, Jay Ellis was the school that served the African American population of Hamilton and Carlyle. Today, Jay Ellis, like so many other schools designated as small and rural, must constantly justify its existence. Because it is just five miles from Carlyle High School and has fewer than three hundred students on its roster, Jay Ellis's students could easily be redistributed into the Carlyle city schools.

This brief introduction of "Down Yonder" could not be complete without mentioning one other persistent daily influence: the media. Carlyle residents have had access to local television for over thirty years. Just twenty years ago, however, the majority of Hamilton's residents had only two fuzzy television stations, ABC and NBC. Now, most families with adolescents have satellite dishes that connect them to dozens of stations, including popular music stations MTV, BET, and VH1. In chapter 6, I will explore how the popular media fits into young people's daily life and social identity.

Investigating "Down Yonder"

My aim in undertaking this project was to produce a "thick" description of a group of people whom I firmly grounded in their structural and cultural environments. Therefore, participant observation comprises the most substantial aspect of my methodology. I spent fifteen months in Hamilton from August 2003 to December 2004. The rhythm of the school year and the school structure, in general, shapes the flow of daily life for young people. Therefore,

I observed one full school year and the first half of a second school year at Jay Ellis.

During the first school year, I volunteered at Jay Ellis two or three mornings a week, tutoring first, eighth, and twelfth graders in reading, math, social studies, and GED preparation. This aspect of my research allowed me to examine the students' attitudes toward school, their behavior within school, those persons who exert significant influence within the school, as well as the political economy of the county system. I continued my volunteer work at Jay Ellis as assistant cheerleading coach from May 2004 until December 2004. This form of participant observation allowed me to collect information about football culture and develop relationships with several female adolescents. In addition, it gave me intimate access to "backstages," while practicing, traveling to games, preparing for assemblies, and hosting activities. During the second year, I also tutored a few students for the ACT during the last period of the day.

I joined one of the two black community churches and attended services each week in addition to visiting other churches. Also, basketball and football games, birthday parties, movies, dinners, funerals, special church programs, school assemblies, and graduations were a central part of my participant observation. In these contexts, I was able to make general observations having to do with family, peer, and community interactions and the role of popular culture in those spaces. Very few of these interactions were tape-recorded; cognizant of the influence of the researcher in ethnographic work, I attempted to emphasize the "participation" more than the "observation."

During the early conceptualization of my research, I imagined that as a young black anthropologist I would "blend in" with the young people in the community. Two short years later, by the time I entered the field, I was almost twenty-five years old and had begun to show the wear of graduate school. Although my adolescent Hamiltonian friends described me as "bubbly" and "cool" on different occasions, I was never mistaken for one of them.[32] My employment at the local Sylvan Learning Center compounded these effects of "mother nature." Initially I was just tutoring there, but then for several months I became center director (I eventually left Sylvan at the end of the first school year). My standpoint in the community most certainly affected my data. I became close with several young people but, as I stated, was never confused to be a "young person." As a matter of fact, for the first time in my life I became "Ms. McMillan" instead of Angela or Angie.

In contrast to some of the obvious drawbacks of having an adult identity, my time at Sylvan furnished me with valuable information. It afforded me entrée into relationships with white community members and youth in an otherwise segregated environment. In addition, through Sylvan, I taught a twelve-week ACT course at two predominantly black high schools within thirty miles of Hamilton. These courses provided another excellent point of comparison because the schools are situated in more middle-class communities. Finally, my role as director of Sylvan enabled me to become familiar with regional schools and school districts, interact with concerned parents, attend PTA meetings, and learn about educational issues in the state of Alabama.

I conducted informal, short, and un-tape-recorded interviews almost daily. In addition, I conducted formal, tape-recorded interviews with fifteen adolescents. These in-depth interviews supplied information about families and households, weekly activities, self-perceptions, religious and political views, and peer relationships. Moreover, in the interviews I inquired about popular culture: what the adolescents' favorite movies, music, and television shows were and why. The interview schedule can be found in the appendix. I also conducted twelve in-depth interviews with community members and Jay Ellis teachers. My goal was to gain their perspectives on a range of local issues that affect adolescents, on specific events that occurred during the year, and on popular culture and the local youth. These interviews were unstructured.

Finally, I "shadowed" three young people; I spent a full day following them from morning until night—sitting in their classes, riding the school bus with them, staying overnight in their homes, and observing all activities in between. This intensive informal contact with several key informants helped me to connect the various aspects of my research in a coherent way. While I was in Hamilton and since I have left, basic contextual information was achieved through collection of census data, newspapers, and various forms of printed material.

Organization of the Book

Each of chapters in *Raised Up Down Yonder* is designed to build an understanding of Hamilton and the young people who grow up there. Chapter 1, "Rooted in Kin," contextualizes my identity in the field and examines the relationship between family name and social interaction. In addition, this chapter highlights the "compound lifestyle." This household pattern found in Hamilton fosters extended family networks and intergenerational activities and reframes the character of poverty from what the general public is used to seeing in popular representations. This chapter also adds texture to young people's family lives by examining the hidden diversity in socioeconomic levels and the prevalence of blended families. Finally, by exploring seventeen-year-old Kelly's family narrative, this chapter contrasts generalizable patterns with subjectively lived experiences.

Chapters 2 and 3 are organized around Kelly's assessment of her school experience at Jay Ellis School, miscast by locals as the "Last Chance School." Chapter 2, "Descendants of a First Choice School," describes Jay Ellis's history and examines the benefits and drawbacks of the small school setting in order to show that the Last Chance School is a new invention and a largely inaccurate description. This chapter shows how the community is historically similar to other African American communities in several ways: the negative impact of desegregation on the school, the dominant character of education as an intimate experience, and the role of a rural/urban dichotomy in the creation of educational patterns. Then, chapter 3, "Educated at the Last Chance School," analyzes the Last Chance School as an ideology that functions to maintain the current social order. This argument is substantiated by comparing the socially constructed caricature of Jay Ellis with the political economic reality in which it is embedded. To conclude, the chapter contrasts the educational system in Hamilton with the racism in the nearby Carlyle school system to show that either option presents limited options for Hamilton's youth.

Then, chapter 4, "Reproducing Misfortune through Mess," focuses on a local linguistic and cultural metaphor called "mess." Invoked on a daily basis, "mess" and "messy" people are blamed for the misfortunate events that take place in Hamilton. I argue that these poetic, yet seemingly negative, concepts provide a number of significant social functions. During the one-year-long social drama that transpired with the football team, mess was used as a coping mechanism; but cultural production theory highlights how mess helped to preserve the status quo. Still, the creative generative aspect of young people's language proves to be fascinating.

Chapter 5, "Resistance and Spirituality," uses Missy's biography to highlight spirituality as an important conceptual lens. Broadening the investigation from school resistance, for example, to this domain of investigation, shows the creative power of young people to negotiate multiple structures and options. Last, in chapter 6, "Not Just Down Yonder," I explore young Hamiltonians' collective identities. This chapter shows that young people see themselves as decidedly rural, albeit in new ways. It also uses moral panics about the negative influence of popular culture to investigate how young people interact with translocal influences. It demonstrates that popular culture is often used to reaffirm rather than destroy the norms, values, and experiences that originate from the local environment. The conclusion, "Going from Home to Home," highlights some of the major findings. It suggests that the young people's rural identities, while significant, may signal a change in emphasis from places to people. It also reaffirms that youth comprise a viable and important ethnographic subject. Finally, it also calls for researchers to continue grounding conversations about youth, writ large, in detailed examinations of their everyday lives.

Many voices are featured throughout this ethnographic portrayal. However, what it means to grow up in Hamilton—navigating complex social structures, making meaning, forming relationships, and beginning to chart a life course—is illuminated largely through the narratives of Sabrina, Kelly, James, Janelle, Missy, and Darnel. I hope that their narratives, with all of their humor, contradictions, insightfulness, and glorious imperfections, succeed in placing black youth in the subjective center.

Chapter 1 **Rooted in Kin**

Arriving in the field in August 2003, the Hamilton landscape seemed so unfamiliar that I wondered how I would bridge the great divide between native and outsider. There were many areas to explore and many people, I assumed, tucked inside the crannies and crevices of rural life. With very few street signs, no streetlights or sidewalks, and few discernible neighborhoods, I knew that my one saving grace was having two insiders as family members to introduce me to community members. I could not have overestimated the importance of this gift. As I would learn in the coming months, family or who one was kin to was absolutely central to everyday life in Hamilton.

My paternal great-grandparents were born and raised in Hamilton. My paternal grandfather remained in Hamilton until he left to attend high school in Montgomery, Alabama, and then college in Tuskegee, Alabama, and college in Hampton, Virginia. He eventually married and moved to Maryland, which is the state where I was born and reared. In my early childhood and young adulthood, however, I visited Hamilton about four times. These visits were my introductions to rural life, and the place absolutely fascinated me. At the time, I did not recognize the role that extended family or kinship played in daily life. When my nuclear family visited Hamilton, we stayed with my great-aunt Sallie, who lived on our family farm by herself, and she did not like to "share us" with our other relatives.

I had, however, built relationships with a few cousins in Hamilton, so when I decided to do my fieldwork there, it was big news in the family. My cousin Jude, who took care of the farm in our absence (my great-aunt passed away in 2000), still did not believe that I was coming (and staying) until the day that I arrived. He still didn't believe I would "last" up until the day I left, one year and three months later. His and others' disbelief that I would choose to come to an empty farm and stay by myself was influenced by who I was, from their perspective.

And after living in Hamilton a short time, I learned exactly who I was from their perspective: I was a McMillan. Whenever I was introduced to someone new, I could see the wheels turning as soon as they heard my last name. Invariably, they would link me to my "family." In Hamilton, kinship is the idiom for action and what gives social events their moral value. In casual conversation I would be associated to "ya'll who live up by them Colemans." Or someone might ask, "your kin still owns that farmhouse back on Jelly Road? . . . Yeah, I remember your daddy when he used to come visit over the summer." The most common references were to my two aunts who lived by themselves for the last twenty years that the house was inhabited. "Oh, Ms. Sallie, she was something else. She was so involved in church." My aunt Edna was described to me as a classy lady. She dressed well, she was an excellent seamstress, and she didn't take any mess from anybody.

The family of my great-grandmother, through whom I can trace the relation to my cousins who currently live in Hamilton, was the second association folks would make. They, as well, were described to me as hard workers, smart people, and in general of "respectable lineage." I definitely was not "fishing" for this information; these descriptions were offered freely and often. It was a nascent experience for me to be in an environment where I gained a default persona just by saying my name. I learned from that point on that I would be proving that I was like or unlike my family, as opposed to starting from a blank slate.

For example, while interviewing one student, Darnel Taylor, I noticed that he was giving one-word answers and being very shy. Darnel was tall, dark chocolate espresso, and ruggedly handsome. He was captain of the football team but too kind and mannerly to be the leader of some "in-crowd." Besides, Hamilton was too small to have an in-crowd. So, I tried to joke with him a little and get him to loosen up; the relationship I attempted to cultivate with the students was informal and humor filled. He told me that he was only being so quiet and "yes ma'aming" me so much because he was trying to be "respectful." After our interview, I linked this almost deferent attitude to something his mother told me one day at Jay Ellis. She shared that she used to watch and admire my aunts when she was a little girl, especially "the way they would carry themselves." Darnel's demeanor then made sense to me.

Thus far, my family depiction sounds favorable, but I knew from the beginning that the connotations of all this "respect" were not 100 percent positive. I was told about the unspoken negatives associated with my family by relatives who did not live in Alabama, my cousin Tiffany with whom I eventually moved in, and Ms. Smith, the guidance counselor and my close informant. The other side of educated, classy, and respectable is "uppity," overeducated, and "too cute." No one in Hamilton actually said that to me because voicing those perspectives would have been considered rude. But one day Ms. Beulah told me in jest about how my aunts would have people come over to their farm and work hard for them all day for free. She said, "You were lucky if you got a glass of water or, on a good day, a piece of cake."

I knew that the perception that my family is educated and uppity was the reason why my cousin Jude was baffled that I could handle farm life. Interestingly, after I did stay and became quite comfortable while I was there, Cousin Jude linked my tenacity to my aunts who, if needed, used to come out on the porch and greet an unknown visitor with a shotgun. Family identity, then, was active in making people who they were, but also it served as a catch-all system of understanding people's behavior, through which most activities could be explained. Some anthropologists, not without controversy, and to various degrees, have examined how systems of internal logic, such as religion, magic, and science, are similar in their ability to explain activities, ascribe them meaning, and chart a course of acceptable social behavior.[1] Being a McMillan helped "determine" people's "social behavior" toward me. And eventually I accepted this. I knew when I interacted with people that I was representing my family and standing for a certain type of person in Hamilton.

More important, I got to see how young people were advantaged and disadvantaged by this system of family identification, in which "social events" were given "their moral value" based on one's family tree. In an interview with my guidance counselor friend and informant, Ms. Smith, we began to discuss a student named Janelle. Janelle was a cheerleader who transferred from Carlyle High because she couldn't stay out of trouble. She had a petite stature, medium build, and cinnamon complexion, and generally wore her hair in a thick ponytail, which she whipped back and forth, animating her every move. I remarked that Janelle was incredibly smart despite her inability to stay out of trouble. During that school year, she "cursed out" the basketball coach, cursed at the principal, and even was removed from school in a police car one day. Ms. Smith's response to my observation was

> And her mother was an excellent student. She's an RN now. She's an excellent student. She's just a nut. And that's the truth! Those Youngs are nuts. They are! *She is crazy.* She can't help it. I mean . . . she actually, she'll tell you. Ask her. Say, "Janelle, who do you act like?" She'll tell you Cheryl, her aunt. She's just crazy as a chestnut. [laughter] I'm not kidding! But she knows . . .

I don't doubt that Janelle knows that people see her as crazy like her family, and if she feels crazy, then why wouldn't her family be an explanation?[2] Unfortunately, Janelle's supposedly inherited crazy gene implies that efforts at reform would be futile. This type of attitude toward students at Jay Ellis was voiced to me again and again. And it was especially cruel to the students from "slow" families or from "lazy" ones. These self-fulfilling prophecies were difficult to overcome and were created by nearly everyone.

According to David Murray Schneider, there are symbols and norms associated with American families:

> "The family" stands for each member and for all members of the family, for how each member of the family should behave, and for how family relations should be conducted by whoever is conducting them. If the "family" were right, then the child would not be delinquent, the marriage would be stable, and so on. This means that if everyone in the family behaved according to the proper standards for family life, all would be well. (45)

Consistent with Schneider's description, family in Hamilton was chief in explaining young people's and adults' behavior. The concept of family truly stood for each member and each member stood for the whole. My identity as a McMillan/Star mediated all of my experiences in Hamilton, from the access I was granted or denied, to the types of interactions I engaged in with people, to the way I saw myself. This was the intimate way that I first began to discover the importance of family as a unit of analysis in Hamilton.

On Saturday, September 7, 2003, my cousin Lewis's wife picked me up to attend her niece's twelfth birthday party. Just beginning my second week of fieldwork, I was eager to meet people and to observe a party for a young person. Carrie picked me up at the farmhouse, driving slowly down my dirt road, so as to minimize the russet dust haze that generally enveloped all vehicles. We shared good conversation about how things at the house were going, talked about Jay Ellis, the school where I would be volunteering, and discussed her family. Carrie was a teacher in her twenty-sixth year in the Head Start program at Jay Ellis. Lewis had already told me that her family "were all teachers, and that's who [I] *really needed* to connect with." Lewis described her family as real good people, crazy, funny, and close-knit. And according to him, I should ask them anything I wanted to know about education.

Before we went to the party, we traveled in the opposite direction to pick up three children whom Carrie promised to drive. They ranged in age from six to eleven years old. From there we traveled back past the churches, near my house, then drove about four or five more miles until a slight break in the road could be seen off to the right. It seemed like we were turning into an area where an industrial plant might be located. Instead, down this rocky dirt road about one mile, the road was suddenly paved, and we immediately turned left into the "Washington family compound."

There were about two acres cleared in the midst of trees and brush, with a big open area in the center and a road constructed right through the middle of it connecting the homes: four trailers off to the left on a hill, each with its own road, and a brick rancher all the way in the back, off to the right. The matriarch and patriarch of the family lived in the brick home where all the descendants had been raised. And each of the four trailers was owned by one of their children and their families. When we arrived, at least five children were outside jumping on the biggest trampoline I had seen, and they stayed on that trampoline for hours. Hamilton was surprisingly mosquito-free, so there was no bug repellent or sunscreen standing between children and nature.

The party took place primarily at Edna's house, the one at the back of the road on the left. Edna was the family auntie; she was unmarried with no children of her own, and a teacher. She took care of, that is, spoiled and disciplined, all of her nieces, nephews, and little cousins. Her trailer home was a three-bedroom double-wide, impeccably decorated, fully contemporary, and very comfortable. The birthday party was quite an affair, that included out-of-town relatives, children of various ages, birthday cake, goodie bags, pizza, music, television (a big screen TV), video games, trampoline jumping, you name it. All of the generations were together. I was quickly introduced to folks as Lewis's cousin. I received hugs, and I was told that I looked cute. In general, they were impressed that I was living on the farm by myself, and they told me (as I heard daily in Hamilton) that I looked just like my cousin Tiffany.

The Washington family compound was clearly a place of love and acceptance. However, jokes about people abounded, and no one was exempt. When one of the older cousins (about twenty-five years old) went to cut the cake, she told the junior guests "raise your hand if you brought a gift. Ya'll can have cake. The rest of ya'll better not go near that cake, and don't even think about a second slice." Then she went around and asked the children (some who were barely old enough to comprehend the joke) what they brought as their gift. She either made fun of the gift, "janked"[3] them and told them they couldn't have any cake, or offered them two slices because it was such a good gift.

The best part of the party was the dance contest orchestrated by an adult who said the youngsters were boring. So she turned the music up—a song by popular hip-hop artist P. Diddy—and made these children, likely aged four through twelve, come down an imaginary "soul train line." They performed all the latest dances, including popping their backs, a dance rife with sexual innuendo. Some were applauded, some were jokingly told to sit down and were booed. At the end of the day, I had met many people from Jay Ellis, and I had gained another adopted family.

I would get to spend many more days at the Washington compound, "visiting," eating, watching *That's so Raven, The Fighting Temptations, Malcolm X*, observing the girls get their hair styled, and even mourning with them, as they lost both their matriarch and patriarch while I lived in Hamilton. People spoke about how close the Washington family was, and in fact, the only slightly negative thing that I heard was from my cousin Lewis, who thought his wife, Carrie, spent too much time down at the compound. She, however, described Lewis as a party pooper because he didn't always want to stay and hang out until the wee hours of the morning.

The Washington family illustrates many shared attributes among the families in Hamilton, including the predominant spatial dynamics and residential patterns, the prevalence of intergenerational activities, the flow of members between households, and the extended family networks. Yet using the Washingtons as a template hides the impact that divorce and the creation of blended families have recently had on young people. In addition, it masks the interrelatedness between family activity and socioeconomic status. Finally, while the experience of belonging to a family such as the Washingtons and having a reputation such as theirs was positive, many young people experience the equally significant impact of a family who does not make them feel great and whose reputation is less than stellar. The remainder of the chapter will focus on these areas of similarity and difference among families in Hamilton, demonstrating that whatever its influence, family is definitely central to life and youth identity in Hamilton.

A Shared Kinship Experience

The spatial environment of Hamilton is the first indication that family is central to young people's experiences. The three major roads or highways that run through the town are county roads 45, 16, and 27. These are winding two-lane roads that flow through Hamilton and connect the community to Carlyle, to the county seat, and to communities west leading all the way out of the state. A small percentage of the Hamilton homes are actually visible from one of these roads. The majority of the families live on a dirt or semi-paved road adjacent to one of the main highways, in a cluster of houses, forming a small community. Two or three groups of families might share a dirt road, and each family grouping might include two or three households. According to the 2000 U.S. Census there are 611 households in Hamilton and the surrounding area.[4] Two hundred fifty-eight (258) of them are households with black members, and 328 are households with white members.[5]

On the road where I lived, my cousins occupy the entrance to the road, visible from the highway, and their mother lives just behind that house. Two small trailers also remain on the property for the seasonal deer hunters who come and stay. Down the dirt road about one-half mile is the "Coleman Quarters." This grouping is comprised of seven homes on one side of the street, the school bus that Mr. Coleman drives next to the homes, one home on the other side of the street, and then next to that home sits an actual permanent pavilion, referred to as "Coleman Pavilion." This structure was built solely for the purpose of hosting family get-togethers; most of the younger generation has migrated north, and when they come back to Hamilton they host huge barbecues in it. Finally, at the end of the dirt road about another half mile is where my family farm is located. It never made it to full compound status, but it was definitely known as the McMillan farm.

Most other family residences mirror one of these models. Some of the more well-known compounds are "Smith-ville," "Fowler's Quarters," and, as mentioned previously, "Washington Compound" and "Coleman Pavilion." These are the ones referred to by actual names in common parlance, but many homes that may not have had names were sprinkled throughout Hamilton. Two variations on this model are having a single home as family headquarters, and having unrelated families who have lived near one another for years and have become fictive kin, of sorts.

In the first example, one family house, usually the one owned by the oldest member of the family or the house where many of the descendants were raised, becomes the headquarters for major family gatherings. This may be the case when a family never has owned the land they live on or may not have had enough land to support multiple homes. Additionally, the descendants might have moved to Carlyle or to some other town in a neo-local residence. So, Sunday dinners or just hang-out time for cousins typically takes place at the headquarters. Many of the students who attend Jay Ellis do not live in Hamilton any longer. However, if they have moved away most of them have at least one family headquarters still in Hamilton where they spend a great deal of time.

The second variation on the compound model is tied to the history of sharecropping and tenant farming in the area. Many of the families in Hamilton are descendants of sharecroppers from the latter part of the nineteenth century and the first half of the twentieth century. When sharecropping or tenant farming for white landlords, families would build small homes or place trailers near the land that they worked. Often, more than one family would build near each other, and they would form a community. The majority of the families now own those small pieces of land, and as a result, neighborhoods have been formed that are comprised of people who have shared space for generations. This makes their interactions very intimate; they hunt together, do yard work together, their children become good friends, and, in general, they keep tabs on all that transpires in the neighborhood households.

Temporary child exchange was another pattern that I observed in Hamilton. In these instances, children were raised in a household that was not their parents' for an extended period of time. In 1999 the black population under eighteen years old numbered approximately 241. Of that number about 30 youngsters or 12 percent were living with a relative who was not their parent or with a nonrelative. When I inquired, these residential arrangements were attributed to convenience, perhaps because of someone's work schedule, because a child expressed desire to live with someone else, or because a particular residence was closer to school or closer to the family headquarters. These arrangements were made often and without fanfare. For example, when Tiffany lived in Carlyle, her second-oldest son George moved back to her parents' house in Hamilton for a little over a year (this was before she moved back and built her house on the family land). Her son was close to his grandparents, so after his grandfather died, he wanted to keep his grandmother's company. He also liked the space he had there as well as country life. Residential moves such as this one involved a flow of money and not just children. Yet, I never heard anyone discuss a formal exchange of money for taking care of a young person.

I also became aware of several instances in which children permanently or temporarily lived between two households or among many. According to Carol B. Stack, in her influential volume *All Our Kin*, "temporary child exchange is a symbol of mutual trust."[6] At the Washington compound, Jessie and Courtney slept most nights in their paternal grandparents' house (their father who was in the army was their guardian, and the children stayed with his parents). But as was stated earlier, all of their aunts raised them, especially Edna, and they often slept at Edna's house or their other cousin's house. Once their grandparents died, everyone in the family pitched in to ensure that their lifestyle was not greatly altered. Because of the short duration of these stays (although they take place frequently), and the often fluid nature of the placement of bodies, the large volume of these short stays would not have been accurately reflected in the census data on household composition.

In *All Our Kin*, Stack also demonstrates how extended networks of kin and friends who exchange "goods, resources, the care of children, . . . [and] acts of domestic cooperation" offset the paucity of resources available due to economic hardship. While Stack's work in "The Flats" depicted an urban setting, financial resources were not abundant in rural Hamilton, either. The median black household income in 1999 was just $14,875 with 55 percent of black people in Hamilton living below the poverty line. In addition, while 44 percent of black youth under eighteen lived in a married-couple family with at least one of their parents (higher than most stereotypes imply), still 7 percent lived with a male head of household only and 36 percent lived with a female head of household only. Although money in Hamilton is limited, one thing folks do have is access to land to grow food that supplements what is bought. These goods are also exchanged.

Extended family networks, prominent in the literature about African American family life, operate in and out of town. The majority of the students whom I interviewed had visited or even experienced extended stays with relatives in Michigan, Illinois, Georgia, Ohio, California, or Tennessee. These trips were formative in helping the young people connect with their family and have experiences that they might not have in Hamilton. In fact, many youth said one of their best friends was a cousin who lived out of town.

Intergenerational activity is another important aspect of family life in Hamilton. As with the Washingtons' birthday party, most activities take place within or among families and include everyone from babies to the elderly. Attending church together, doing outside work, hunting, farming, watching television, going to Tuscaloosa, Alabama, or Meridian, Mississippi, grocery shopping, watching children, and attending special events such as football and basketball games are just a few examples of family activities that include many generations. Attending Jay Ellis School cements family ties and fosters intergenerational bonding as much as, if not more than, it creates peer relationships.[7] Because the school is a small kindergarten through twelfth grade school, students ride to school on buses with all ages from five to eighteen. Additionally, most after-school and extracurricular activities (because of the small nature of the school) depend on participation from many, if not all, grade levels. It is not uncommon to see a fifth grader after school conversing with a group of his tenth-grade cousins.

Friday night football games are an excellent example of the prevalence of intergenerational family activities in Hamilton. At Jay Ellis, the Friday night games look more like family reunions than ball games. Little babies are carried around by parents, grandparents, siblings, cousins, and so on; children play together behind the bleachers until they are told to come sit down, and teachers bring their children with them. In fact, whole caravans of families come to games together. The football field, itself, is mixed with puny seventh graders and burly twelfth graders; many of them are related. And while the

young people may roam off together for a while, it is not in the stereotypical way that adolescents are depicted in which they are embarrassed to be
seen with their families. These young people *are* their families, and trying
to separate from them would lead to isolation from their life blood, identity,
network of meaningful people, most of their friends, and their school.

Activities that contribute to supplemental income constitute one large category of activities in which Hamilton's young and old participate. In addition
to people growing their own food, as mentioned above, various programs
geared toward low-income families help to supplement their monthly income. For example, Helping Hand, a program funded by the State of Alabama, through the Health Department, supplies USDA-prepared frozen dinners, drinks, and snacks to qualified elderly and disabled people. The amount
of food that this one program provides trickles down to significantly offset
food costs for Hamilton families. More important, rifling through these dinners for what is edible was actually an enjoyable group activity. We spent time
carefully selecting, "doctoring up," and eating these "dinners" at my cousins'
house on many occasions. One family, for whom these glorified TV dinners
were an insult to southern home cooking, passed them on to me. And as a
"poor" researcher I was grateful to eat and share them.

A similar program administered out of the local community center provided free lunches to children over the summer. Getting the lunches was a daily
ritual in our family compound. My cousin Janie, Tiffany's eighty-two-year-
old mother, would start to call the house at about 7:30 a.m. to wake up the
boys and tell them to do one thing or another: come pick up her chicken eggs,
go over to Ms. Susie's house and help her pick some beans, crack the pecans,
feed the dog . . . whatever she could use to get them to come and spend time
with her. My two cousins, thirteen-year-old Jonathan and seventeen-year-
old Justin, were adept at ignoring her until about 11:30 a.m. when it was time
to get the lunches. At that point, either Justin would drive his car around the
corner to get the mail from the post office and fetch the lunches, or Jonathan
would be driven around the corner to the community center by Cousin Janie.
Jonathan would pick up the lunches, sweet talking the school-aged workers
to get as many as he could, and then they would stop by the post office. When
we all met back at the house, we would choose whether we wanted bologna
with or without cheese, which snack we wanted, and which flavored juice
was the most desirable. This was an everyday feature of the summer. Despite
my little cousins' protests (including stomping, sucking teeth, "ahh man"ing,
declaring that "grandma" was evil), this ritual was a significant part of their
lives. And old cousin Janie was smart because the lunch ritual was the only

way she got them to stop playing video games and come down to her house and spend time with her.

A local Carlyle Episcopal church runs a free weekly pantry for 345 elderly residents who qualify.[8] This, as well, involved a ritual. An elderly person or his "scout" would have to get to the church early Tuesday morning to stand in the long line, awaiting the opening of the pantry doors at 8:30 a.m. as if it were a rock concert. After the doors opened, and they moved through the line, recipients' names would be checked off and they would receive a brown paper bag full of goods from cookies to canned meat to juice boxes. Many a Tuesday morning, we (the cousins) sat around Cousin Janie's small kitchen table, pulling each item excitedly out of the brown paper bag as if we were diamond mining rather than going through our bag of fifteen dollars' worth of soon-to-be-expired groceries. We even bartered for our favorite snacks.

According to sociologist William Falk, poverty and family life have commingled for so long in the rural South that being poor can hardly be extracted from the day-to-day character of life.[9] Things that might come under the heading of "making do" (swapping children, growing and exchanging food, taking advantage of local programs, constantly participating in the informal economy) deceptively lose their structural impact because of the way the local culture so beautifully glosses over them. I found it to be amazing that some people seemed concerned about my well-being more than I was concerned about theirs—to them, I was just the struggling student away from my real home.

The point I wish to make here is that the majority of people in Hamilton don't walk around feeling poor, despite the fact that the U.S. Census may deem them to be so. For many, poverty is picking beans, diamond mining for free pantry items, staying at their cousin's house, shooting at dogs that eat their live chickens, buying barbecue from a family who has a freshly slaughtered hog, or stalking the sale items at CVS, Food World, and Piggly Wiggly. In fact, according to relative deprivation theory, which argues that people judge how they are doing in contrast to those in their environment, adolescents may have felt the poorest when they watched MTV *Cribs*, a show that featured the decadent mansions of singers, actors, rappers, ball players, and other celebrities.[10]

A More Nuanced Portrait

While the overall patterns of residence, household composition, extended family networks, and intergenerational activity may be shared among young people in Hamilton, the character of specific families differs greatly. Socioeconomic status even among the poor does vary, and it helps shape the form of family interaction in particular ways. Further, the existence of blended families due to divorce adds a layer of dimension to the depiction of Hamilton families. Finally, viewing family from the perspective of one adolescent reveals that whatever the patterns are, one must listen to individual perspectives to understand the significance of the patterns.

Young people in Hamilton lived in households at a variety of socioeconomic levels. They ranged from living in a household with, for example, (1) five members—one mother disabled on public assistance, a cohabitant who was also on public assistance, her boyfriend, her sister, and herself; (2) five members—one father who drives an interstate truck, one mother who works at a clothing factory, an elementary-aged niece, an elementary-aged nephew, and herself; (3) four members—one mother who works at a clothing factory, one father who works at a paper mill, one sixth-grade niece, and himself; and (4) two members—one divorced mother who has been a registered nurse at a hospital for over twenty years and herself.

The 2000 U.S. Census reflects this level of diversity. Among black families in Hamilton 29 percent earned a total yearly family income of less than $10,000; 11 percent brought in a total family income of $10,000–$14,999; 22 percent obtained a total family income of $15,000–$24,999; 14 percent earned a total family income of $25,000–$34,999; 20 percent earned a total family income of $35,000–$59,999; and 4 percent brought in a total family income of $60,000 and above.[11] While the figures seem to lean heavily on the side of lower socioeconomic statuses, a five-thousand-dollar difference in income in a rural community such as Hamilton is mammoth. It could amount to having a working vehicle; being able to visit out of town relatives; having the money to purchase items for extracurricular activities; or being able to afford a tutor for a child's school subjects.

To further highlight the economic diversity among families in Hamilton, one of the seniors during the 2004–2005 school year received a 1998 red Chevrolet Cavalier from her parents (although she had an after-school job to help pay for it), while in 1999, 98 black households (20 percent) reported having no vehicles available; 43 black households reported having no telephone service; 15 black households lacked complete kitchen facilities; and 8 lacked complete plumbing facilities. The greatest diversity in socioeconomic status won't even be evident in the population at Jay Ellis because those few families in the upper-income brackets choose to send their children to the integrated Carlyle school system. Actually, one wouldn't meet school-aged children of some of the higher socioeconomic status black families because the younger generations have out-migrated all together.

In order to understand how these variant socioeconomic statuses correlate with family life, one must acknowledge that money, alone, does not account for the differences. The type of job one has dictates the hours that members of households are at home, the regularity of their schedules, and the level of emotional availability that a member of a household might have. For example, the two men I knew that worked on jobs at the nearby paper mill had nuclear family lives with a great deal of regularity, pattern, and stability. These were considered "good jobs." They paid well, provided good benefits, and not many black men worked at the mill, so there was a level of prestige associated with these jobs.

However, the two families that I knew in which the father drove trucks out of state experienced less regularity than the families just described. The young people in these households were involved in more shenanigans. And although these families had just as much money (and likely benefits) as those working at the mill, the prestige of truck driving was not as high. When I told one teacher at Jay Ellis that a young man whom I was tutoring wanted to drive trucks (in a conversation about his progress), he replied, "Well, *you know* his father drives trucks . . ." The tone was not quite condescending, but neither was it hopeful.

Interestingly, adolescents expressed great admiration for the fathers in these truck-driving families. The truck-driving lifestyle created a "knight in shining armor" motif for the two young adolescents whom I knew in these households. The son of one truck driver would tell me about what his father was going to bring him when he came home, and he told me about how he loved when his father let him go on a trucking excursion with him. The daughter of the other truck driver would gush about her "daddy." In her narratives, he always provided money for her and gave her what she wanted when he came home. The truck-driving father gave these young people financial resources, freedom from daily regulation, and emotional love untainted by the day-to-day chaffing associated with child-rearing.

Moreover, popular media and common parlance abound with disdain for citizens who collect unemployment compensation, public assistance, or disability pensions. From my observations, disabilities affected family life in Hamilton in two ways. Those who received benefits either displayed intensified involvement in family, community, and school life, or it made people with disabilities withdraw and have limited interaction with others. One mother who was recently unable to work due to a disability used her extra time to volunteer at the school, support her sons in all their sporting events, and volunteer at the church. My cousin Lewis, who has suffered with kidney disease all his life and received a kidney transplant a few years ago, is "rent-a-relative." A former high school basketball star, his physique, energy, and broad smile hide the extent of his health challenges. Yet, he opens and closes the church, serves on the deacon board, takes care of his mother, interacts with the young people in his family, coaches the Jay Ellis girls basketball team, drives people to and from Birmingham to the airport, serves on the school board . . . basically does any and everything that people ask of him. His labor power enables him to be the community glue to hold everything together.

Yet, one of the prominent compounds in Hamilton is "Johnsonville." Although I never went inside any of the houses (I dropped one of the senior boys off there one day), community lore is that the family—multiple households—receives disability pension for extreme obesity. On more than one occasion, I heard jokes about the family, that is, about how they would dine in their compound eating prime rib every night on the government. Some people would tease that they, themselves, might eat better if they didn't work. In actuality, these tales helped establish the boundaries of acceptable community behavior. Clearly this family was not within those boundaries. Sadly, one weekend that I was out of town, one of the members of the compound— only thirty years old—died of massive heart failure. The mortician estimated that she weighed close to one thousand pounds, and informants reported that they had to lift her body out of the house with a crane.

As mentioned above, social science research on African American families has been instrumental in highlighting the informal flow of people among households. The data on male/female partnerships, in particular, might lead one to believe that the breakups and reunions frequently reported in rural African American fiction and nonfiction take place outside of the confines of marriage and are nestled largely under the umbrella of "female-headed households." This may have been truer in the past when a lack of resources and historically derived constraints (from slavery) led people to cohabitate for long periods of time in a committed relationship, without a marriage license.

I was shocked to learn that in Hamilton this is not the case; marriage and remarriage are the norm, and the exchange of young people among households is sometimes complicated, inorganic, and consequential. In fact, many adolescents whom I interviewed and got to know were in one or more blended families wherein the concept of divorce and its legalities and emotional ties were very present. Virginia Heyer Young, distinguished anthropologist and lecturer emeriti from the University of Virginia, conducted research on African Americans in a small southern town in the 1970s. She discovered that in thirty-eight out of forty-one lower-income households men were the main providers. The findings from this study contradicted the prevailing stereotype of the female-headed household. According to Young, not only were the households two-parent, with men as the chief financial providers, but

> family ties through men and emotional attachments to their kinsmen are socially important in this town, as well as mother-daughter ties. At the same time there are many illegitimate births, multiple sequential marriages, and frequent dissolution of marriage.[12]

The same "emotional attachments" to paternal kin coupled with illegitimate births and dissolutions of marriage, which Young mentions, still exist;[13] they create emotionally charged environments for some young people in Hamilton. These complications usually remain veiled in the public domain, overshadowed by the overall "closeness of family." After completing my lengthy formal interviews, however, I discovered that only two out of those fifteen students were in a family or household that was not shaped in part by divorce and/or remarriage.[14]

The way that the students talked about their family compositions in their interviews ranged from peripheral references, to intentional terseness laden with emotion, to central thematic status. When I interviewed Darnel, one of the two students who did not belong to a family in which official divorce and remarriage was a feature, he casually answered the questions about family without much emphasis.

Who lives with you here? My sister and my mother. *And, have you all always lived here or did you used to live somewhere else?* We used to live with my grandmother 'fore we moved down here. *When did you move here? . . .* Eight years ago. *And at that point who was living with you guys?* Me, my grandmother, my aunt, my cousin, and my mother. *What does your mom do?* She's a manager at Jay Ellis in the cafeteria. *And what about your dad? Is he around?* Yes, he's—nah he lives in Atlanta. *Oh he lives in Atlanta? And what does he do?* He works, I think he's the manager at Home Depot. *Do you see him often, or . . . ?* Every now and then. *Were your parents married before?* No, ma'am. *And did you ever live with him?* No. *Do you have any siblings on his side?* Yes, ma'am. Two brothers. *How old?* One is fifteen, and the other is a year. *And, do you see them?* Every now and then. *I know your grandmother is alive because I met her. Are any of your other grandparents alive?* No. *Are you close with your grandmother?* Yes, ma'am, VERY. *Very close, O.K* [laughter].

Rather than being moved one way or the next to discuss his nuclear family, Darnel was much more interested in talking about his grandmother. The summer before I completed the interview, his younger sister was supposed to go and stay with their father in Atlanta for a while. That trip never happened, and for his sister, at least, it seemed to be a sore subject.

Families that involved remarriage evoked more thorough analyses of the situation by the adolescents. Missy, whose interview is quoted in depth in chapter 5, told me about her father's outside children and her blended family. One can observe how she uses humor to discuss her family composition, although it has impacted her greatly. I begin this excerpt by asking her if she is close to her father's stepdaughter, who is in her Jay Ellis graduating class of twenty-eight students.

> *Oh so are you close to Janice, are you close to your stepsister?* I mean we cool, but we can't be [unclear], because her mother makes it seem like my mother is a bad person because she wants so much from my dad . . . *So how many stepsiblings do you have?* Well, my mother, she had two stepsons and a stepdaughter and my father has two stepdaughters and a stepson . . . And my dad's got seventeen kids spread across the U.S. [laughter]. He finally admitted to it last year. *Oh goodness. Really across the U.S., or . . .* Really across the U.S! I'm serious. *Do you all have a big family reunion?* Umm, the people from Michigan, but he's never taken any of his outside kids, never. *Do all his stepchildren, do all of your mom's, do they all go to Jay Ellis too?* No. Actually, one of my dad's kids—do you know Ticia? She's in the fifth grade. That's his daughter. *Oh, OK.* That's his daughter. And she just came to Jay Ellis. That's like the only one I'm really close with. She talks to me about anything. And, she talks to me about why he, ummm, don't come around as much. And then I was like, he has a family just like your mom has a family. I have to explain that kind of stuff to her. And, she real cool, she a lot like him. As far as getting mad and flipping out, she's a lot like him. And, let me see, she went to family reunion for the first time last year
> . . . *The one in Michigan?* Yes.

"Yard children" are a phenomenon in Hamilton. I regularly had conversations with adults and young people in which yard children or "outside kids"—that is, children conceived outside of marital unions—were topics. Infidelity was such a verbalized part of life that I began to question whether that should have been my research topic. I would characterize infidelity as a supposedly contentious part of life in Hamilton, but in actuality it is quite normative considering the frequency with which it happens and its predominance in the local discourse.

Another Jay Ellis senior was impacted greatly by the ups and downs of her parents' relationship. In the following section, I will present the story of Kelly Lawrence. On one level, the excerpts from Kelly's interview help us to understand how socioeconomic status, residential and household composition, extended family networks, divorce, and infidelity intertwine and take root in the life of one adolescent. On another level, Kelly's story is compelling because she is one of the students who, after knowing her for a year, I deemed to be relatively "spoiled," carefree, and happy. Only after completing this interview did I really begin to understand the complexity of "Kelly's heart."

Kelly's Heart

I got to know Kelly when I was co-coaching the cheerleading squad at Jay Ellis. Not only was Kelly on the team, but also she had been cheering at Jay Ellis ever since the sixth grade, and she eventually became team captain because of her dedication. Kelly was full: full face, full smile, full figure, full of laughs, and full of life. She was always laughing, acting "goofy" (in her own words), and in general lighting up a room. In addition, she had become known at Jay Ellis as one of the students who did her work and stayed out of drama. She later told me that staying out of drama was intentional, and sometimes she had to pray and ask God to help her not to fight.

When I interviewed Kelly in September 2004, I discovered that her bubbly public demeanor hid much depth. We sat down to talk in my placid living room, which smelled stale as if no one lived there, no matter how many months I stayed, how much I painted, or how many candles I burned. During our interview, Kelly opened up about her family and allowed me to meander from my interview questions. I truly appreciated her openness and willingness to share with me. She helped me to understand what it *feels* like to be at the intersection where kinship patterns collide. The following are excerpts from our September 5 interview. Kelly's manner of speaking was slow and her country accent was one of the heaviest of any of the students I knew. So the interview should be read in that way. Where "laughter" is written in brackets [], it mostly indicates that Kelly and I were laughing or giggling. I use parentheses () to indicate when Kelly was not joyfully laughing. It should be interpreted as the type of laughter that prevents tears.

Kelly, what's your [full] name? Kelly Isabelle Lawrence [big smile, laughter]. *Nice smile!* That's my grandmother's name. *Oh . . . Kelly or Isabelle?* Both. *You're named after your grandmother; that's so sweet.* Great-great-*great-great*-grandmother! . . . [laughter]. *Your great-great-grandmother's name and your grandmother's name?* And my momma's name. But my momma is Beverly Isabelle Kelly Lawrence. *That is so cool. So you are keeping the name in the family. I want to do that too.*

So when were you born? September 13, 1986. *Where?* John Banks Memorial Hospital. *So that makes you seventeen . . . and were you living in Hamilton when you were born or you were living in Carlyle?* In Hamilton. On an old country road. The house in the back of the woods, the last house. *Right here in Hamilton or in Spring Grove or Fowlcreek?* When you come off 27, it's an old dirt road on the left. *Uh, huh. When you come off onto . . .* Before you get in the deep curve [to] go around to Hamilton, it's a road on the left.

  Is anyone back there now? All my kinfolks, my daddy's folks, my aunties, and uncles—all the Smiths—and some more folks. *And when did you move to Carlyle?* When I was . . . sixth grade. So, I was what, thirteen? Fourteen? Something like that. *How come you moved to Carlyle?* Me and my momma moved because . . . they got a divorce—my mom and my dad. And my brother was already out the house. *So the two of ya'll moved?* Yeah. *And your dad stayed?* Yeah [unclear] . . . *Is it because you all wanted to move or . . . ?* We wanted to move. He wasn't doing right. So we moved—we left—I told her to leave. *And at that point you were only in the sixth grade?* Then we moved BACK down there [to Hamilton] . . . then came back to Carlyle. *OK.*

The initial paragraph presented here includes the first words uttered when I turned on the recording device. Almost instantly, we get to see how embedded Kelly is in her family, just as most Hamilton youth are. In her case, she not only bears her paternal surname, but she is literally marked by bearing the name of several generations of her maternal kin—a fact that she was quite proud of. In only two more paragraphs, her demeanor changed dramatically when she mentioned her parents' divorce. Her pace of speaking slowed to half time.

Kelly was one of the students at Jay Ellis School who lived in Carlyle and chose to go to Jay Ellis. In the field, I had learned that this usually meant the student's family had originally come from Hamilton, or that they had some family tie to the school. The other option would be that a student was expelled from a Carlyle school or was habitually getting into trouble, and Jay Ellis admitted the student to boost its enrollment. I knew Kelly had been at Jay Ellis since Head Start; now, I learned her connection was her father's family, and that she used to reside in Hamilton.

Kelly's interview, up to this point, paints the portrait of a typical residential pattern in Hamilton—that is, what it sounds like for someone to describe where they live and with whom. "The deep curve" on County Road 27 might as well be an official landmark. It was certainly a reliable way to give someone directions. The fact that Kelly moved back to Hamilton a second time, before finally settling in Carlyle, disturbed her, and provided a context for how a body in transit might feel.

  So tell me about your family, I know you have two brothers . . . Got two brothers. Before my daddy met my mom he had a daughter: my sister Barbara. And then, he got a little girl, now. *Is he remarried?* [some sort of gesture no, very uncomfortable]. *OK, moving on (laughter). I take it that this was not a pleasant divorce.* It was bitter. It was blah . . . blah.

So the family members that don't live in your household . . . you have two sisters, one younger, one older and where do they live? My older sister lives in Cleveland, she's thirty. And his child stays with him. *Right around the corner, right here?* Mmm hmm. She's in preschool . . . *Her mother's staying there, too?* She ditched [him]. She stays in Birmingham or somewhere. She don't care about her kids. *Do you have a relationship with your little sister?* We try . . . not really. *But you know her if you see her?* Yeah. I don't call her as my sister, though (giggle).

What are your parents' occupations? My mom works at the hospital, she's an RN. She delivered just about everybody in my classroom. And my daddy, he's a carpenter. *And is he self-employed or does he work for somebody?* Self, self-employed. And he's a farmer [giggle]. *In the way that everybody in Hamilton is a farmer . . . they all have okra*—and cows and he got, what . . . three pastures? With about ten or more cows on them. *Well, he's a farmer then. He raises cows . . . does he raise any crops or anything?* He raise greens and corn, he was doing squash then he started doing watermelon and plum trees and peach trees and, uhh . . . muscadines. *So, you're a bona fide country girl. You're just masking as a city girl.* [laughter] From da countre [exaggerated accent] . . . .

How much money do you think your parents make a year? I don't know about him, but my momma probably make over thirty thousand. Something like up there . . . between thirty to thirty-five. Maybe forty [laughter]. If she put in some overtime, I'll say. *And I know you have a job now, where do you work?* Family Dollar. *Family Dollar, good ole Family . . . and how long have you worked there?* Since June, the end of June. June twenty-seventh. *Is that your first job?* No, I was working at Pizza Hut in January for just about four weeks . . . But she wouldn't give me no hours and then they was taking money out for me being a waitress. *Mmm hmm.* So I didn't like that. So I put in another application. Got hired at Family Dollar. *Do you work at your job for "spending money" or to contribute to your family?* For spending and contributing. Both. *So you do give some to your mom?* Yep.

Alright. Do you know anything about your relatives and how they got to Hamilton? Even like your father's family? Your mother's family? My . . . the folks that down here is my daddy's family. Tell you the truth I don't know how they got here [laughter]. *Do you know how long they've been here?* Uhh Uhhh. All I know is my, my great- my great-great granddaddy was a Indian chief. He was a Cherokee. And they moved from Mississippi, I think. *Hmmm.* Or something like that. *That's on your dad's side or your mom's?* My daddy's side. All my daddy's folks down here. My momma's folks in Cleveland and Georgia.

How did your mom get down here? She met—he had some folks in Cleveland, too. And she met him at a bar. And I . . . I don't know how they connected 'cause she never did tell me the story. And so they got married, and she moved down here. *Wow. A real live import!* He brought her down to the country. *Do you visit Cleveland much?* Yeah. Bout once or twice a year. *And you have cousins up there?* Cousins and aunties and uncles, nieces. *Are your grandparents alive?* My momma's momma. She is eighty-six and she claims she is seventy-two [laughter]. But we found her birth certificate, and she eighty-six. And she keeps saying she's seventy-two. *And she can pass for seventy-two?* She look like it. She love to dress. *And what did your grandmother do for a living, do you know? Did she work outside the home?* She works for, uhh, the elderly people. *Still?* She sits in the home. She used to be a housewife till my granddaddy died. *Yeah?* Cause my granddaddy was a pastor and he died of a heart attack. *How long ago was that?* My mom was fourteen, and she's turning fifty in January, so that's a long time. *Cool, so do you have a close relationship with any other older people?* Nope . . . Just my momma and her sister, my auntie. That's about it. *Your mom's sister lives here?* She stays in Cleveland. *But you see her often?* Mmm hmm.

Do you have any cousins that live around here? My daddy people. But I don't talk to 'em that much. The only ones I talk to is like twenty to thirty something. *Do you have cousins at Jay Ellis?* Yeah, a few of 'em. *But not like "the Youngs?" . . . "the Jones?"* . . . Those are my cousins, Missy, Quenita . . . *Missy who braided your hair?* James Riles and Donnel Taylor. Yeah. Can't think of nobody else right now. Maybe some on the elementary hall. But most of them transferring to Carlyle . . .

Who are the most important people in your life? My mom and my nephews. My sister has a little girl and a boy but I ain't too close with them like I am with my nephew, my oldest brother's child. 'Cause I stayed with . . . well, I used to stay with them all the time and he comes stay with me. *Your oldest brother is the one who drives trucks?* Mmm hmm. *And he's the one who is also now remarried. And these are the children from his first marriage?* Yeah, well, he's got one from the ex-wife and now he got one with the new wife.

Kelly's family socioeconomic status placed her in the middle to upper segment of Hamilton society. This was due to the prestige of her mother's job, and the fact that her father owned land and cows. Her relationships with her extended kin were also representative of the average adolescent in Hamilton. She went to school with her cousins, she used to live on the road with her father's kin, and she visited her out-of-town relatives every year. One thing that made Kelly unique, however, was her knowledge of her own family history and her general ability to convey details about her grandmother's life. I found most of the adolescents' cognizance of family to be intimate but largely ahistorical.

Another thing that distinguished Kelly from many of her peers was that her maternal kin resided entirely in Cleveland and Georgia. One can only imagine the added emotional strain this caused when the relationship between her parents disintegrated. The people Kelly listed as living on her dirt road—"all [her] kinfolks, [her] daddy's folks, [her] aunties, and uncles . . . and some more folks"—were connected to the person who caused her so much pain. Furthermore, it becomes clearer why she and her mother moved to Carlyle, while he stayed at the family house. At that time, Kelly's father inhabited their old space, which, by her ability to easily rattle off the crops he grew, leads me to connect that physical landscape to her identity. To make matters worse, his "illegitimate" preschool-aged daughter was being raised by him in *her* former domain.

One conundrum of the small school model in Jay Ellis is that students say that they love to be at school with their friends and cousins. But that same feature has just as many complications as it does benefits. Kelly's father's daughter attended preschool in the same small building where Kelly went to school. I saw him dutifully pick up his young, very fair skinned daughter (possibly of mixed racial ancestry) from school on more than one occasion. It is no wonder that Kelly felt conflicted about building a relationship with her; it is only more difficult to imagine when she later in the interview lamented how distant the relationship with her father had become since the days when they used to go fishing together.

The following excerpts come from the end of the interview, after we had spent an hour discussing school, church, recreation, and other topics. Most of the students I interviewed had to think hard about a time when someone hurt them, but the answer was easy for Kelly. And she seemed relieved to be able to fill in the details for me—to justify her feelings of bitterness, betrayal, and ambivalence.

> *What is one time that someone really hurt you or broke your trust?* When my dad cheated on my momma. There never is, nobody ever did nothing to hurt me, but it's like when somebody do something to my momma, it hurts me too. *How did you find out?* The lady called the house and she thought I was my momma and she cussed me out and called me all kind . . . well she thought she was talking to my momma 'cause she was calling her all kinda names . . . and what she was going to do with my daddy and all that. And I cussed her out and then gave the phone to my momma. And by the time she got the phone, she hung up. So I went down there and I wanted to cuss my daddy out, too. But mom said, "You just a child you don't do that, you don't talk to adults like that." And then she did it (laughter). So, ever since then, I got respect for him, but ain't got respect for him like I used to, like I was a little girl gettin' on his back going to the fishing pond, and all that stuff.
>
> *Do you see him?* Every day . . . Every day. *Where do you see him every day . . . you go by his house every day?* Noo . . . he comes to our house every day. He act like he can't

let go even though he know he did something wrong, but he can't let go. "I want my family back, blah, blah, blah, blah . . . stuff like that." *And you don't want them to get back together?* NOPE (giggles, cuts me off). Nope. *Why?* 'Cause he did the wrong, and he didn't say he was sorry. Well, yes he . . . he told her it was a mistake. And so that's why we moved back down there. And he still was messing with another girl. That's how he got his little girl, now. So, we moved back to Carlyle. I said, "Ma, you move down there one more time, I'm leaving." (laughter) I was gone. I ain't want to move down there. I told my momma I was gonna run away. And I was—And she said, "Don't leave me [imitating her voice]."

Did that affect your grades or school [work] at all? When I got to the seventh grade, I had Fs in about three classes [giggles]. *Really?* Yeah, I know I had Fs in math, 'cause I wasn't sitting there trying to do it. I had an F in science, 'cause I wasn't try to sit there and figure it out. And it was another class . . . Actually I take it back I think they were Ds . . . Yeah, my momma had . . . she was trying to talk to me, and . . . I brought 'em back up to Bs. Some. Two were As. I ain't never had no A in no math [laugh].

What are your favorite parts about yourself? My heart. *Why do you say that?* Because . . . uhh . . . I hold a lot of stuff in and don't let it out, I'll say. Then I be crying if I get to startin' talking about it, and all that stuff. Feelings are deep. *And you like that about yourself.* No . . . *What are your least favorite parts about yourself?* My heart. 'Cause I hold too much stuff in (giggle). *What kind of stuff do you hold in? I don't want to make you cry.* Things that I want to say, but I can't say 'cause they are adults. *Like things about your parents divorce?* Yeah. That, and . . . and . . . uh stuff I want to say to my brother, but ain't no need in talking to him 'cause he ain't going to pay me no attention and nobody else attention, 'cause he gonna do what he gonna do. And . . . how can I put this? I can't put it into words right now . . . I'm always caring for folks, I'll say. And then, half the time they don't care about you. So, that's another big thing. I get it from my momma. *How do you think other people see you?* Goofy [giggle]. If I ain't smiling something's wrong. But most folks see me smiling, and talking too much.

Kelly's heart is a poignant symbol of the tension that many young Hamiltonians feel. The tension in large part derives from structures that include them, kinship in this case, but in which they have few culturally normative avenues to exercise agency. Kelly was the central figure in the story of how she found out about her father's affair. She received the phone call, she was "cussed out" by her father's lover, she gave the phone to her mother. Still her mother explained that she had to show her father "respect." In Kelly's words, there are "things that I want to say, but I can't say 'cause they are adults." She certainly couldn't control her and her mom moving back to Hamilton; she was just a body in transit. However, she did exercise agency when she refused to move back to Hamilton the second time.

Kelly's heart, as both her favorite and least favorite part about herself, performs many functions. It connects her to the people she loves, yet it allows her to be hurt by these same people. It mediates her knowledge of what's right and wrong but restrains her from enforcing those beliefs. Finally, Kelly's heart helps her to survive by bearing all of her hurts so that her public persona can be "goofy," "smiling," and "talking too much." I think it is rather ironic that just as Kelly's nuclear family was falling apart, cheerleading emerged as her favorite activity. As a cheerleader, Kelly was able to "care for folks," that is, her team, through a role that involved no expectation of care in return, and thus little risk of being hurt.

The last excerpt introduced the theme that she develops more below: how she sees herself reflected in her mom.

> *The person who inspires me most is* . . . Umm, I was fittin to say my momma, but I don't want to go through the things she went through, so . . . uhh. I don't have anyone to follow. I used to say my momma . . . But I don't want to go through what she went through.
>
> *Um the biggest block to my future success will be* . . . I was fittin to say my momma again, but she tryin to push me out. She's like "you goin leave me?" I'm like, "Yeah, momma I'm gonna leave you." And then, I don't know. She's like, "You gonna come back?" But I'm like, I know I'm gonna come back to see momma. I ain't got no big block, it's just I'ma miss momma. But you got to leave momma one day.

I interpret Kelly's mother to be a symbol of her own self and her own future potential for agency. Although it is her father who has hurt her, and her father who ignores her, the one thing Kelly would change is her "mom's way of seeing things." In fact her biggest role model is her mother, with the exception of one thing: she doesn't want to go through what she went through. Kelly sings beautifully; it is one of the aspects of herself that she likes most. When I asked her earlier in the interview where she learned to sing, she replied: "My momma . . . She sings. I grew up in the choir. They said no kids in the choir, but I was in the choir ever since I was little . . . a arm baby. And ever since then, I just been singing. Hear my momma sing, I just be trying to sing like her. If folks on the radio sing, I try to sing it like them. Now I got my own voice."

In an effort to find her own voice, Kelly had to go through the process of distinguishing herself from her mom. Kelly shares her mom's name, her voice, and her ambition, but she does not want to be abused. One behavior that she said they share in common is "always caring for folks . . . and then, half the time they don't care about you." Through the metaphor of breaking away from momma and going off to college, Kelly was figuring out what lessons her family had taught her. And, in the process, she was negotiating who she would become.

Conclusion

Family in Hamilton remains unparalleled in its influence on young people's lives. From the time they are born, young people are socialized as members of families; and their membership in these groups, whether they be nuclear families, extended families, blended families, kinship groups, or households, tells people in the community who they are and, unfortunately, who they will likely become. Sylvia Yanagisako's ethnographic work shows how family for Japanese Americans often takes precedence over individuals as significant units of analysis.[15] Through the process of conducting her fieldwork, Yanagisako discovered that "the act of constructing a list of one's 'relatives' was interpreted by [her] informants as being an 'American' phenomenon in which the appropriate units are 'persons' rather than 'families' and that entails choice rather than ascription."[16] Like Yanagisako, over the course of my fieldwork, I learned that young people and adults in Hamilton recognize families as ascribed wholes, and therefore constitute relevant units of analysis in and of themselves. As a member of a Hamilton family, I had to manage the perception of my ascriptions daily.

Hamilton families exhibit similarities in their patterns of residence, household composition, extended family networks and intergenerational activities. The compound lifestyle, where many related households share the same space (often on a dirt road), creates close-knit kin groups who spend a great deal of time together, intergenerationally. The prevalence of permanent and temporary child exchange that I observed is reminiscent of earlier ethnographies on African American kinship, such as Carol Stack's classic text, *All Our Kin.*

The character of Hamilton's 258 black households (or 189 black families) varies greatly. While 55 percent of black people in Hamilton live below the poverty level, there is still a great deal of socioeconomic diversity that affects everything from mealtimes to relationships with parents. In addition, "blended families," or families where legal divorce or remarriage has taken place, complicate the landscape. While Stack perceptively and justly concludes that the "highly adaptive structural features of . . . black families comprise a resilient response to the social-economic conditions of poverty,"[17] focusing on the actual young bodies in motion reveals these features to be meaning-laden, and carry with them discomforts, contradictions, and emotion.

One seventeen-year-old young woman, Kelly, gives us a glimpse into what belonging to a family can feel like—the ups, downs, closeness, and distance. Kelly helps us to comprehend that education, especially education about identity, begins "at home." As her story illustrates, all other lessons she learned at school, in the community, at church, and from popular culture were filtered through the lens of her family circumstances and the lessons that *they* have taught her. Kelly's story alludes to one central element of adolescent identity in Hamilton: the tension between the structures as they exist, and the avenues for expression that they provide youngsters. These themes will be addressed more fully in chapters 5 and 6. The next chapter, however, will proceed with Kelly telling us about her formal education at Jay Ellis School, "The Last Chance School."

Chapter 2
Descendants of a First Choice School

Do you like Jay Ellis? It's alright . . . I been there every since I was three . . . and since
we was staying in the country already, I wasn't going to go to another school. Till
when we moved and my mom was going to make me go to Carlyle. But I didn't want
to go, 'cause I didn't know nobody. Then, I thought if I was going to go up there, my
grades was going to drop 'cause they on another level than Jay Ellis classes are. So
I stayed at this one. But it's an alright school. It just needs some improvements in
different areas . . . To me, they need a music department. We got a sometimey choir
. . . And need a library, need more books, more activities for students to do, instead of
them hanging in the gym all the time . . .

Do you think people have a good opinion about Jay Ellis? Not everybody. Not even
some teachers at Jay Ellis . . . Some people say Jay Ellis is at the bottom, and we don't
learn nothing . . . and we don't have nothing, and stuff like that. *Do you think it's true?*
. . . I can't put it into words. Like Carlyle, they have, they get more stuff than we do,
because they have more money supplies, say, from the parents and our parents don't
too much put in money at the school, 'cause they don't come to PTO meetings. No
support. I'll say, no support. *Why do you think parents don't go to PTO meetings at Jay
Ellis?* Some either be at work, some say they just don't care . . . my momma be at work,
though. She used to go, but she working in the morning or in the evening. When she
working in the morning, she get off in the evening and she be tired. So, she usually
just ask Ms. Samuel what happened, and what they talking about, and what's going
on at school . . .

Do you think Ms. Moore's a good principal? In a way . . . she has uhh . . . to me she has
a little slight favoritism to some folks. Then, she's kinda too nice to some folks. She
let a lot of folks in the school trying to give 'em a last chance. Cause that's what some
folks call Jay Ellis, "Last Chance School." And then she find out there are like bad students and she don't want to kick 'em out, so she'll wait till they do something wrong
too many times. Then she'll want to put them out. She's a nice person, I'll say. In a way.

Jay Ellis School is the small rural school that most of the black children from
Hamilton attend. The school includes all primary and secondary grades—

from the Head Start pre-kindergarten program all the way up through the twelfth grade. The central place that Jay Ellis occupies in the lives of young people and within the Hamilton community cannot be overstated. Not only is Jay Ellis the place where children spend half of their days for up to fifteen years, but this structure has become the public representation of black Hamilton, itself: its history, its future, and its residents.

Race and racism are two things that polite southerners do not often make time to discuss, especially in an environment that is dominated by the richness of black life. But when their children attend Jay Ellis, Hamiltonians cannot ignore race.[1] Omnipresent football culture places the unequal distribution of resources under a stark light, newspaper articles bring white public opinion of Jay Ellis into plain view, and national "No Child Left Behind" policies and statewide graduation examinations thrust Hamilton children into comparison with an imaginary "mainstream." Jay Ellis, then, is not only directly influential in the lives of adolescents, but the discourse in which it is embedded indirectly impacts these adolescents and provides their families with an entrée into discussions of race, racism, economic disparity, and public representations of self. Jay Ellis, as a contentious space, embodies these issues when it is discussed around kitchen tables, in newspapers, among white community members, and at football games, among many other venues.

Kelly Lawrence was a senior when she described Jay Ellis in the preceding excerpt, having attended Jay Ellis ever since she was three years old. Her portrayal of Jay Ellis as a place that she wanted to attend, but that was rife with problems, is strikingly similar to the way the other adolescents whom I interviewed and had informal conversations with described it. Using Kelly's voice as a backdrop for the next two chapters, then, reveals that Jay Ellis students have a perceptive grasp of the many facets that comprise their schooling situation, even when they don't realize it. Kelly's depiction encapsulates many of the central themes that I will address in the forthcoming chapters. All of these themes explore the same question: How does the Jay Ellis school structure and the larger school system educate Hamilton's youth, impact their identity, and influence their life course? The first aspect of the school that impacts the students' social location, whether or not they know it, is its history.

Jay Ellis: The First Choice School and Its History

Thankfully, before I got to know Jay Ellis as the Last Chance School—before I started reading newspaper articles and overhearing conversation about it, before I talked to parents and burned-out teachers, before I knew who the superintendent was, and before students confided their unmet hopes in me—I was fortunate to experience Jay Ellis with fresh eyes and ears. Thus, my first, rather naïve, impression of Jay Ellis was that it was a bucolic country school, where positive self-images were formed and where black students and a predominantly black teaching staff worked together in a safe space.

My cousin Lewis and his wife, Carrie, whom I described in the last chapter, were instrumental in integrating me into the Jay Ellis community. Before I went to the school during the school day, they invited me to a Friday night football game held at the school. And when I arrived, I was astonished. For a regular high school game, it felt like a major event. Not only were the stands packed with the family members of the players, but, more surprisingly, community members who had no children at the school were cheering and chanting just the same as the parents. There had to have been over two hundred people on our side of the field. The snack stand sold hot dogs, popcorn, nachos, candy, and beverages to all of these guests. Overall, the energy was kinetic. From this football game on, I was captivated by Jay Ellis.

That night, under the dim little light next to the side entrance of the school, my cousin Lewis introduced me to the guidance counselor, Ms. Smith, and told her that I wanted to do research about the school. He also told her that she should expect me to stop by the school sometime during the next week. The air was moist and heavy, filling the space between us. I was nervous because I didn't want people to be suspicious of my intentions or hesitant about my impending intrusion. But I can remember that, although it was dark and I was slightly discombobulated, trying to take it all in—the lights, the smiles, the faces I would likely see again—Ms. Smith welcomed me, an outsider, into the community without hesitation. And she immediately began to talk about how beneficial my presence could be for the students.

The next week, I had Lewis meet me at the school to reintroduce me to Ms. Smith. In the daylight, I had the chance to examine the school anew. I drove through the rocky driveway and parked on the paved parking lot in front of the school. The school building is a neat, simple brick building, with two long halls. From the outside, it is shaped like a right angle, and the main entrance to the school is almost at its vertex. Once one opens the main doors, to the left down a single hall is the "high school hall," where all of the classrooms for the upper grades are located. Straight ahead through the doors is the cafeteria/gymnasium/stage. And to the right are a small main office, a library, and then "the elementary hall" down the vertical side of the right angle.

During that initial daylight introduction to the school, I visited with Ms. Smith in her office, which also doubled as the computer room and hosted keyboarding class. In the light I could see Ms. Smith up close. She had a light, honey-brown complexion and a short tuck-under hairstyle, one of the few things that revealed her age (her hair looked too neat and well coifed for her to be as young as one might think). Ms. Smith was still bright eyed and perky, despite how long she had worked at Jay Ellis. As she greeted me with a warm smile, she inquired about my family connections to Hamilton and shared what she knew of my family; let me know that she understood that Brown University was an Ivy League school and what "that meant"; promised to find me a home in the school; and volunteered to talk to the principal about what I could do in the school.

Throughout our interaction, I witnessed the organized chaos typical of her office—the phone ringing, teachers stopping by for coffee, and students wandering in to ask her for one thing or another. The dust in corners and on her desktop trinkets revealed that it was a space of haste and action, not of fiddling and mulling. I hardly remember a day that I actually saw Ms. Smith sitting down in her office. She was warm and cordial with the students and her intimate relationship with the students was apparent; they trusted her and she loved them. I quickly learned that Ms. Smith was an institution at the school. In my mind, I had already written my ethnography. The school chapter, at least, was going to focus on the benefits of the small school model. Much of the literature about urban education was pointing in this direction. I thought, "what amazing lessons we could learn from a rural school in which children are treated as family members."

After leaving Ms. Smith's office, I stopped by the Head Start room in the elementary hall. This is one of the federal Head Start programs, housed at Jay Ellis, although not technically run by the school. Lewis's wife, Carrie, had been a teacher there for sixteen years and is another "institution" at Jay Ellis. When I knocked on the door, she welcomed me and introduced me to the students, some of whom greeted me with a hug. They were an energetic group of three-, four- and 5-year-old children. And I got a chance to witness my first "Walk the Walk, Talk the Talk" game. In this game, the students were required to sit in a circle and each one had the chance to walk down the middle of the circle where big laminated numbers, shapes, and letters were arranged in a straight line on the floor. As they stood on each item, they had to identify it. If they got stuck and couldn't figure it out, the students clapped their hands one time and yelled out, "Walk!" If they completed their path, the students yelled out, "Walk the Walk and Talk the Talk!" The game included everything from pensive facial expressions, to giggling, to hitting. I tried to catch as many "Walk the Walk, Talk the Talk" games as I could because I was fascinated by a game that was so much fun and reinforced the major educational targets at the same time.

The Head Start room was brightly decorated and well stocked with toys, games, workstations, crafts, letters, and numbers. I was thoroughly impressed. Over the course of my time at Jay Ellis, I stopped in to visit and observe the Head Start room many times. One day, a well-dressed child named Derrick told me "look at my bling," while pulling at his mini-designer shirt. Another day, I watched a little boy whom Carrie and Sheila described to me as a "drug baby" punch a little girl in the face and show no remorse at all. It was never dull in the Head Start room because it was always organized, always exciting, and I always left feeling that, despite whatever stresses Carrie and Sheila experienced, the students were getting such a great start with them.

My somewhat ignorant, uncomplicated early assessment of Jay Ellis must be understood in terms of my background. Having conducted research in urban schools in Providence, Rhode Island, and having some experience in urban schools in Baltimore City, the school seemed ideal. It was so safe that people wandered in and out of the school building without being stopped or asked to go through a metal detector. Teachers not only knew the students, but also knew their families, and the life of a student seemed relatively uncomplicated.

Carrie was the first person who, within my first week at Jay Ellis, let me know that my perception of paradise was just an illusion. She explained that she and others did not like the principal, Ms. Moore. Ms. Moore was younger than she looked. A dark-brown-skinned woman with short hair and an angular face, she generally wore a dress and shoes that could double as nurse's shoes. She was sturdy, but not large, and her body language made her seem more suited to being the manager of a nursing home than the principal of a school with rambunctious kids. When she came to football games, she looked uncomfortable, as if she borrowed someone else's clothes. According to Carrie, Ms. Moore admitted anyone to the school, picked and chose favorites, and had no control over student discipline. Carrie was the first of many people to tell me that the school would do better with a "strong man" as its principal. Ms. Smith weighed in with similar assessments, and soon, by virtue of my sheer excitement over the school, teachers, parents, and students found it necessary to let me know, "you'll see," meaning that you'll eventually discover the downsides of Jay Ellis. And I did. But before I highlight all of the complications and contradictions that I observed over the course of my fifteen-month field experience, I must give attention to the benefits of Jay Ellis, especially since these are the least espoused truths.

As I remarked in the introduction, Mr. Edwards, the high school English teacher, was the first one to give me a copy of the infamous No Child Left Behind article written about Jay Ellis in the spring of 2003. The students told me that Mr. Edwards "didn't play," but they didn't have to tell me, I already knew that just through osmosis and observation. "Janking" is a term that means telling jokes about someone, similar to playing the dozens, a well-documented feature of African American vernacular English. I witnessed Mr. Edwards use this technique, quite effectively, to relay his subject matter to the students and maintain order, but this smile could turn straight in a second, and that round body could go from jolly to stern. Hearing his concerns about the article broadened my point of view and encouraged me to investigate the history of the school. According to Mr. Edwards:

Well, I don't know how we were chosen. I don't have any idea. But the lady came last year . . . and umm did the interview, and she basically interviewed most of the staff, students, parents, and community members, different people or whatever. And honestly speaking, when she interviewed us, I was not . . . I didn't know her total motive for interviewing. I just thought it was about a struggling school or a school that may not have been doing all it could do and blah, blah, blah. So, my opinions were honest, genuine, about that school—[for example] since I've been here, what we have been able to achieve in spite of the things that may or may not be available to us.

And that we have been able to succeed academically. And some of the most prominent people in Carlyle, business owners, otherwise, are graduates of Jay Ellis. We have graduates in all fields all over the country. And, ummm, she was concerned about the physical plant. And, so I told her that in 1966 when this school was built most students were living in trailers, or substandard housing with outdoor toilet facilities and all those things. So even with this school—the way she was trying to make the plant be or whatever—I said this was a safe place for them because this was so different from home. But, she just decided that she was going to rework the article to make it seem as if there was nothing, nothing good ever came out of Jay Ellis.

I was glad that Mr. Edwards, early on, called to my attention the importance of the history of the community in understanding the education of Hamilton children. It led me to discover that irrespective of my own somewhat naïve appreciation of the school, Jay Ellis was not always a "Last Chance School," not even to the indigenous community members. In fact, the recent incarnation of this last chance identity largely disregards the history of the school and fails to place the education of rural African Americans into historical context. Over the course of my fieldwork, I learned that for generations of Hamiltonians, school signified a departure from the former generations' lot of picking cotton and represented a chance for them to achieve success and gain dignity. Moreover, my informants described the schooling of rural African Americans in Hamilton as an extension of family and community activities. From their recollections, it seemed that formal education was not distant, institutional, and assessment driven; it was an intimate experience in which individual African American youth, side by side with their closest friends and family, went to a place that they believed could genuinely improve their lives.[2]

I would characterize formal education in Hamilton as having gone through three distinct periods: the one-room schoolhouse grassroots phase, the Rosenwald School secondary education era, and the current Jay Ellis School chapter, marked simultaneously by the greatest potential and most constraints. The first phase actually began in the early twentieth century when Hamilton's small children were educated in one of the local churches. Then, in the 1930s the African American community members built their own one-room schoolhouse, which they refer to as "The Hamilton school." When the Hamilton School was built, only two black families owned cars, so together children walked to school. The school was located right in the center of Hamilton a few yards from the two churches and around the corner from the two local African American country stores. That site still stands and was renovated several years ago and made into a community center that distributes lunches over the summers, hosts community meetings, and can be rented for private functions.

Retired sergeant Jacob Daniels described his experience in the one-room school:

So when you went to the Hamilton school, you went there from kindergarten through sixth grade or through fifth grade? I went there from second grade through the sixth grade. Cause I went down to Moscow [church] for two years. *And what was school like at Moscow and then at the Hamilton school?* We was required to get our assignments and we was also given homework to do. Not just once a week, but every day. We would have to—they would give us something particular, like speeches and things of that nature. In fact, its one of the things Ms. Arrington made us do . . . [recites impromptu Sam Walter Foss's iconic poem, *House by the Side of the Road*] . . .

We had to learn not only that, but other things that build, to me, as I've learned, build character and understanding among your fellow man.

And was it a one-room schoolhouse? Yes. One-room schoolhouse with a big pot heater sitting in the middle. And we had to go and get the wood to keep warm, to make a fire to keep warm. The school board only supported the white people. They didn't support the black people. So in other words, we'd be walking to school. And they'd pass us in their school bus going to school. *How did that make you all feel?* We didn't think nothing of it. We figured that it was a system, a way of life. And we lived that way of life as long as they didn't mess with us. And we didn't even worry about it, see.

So when you were in school in one room, were you divided off by ages or everyone was all together? Uhh, in the elementary you was divided by ages, see . . . As you advanced in grade, then you were divided by grade. *And there was a different teacher for every group or . . . ?* No, you had two teachers, and they would teach in one class . . . *So you all were just well behaved, you would sit and do your work? Did you cut up?* Well, we had fun [laughter]. But, once you got in that classroom, the teacher had your attention cause if he didn't [smacking noise] . . . *you would get wacked.* Once you got in that classroom, Ms. Arrington didn't play. Period.

It amazed me while I was in Hamilton that this part of its history was not invoked more at the school or in conversations I engaged in about education. A retired teacher, who returned to Jay Ellis to teach the high school students a supplementary English class and various elements of black heritage, used to mention this sort of history in his class. But I never read about it in any printed material. Nor did I hear it mentioned at a school assembly or at a graduation. I certainly didn't hear about it from the white community members who criticized Jay Ellis. I never heard a student describe or mention this history to me, even when I asked about Jay Ellis. For me, it was sobering to realize that less than one hundred years ago the formal education of blacks in Hamilton was completely self-determined and community driven.

The second period of schooling for black Hamilton youth came about with the creation of one of the famous Rosenwald schools, on the land where Jay Ellis now rests. The Rosenwald school building program was founded by Julius Rosenwald, president of Sears, Roebuck and Company from 1908 to 1922, and Booker T. Washington, principal of the Tuskegee Normal and Industrial Institute. Washington, who devoted his life to self-help for African Americans, approached Rosenwald in 1912 about providing matching teacher-training grants for schools that followed Tuskegee's model. When the funds had been distributed and there was a $2,800 surplus, Rosenwald agreed to let Washington use the funds to build six rural schools in Alabama. In 1914, Rosenwald gave $30,000 toward the construction of one hundred rural schools, and in 1916 he aided in the construction of two hundred more. Each of these building grants was $300 and had to be matched by funds that the communities raised.

Over time, the Rosenwald fund underwent many internal changes. For example, the fund began to require a minimum school term in order to qualify for its matching construction grants. This encouraged school boards to extend the school year for African Americans (it was usually truncated) and bolster teachers' salaries. What remained consistent throughout the variations in Rosenwald's agenda was the concept that personal sacrifices and self-help were essential to the survival and effectiveness of the schools. By all accounts, his and Washington's vision was successful. According to the National Historic Trust for Preservation:

> By 1928, one in every five rural schools for black students in the South was a Rosenwald school, and these schools housed one third of the region's rural black schoolchildren and teachers. At the program's conclusion in 1932, it had produced 4,977 new schools, 217 teachers' homes, and 163 shop buildings, constructed at a total cost of $28,408,520 to serve 663,615 students in 883 counties of 15 states.[3]

Hamilton is a part of this critical historical movement. According to Sergeant Daniels, the land for the school was donated by Jay Ellis, a white man who may have been sympathetic to blacks because he was married to, or at least permanently partnered with, a black woman. When the Rosenwald School was built, it was a beacon of hope for the black community. Students took pride in traveling several miles by foot to attend high school. Sergeant Daniels fondly recalled the going to school ritual, as well as his and his peers' mindset at that time:

> We had to walk to school. Your parents bought you your school clothing, church clothing, and everyday clothing. You had one suit, or whatever you wore to church, that's what you had. You had your school clothing. You had one pair of good shoes. And some other clothes and things you worked around the house in. And the point is, like, in summer time we didn't wear shoes, we went barefooted. [laughter]. So we just had . . . just had a lot of fun. And we had to walk to school when school started. *How far was school from where you lived?* OK, from Hamilton, to Rosenwald, I walked that everyday. That's about three . . . about four miles. *Wow . . .*
>
> It would just be a road full of us. *How long does four miles take?* I don't know, well shoot, we would start out—I guess school would take you in at eight o'clock, and we'd start out at about 7 o'clock and we'd be there. Yeah, see that's another thing: time. We didn't worry about it. We just knew what time to get up and get ready. We knew we had to walk to school. And the children . . . well, we were just like one big family in Hamilton. You had the Stars, the Washingtons, the Daniels, the Jones. Then you had the Turners, the Clearwaters, the Ellises, and the Thomases . . . And we, you see all of the young people in church now? You see I went to school with their mothers and fathers . . .

The feeling of family and community, then, continued, even as the school moved farther away from the community's center. All of the Rosenwald students made the trek to school together. According to my informants, at that time, many of the families were still sharecropping land for whites, or planting cotton on their own land. The school year would begin late, in October, because youngsters were required to harvest cotton. One student James said his grandmother tells him, "how they used to pick cotton and stuff. Tell us we got it made cause we ain't got to do all the stuff they used to do."

The third and final significant juncture in education for blacks in Hamilton began in 1966 when the Rosenwald School burned down, and the county erected Jay Ellis School in its place. The stone marker outside of Jay Ellis reads in big bold letters, "Jay Ellis School, 1966, George C. Wallace Governor." Wallace is the infamous governor who stood at the door of the University of Alabama to block two black students from attending three years before Jay Ellis was built. The placard that bears his name is an apt symbol of the many struggles the school has faced since that time and the many complications it continues to work through.

By the time Jay Ellis was rebuilt by the county, several key events had taken place nationally and locally that impacted Hamilton education. Most significantly, the landmark *Brown vs. The Board of Education* Supreme Court decision, which deemed that the previous "separate but equal" Jim Crow precedent was unconstitutional, had already transpired in 1954. By 1966, the county had assumed responsibility of Jay Ellis, and it was brought under the county umbrella with the other four county schools. When Jay Ellis was rebuilt, then, it remained a fully black school because the white children in Hamilton had long since attended the high school in Carlyle. But this meant that Jay Ellis, which was "naturally segregated," had to be built to equal the quality of the white county school about forty-five minutes away. The physical plant that is so derided now was a major upgrade in 1966, and, as Mr. Edwards pointed out, it was far ahead of most other physical structures in the students' immediate lives.

School integration was not fully enforced until the 1970s, and for Jay Ellis that just meant faculty integration. As Ms. Smith and others described it to me, during the first years of the new school building, Jay Ellis was the premier place for black Hamiltonians to be educated. The stories that residents shared from that era made it sound as if the late sixties and seventies were the glory days. Ms. Smith recounted how she loved teaching at Jay Ellis in her early days there. She came as the business teacher in 1973 and became the guidance counselor in 1977.

How did you like it when you first got there? When I first got there? I LOVED it! It was nice. We had about seven hundred students for one thing. *Seven hundred! Oh my goodness.* When I got there, I taught typing and shorthand, business math. I didn't miss a day for the first five years. *Wow.* I liked it just that much. And it was always—we were always short of funds. We needed more of everything. But, people worked well together. It was just a different atmosphere . . .

Ms. Carter, myself, and Ms. Lamont, we all came at the same time. And we were the last of that group. But people were, you know . . . people. They would tell you off. They'd just tell you what they were thinking. And you would fuss and carry on, but then that would be the end of that . . . And we accomplished a lot with the little we had. The kids learned, they went away to school, and now you know they come back and they've done relatively well.

Who were some of the graduates you can think of? We have five people that work at the Redstone arsenal in Huntsville. That's the Rocket Center. Tennessee Valley Authority: there are three that I know of. We just did well for the little bit [of resources] that [we had] . . .

Ms. Smith was able to rattle off a detailed list of several Jay Ellis alumni and the occupations they have held over the years: including a local mortician, a doctor, a lawyer, an engineer, several social workers, a bank officer, and other successful alumni. She went on to say:

I'm just going to tell you the truth. Most of the black people doing halfway well in Carlyle came from Jay Ellis. Maybe with the exception of Samuel Lambert, who went to Carlyle High. Mitch Bailey from city council went to Jay Ellis [too].

Not only did Ms. Smith relish listing some of the prominent Jay Ellis graduates, but she enjoyed describing in vivid detail the activities the school used to provide for the students. They used to sponsor, for example:

[The] 4H [club], science fairs . . . I always had what we called pride week. That's a week-long program of activities, and I'd invite somewhat successful students back. And they would talk to the students about what they did, and how they got to be where they were. I'd have people from the community come in. Just quilting, crafts, so they wouldn't lose all of their little heritage. Ladies showed them how to do quilting, syrup making, basket weaving. I can't remember now. Stuff like that. We took a day for careers, a day for talent and fashion, especially when we had home economics, they got to do their little fashion show with whatever they had made. They had food shows. Different ones made different things. You could get a little taste of this, and a little taste of that. Umm, that's about it.

We had a sports day, of course. We even had one man from the community . . . I forgot his name now, but he played in the old negro leagues. We got a lot of different paraphernalia. Stuff like that . . . *Mr. Edwards was telling me that the classes used to compete a lot more, too* ... Mmm hmm. We used to have little bowls, academic bowls, and they wanted to learn. Now, there's no desire to learn. Well, I won't say that. You know there's some. But not the way it was then ...

I think that one of the issues now is that teachers don't have to do clubs. Principals used to assign teachers things you had to do. We even just tried to have things like talent shows, fashion shows, just for entertainment. We used to have beauty walks. Most of the time that was Ms. Carter and myself. We had fall festivals, you know for the kids, spring festivals ...

Ms. Smith retired at the end of my first school year at Jay Ellis in May 2004. To me, her retirement marked a major transition from a particular era at the school. By that time, I was well aware of many of the political situations unraveling at Jay Ellis, some of which had contributed to her departure. But over the course of that year and the next, I still saw the tangible benefits of the small school. We didn't have the hustle and bustle of seven hundred students, but the school held a fall festival in the gym with music and vendors. The retired coach for whom the school stadium is named organized monthly character assemblies. Although they were a little lackluster, I did hear a few good speakers, and students seemed to remember them for at least one day. Homecomings and graduations were filled with excitement. As a matter of fact, the graduations (held in the gymnasium) were packed, with over two hundred attendees, standing room only. Both years that I attended the commencement, the speeches given by the valedictorian and salutatorian were thoughtful and well delivered.

One of the things that stood out most, to me, as a benefit of the small school is the ability to solve problems creatively, on a case-by-case basis. The valedictorian of 2005 was a bright, focused young lady from Carlyle named Sabrina. A resident of Carlyle, she had one problem; her temper kept getting her into trouble. When I came to the school in the mornings, Ms. Smith often reported what had happened while I was gone between Sabrina and someone at the school. Sabrina was a live wire, a light-brown bundle of energy in a miniature package. She competed in the Miss Christmas Carlyle pageant while I was in Hamilton and was crowned "Ms. JEH" in her senior year, but she was not a stereotypical beauty queen. Rather than pamper her natural beauty, she preferred to study, and study diligently.

Well, Ms. Smith arranged for a professional to come and conduct an anger management workshop, and that promptly ended Sabrina's problems. Not only did that arrest her anger issues, but she thanked Ms. Smith for stopping her from going down a destructive path and was happy to share her progress with me. Ms. Smith and Sabrina had an amusing relationship. Sabrina often appeared in Ms. Smith's office to ask to use the phone or to request some other favor. Most of the time, Ms. Smith obliged, but not without giving her the "once over" first and letting her know if her hair was "a mess" or her clothes looked disheveled. Ms. Smith told me that over the years she has "combed heads, ironed clothes," and done it all. That was precisely the beauty of her role in the school.[4]

When I asked students whom I interviewed whether they liked Jay Ellis, responses ranged from "yes," to "it's alright," to "it's OK." Sabrina described the feeling of Jay Ellis this way:

> I think for areas like this, a K–12 school is good for like anybody 'cause it gives you a feeling of going from home to home. Instead of calling it school it's more like a home, because you learn but at the same time you're getting a family environment.

Darnel Taylor, the captain of the football team, also said that he liked Jay Ellis because it is small.

> *Do you like school there?* Yes ma'am. *Why?* Cause I—it's a smaller school and you can learn more, smaller classes rather than bigger classes. And we have fun. Enjoyable. Enjoyable school. *Have you always been at Jay Ellis?* [Yes, I'm a] Head Start baby . . .

Darnel's opinion that a smaller school was more enjoyable was echoed by the students again and again. Missy, who attended another school for a few years, put it this way:

> *Do you like it?* I love it! [Laughter] *You love it—why do you love it?* Umm, it's small, everybody knows everybody, it's not who did this, and who is that, and who is that? With a lot of new students coming, we still get to know them, 'cause it's a small atmosphere. *Like compared to Livingston, you like it better than Livingston?* Yes. Cause some of the classes be downstairs, some of them be upstairs, some of them be in another wing. And they be like "who is the new girl, who is the new girl?" When I first got there, they was like, "who is that, who is that?" And I was like I don't like that. At Jay Ellis, you just sit down. You be right by the office and the gym. You sit down, go to the office or the counselor's office and be like "this the new girl." And then somebody will go ask for her name and they'll spread the word.

I sometimes felt that when I asked students if they liked Jay Ellis, they were so used to defending the school that they were self-programmed to say yes; the default answer was, "I like it because it's a small school and you can learn more." Students repeated that mantra even when their faces looked pained to utter the words. This is why I believe Kelly's response to the school best integrates students' true feelings about the school and the reality of the Jay Ellis experience: "*Do you like Jay Ellis?* It's alright . . . I been there every since I was three . . . and since we was staying in the country already, I wasn't going to go to another school."

These phrases reveal the simple, profound truth about Jay Ellis: it is a country school designed for Hamilton's black children. Many of them "been there ever since [they] was three." Some of the students told me that they are uncertain if it's the "best" education, but that it's comfortable. And most of them said they like going to school with their family members. During fifteen months of participant observation, I saw students benefit from and respond well to the small school environment. And at other times, I witnessed them be disappointed by the system and feel trapped by their limited options. I think that despite whatever frustrations students feel at Jay Ellis, they sense that Carlyle High is a city school designed for white students, not for them.

In the final analysis, whether students say they like Jay Ellis or do not, by attending it they become part of the living history of African American schooling in the rural South. Education as an intimate experience is part and parcel of what it has meant to be a rural, southern African American over the last one hundred years,[5] especially in Hamilton. In fact, in order to fully understand "The Last Chance School" as an intricately composed public identity, which is negatively impacting the students' education, one must first acknowledge how the school is interwoven with the history of education for rural southern African Americans. Upon recognition of such a rich history, both the naïve observer, like me, and the truly entrenched community member, like Mr. Edwards, must appreciate that Jay Ellis is far from the last choice; for many in the past and present it indeed has comprised a worthy first choice. Mr. Edwards summarizes this argument well:

To me, that's the whole story behind our race. We may have had the most rough or the lowest upbringing, you know what I mean? Just minimum to eat, minimum to wear, minimum place to live. But that didn't stop you from wanting something in life and succeeding . . . Out of all we may not have gotten done, in the physical plant, we have offered advanced diplomas, our kids have gone to college, we have doctors, lawyers, pharmacists, chemists, engineers, school teachers, principals, you name it, people with ranking position in the military. You name it, we have it—business owners, major players. And they totally ignored all that in the article to paint a picture that we were the worst school in the United States. And that really just bothered me, 'cause I know schools that are in worse shape than we are.

But There Are Limits

As important as it is to highlight a few of the many positive aspects of the Jay Ellis experience, it is equally as important to tell the truth about the limitations of the small school model and pinpoint the historical reality in which the school size is embedded. In the last section, I described the final phase of schooling in Hamilton as marked by the erection of the new school building in 1966, after the old Rosenwald School had burned down. As I indicated, the enhanced facility was both a symbolic and a tangible leap into a new league of education for Hamilton's adolescents.

That juncture in Jay Ellis's history coincided with a significantly more pronounced sense of school options in education. Prior to the gradual enforcement of desegregation, white students in Carlyle and Hamilton attended Carlyle High School; black students in Carlyle went to A. J. Cobb, which is now an integrated middle school, but was then the K–12 school for black students; and black students from Hamilton attended Rosenwald.

There was some choice, however, involved in which school black students from Carlyle and Hamilton attended, even during segregation. I heard of a few cases in which black Hamiltonians sent their children to A. J. Cobb. But prior to the forced integration of the Carlyle school system, the exchange operated much more in the other direction. Frustrated with racism and the blatant Jim Crow Carlyle school system, black parents in Carlyle sometimes chose to send their children to Jay Ellis. One black studies professor, who wrote an autobiography of her life, including her time growing up in Carlyle, described one such instance that involved her brother. She described her brother as quiet and shy and said that when the black principal of A. J. Cobb began to take issue with him, as he had done with her and her older brother, her younger brother made the decision to go to Jay Ellis, despite her mother's concern about the family reputation.

Her brother, Saul, graduated from Jay Ellis in 1962 as valedictorian of his class, one of the many members of the class who chose to commute from Carlyle. In 1975, however, school choice was taken away from Carlyle residents and left solely to Hamilton residents. This sudden power shift worked against Jay Ellis. The school enrollment dropped almost instantly, changing Jay Ellis from a small school to a very small school and severely curtailing its resources. I asked Ms. Smith about the decrease in enrollment, which was a well-discussed issue at Jay Ellis:

When did the enrollments drop? Was it steady over the years or did it all of a sudden drop?
No, it all of a sudden dropped in about 1975. That's when the courts said that students could travel in to Carlyle, but they could not travel outside of the city school system

into the county school system. Now, the Carlyle school system pushed for that, you know, because they were losing a lot of students. *Oh they were?* Mmm hmm. All the black students were coming out to Jay Ellis, because they made A. J. Cobb, which had been the all-black high school, into a middle school. *Right.* That was forcing them to go to the white high school.

You know you get paid money depending on your average daily attendance. And if most of your students are going out, then they [Carlyle city schools] were losing quite a bit of money. So once they [black Carlyle students] couldn't ride the bus anymore, they didn't have transportation. *So they stayed in Carlyle?* Mmm hmm. *Oh, so a lot of our students were from Carlyle and they weren't allowed to go to Jay Ellis?* They were not allowed, plus they didn't have transportation. Sometimes if they had transportation they would try to come. *So then in 1975, 1976, it went down to how many from seven hundred students?* It slowly dwindled off to about four hundred something, then three hundred something. And at one time we got so—I don't know whether we had two hundred and fifty students. And then, of course, we lost a lot of teacher units. And then we didn't really have enough teachers to do anything with. *You lost teacher units, what does that mean?* The numbers of teachers you have is based on your average daily attendance. So if your average daily attendance drops, then your number of teachers drops. A teacher is one unit.

Two major changes transpired as a result of the dramatic decrease in en-rollment. The first, most obvious, one is that the school's capabilities be-came limited because it could not afford to support many of the activities it used to. Gradually the fairs, programs, and speakers that used to abound dwindled. Moreover, Jay Ellis became handicapped in terms of financial and human capital. Not only did the overall school tax dollars decrease, but also teachers were stretched thinner, with each teacher taking on more subjects, even though there were fewer students. And the effect snowballed such that Hamilton parents began to send their children to Carlyle High because of the decrease in Jay Ellis's resources. Naturally, every element of the school suffered, including its morale.

The second major result of the decrease in enrollment because of Car-lyle residents' forced attendance of Carlyle High, was that the gaze between black city and country folks that had always existed became more malicious.[6] As a result, the social ties that united people in the struggle against racism dwindled. In her autobiography, the same black studies professor who was mentioned above alludes to this love/hate relationship between black folks from Carlyle and Hamilton. She described her own experience growing up, laughing at the "country" folk, who she now deems to have been superior. She writes that, in hindsight, those country children had arisen at 4:00 a.m.

to do chores before school even started, and that her brother did the best thing to go to Jay Ellis where he was respected and made real friends.

Prior to the enforcement of Carlyle students' attendance of city schools, exchanges like this one provided social cohesion between blacks from the city and country. Even though the tendency might have been for the city residents to judge the country residents, that instinct was tempered by the exchange of resources that took place. It is more difficult to marginalize another group when one needs its resources. In addition, when Carlyle students attended Jay Ellis, shared race and coping with racism were the axes of commonality.[7] Over the years, class has overtaken race such that black students in Carlyle feel pressure to identify with white students at Carlyle on the basis of "supposed superiority," rather than identifying with Jay Ellis students based on race. Much more will be said about this phenomenon and its current impact on Jay Ellis in the next chapter. The important point here is that the decrease in school enrollment changed Jay Ellis from a small school to a "too small school." The reason behind the decrease in enrollment changed it from a small school, to an under-resourced school, subject to the scorn of city-dwelling blacks more than ever.

During the 2004–2005 school year, Jay Ellis's average daily attendance according the board of education was 230.3 students. This number is unrepresentatively low because it is based on the first forty days of the school year and many students begin Jay Ellis after that time, having transferred in from another school. But whatever the technical enrollment number was, during my time at Jay Ellis there were approximately three hundred students. In 2004–2005, the teaching staff was comprised of 17.6 teachers for the entire school, kindergarten through the twelfth grade. In this environment, the benefits of the small school are dwarfed. Yes, people know each other well in that environment. Yes, students might feel less stress and pressure to dress and to speak in a certain way. Yes, problems can be creatively solved on an individual basis. But, as I observed over the course of my fieldwork, this size is stressful on the administration and faculty members.

The principal, when describing the lack of resources, often pointed out that with just her and the secretary as the administrators in the school, when one of them went to check lunch tickets, the other one had to cover the phones. In fact, the principal's job seems nearly unmanageable when one considers that she had to complete all of the requisite paperwork for the county board of education, the paperwork for the state board of education, and the paperwork for the national No Child Left Behind Act related to standardized assessments by herself. A chance to carve out a vision for the school was eclipsed by mundane tasks that no one else could do.

The teachers on the high school hall endured the most stressful, overworked conditions. The social studies teacher, for example, taught six different grades (seventh–twelfth), and therefore six different subject matters each day of the week. In addition, he was the assistant coach of the football team, which held practice every day after school and played games every weekend. During the regular season, football games could be held up to an hour away, and he spent time making all of those journeys. Unfortunately, I observed that some of the teachers maintain their sanity by limiting their after-school involvement to almost no involvement and assigning "seat work" or "book work" many days in class.

The drawbacks that Kelly mentions in her assessment represent the students' desire for more resources and activities for themselves. For example, Kelly called the choir "sometimey," alluding to a desire for more regular choir rehearsals because she loved to sing. Her description of the choir was an understatement. In my two years there, I heard the choir sing only once, and Ms. Moore, the principal, held practice with the "members of the choir" the day before they sang. Kelly also said they needed more books and activities. Many students with whom I parleyed said they wanted a music department, but the school can neither afford instruments nor attract (or afford) a qualified music teacher. In consulting students, the issues that came up again and again were a need for more books, more school subjects, upgraded computers, a new gym, more teachers, televisions in every classroom, a band, sports other than football, basketball, and cheerleading, and more after-school clubs. Missy thought that students should have thirty minutes a day of counseling to talk about what's going on in their lives, an innovative but unlikely proposition.

The school facility, which was more than adequate when it was built in 1966, is still not dilapidated by any means. However, it cannot compare in quality or grandeur to the predominantly white county school that I had the opportunity to visit, which had a huge library, an open atrium, and quality televisions and computers, just to name a few of the differences. Overall, it has the look of a first-rate twenty-first-century school, while Jay Ellis has the look of a one-time first-rate twentieth-century school. James states it this way:

> *What other ways do you think it's a good or bad school?* It's a good school 'cause the
> classes real small and the teachers you know can explain better. It's a bad school
> 'cause of the facilities we got. We ain't advanced, with what all the other schools got.
> So there's good and bad.

One thing that I was able to witness first-hand was the disproportionate impact that single entities can have on the education of students at a small school like Jay Ellis. A highly ineffective mathematics teacher who taught at the school my first year successfully befuddled six grade levels' worth of math students. At first, I assumed that students exaggerated about this teacher picking favorites, talking about his personal life during class time, and teaching poorly. I became a believer after he accosted me in the hallway one day to tell me about the thousands of dollars he had spent gambling the previous weekend and how he had to find a woman down at the slots (not his wife) to console him. This was just one of many of the inappropriate conversations that I had with Mr. Buford, who was obviously addicted to gambling. Sadly, because mathematics learning is cumulative, the skills that students missed while in his classes had to be made up for somehow.

The incredible influence of individuals like the guidance counselor, Ms. Smith, might seem to be a positive element of the school. Indeed, she was able to do a lot more at a school like Jay Ellis, since she had a higher degree of autonomy and creative problem-solving ability than she might have had at a larger school with more bureaucratic restrictions. For example, within one week of when we first met, she consulted with all of the Jay Ellis high school teachers, got a list of the most problematic students on the high school hall, and arranged to have them meet with me twice a week, as a group, for tutoring sessions. However, it is precisely because of the magnitude of her influence that the school really lacked a valuable resource once she left.

The school experienced a similar setback with the departure of Mrs. Jimenez, the high school science teacher. She also was one of the prominent figures at Jay Ellis during my first year; she was easily noticeable because of her Cuban accent and her very energetic personality. As the only teacher at the school who hailed from outside of the United States, and for whom English was not her first language, the students learned a lot from her about diversity and appreciating various cultures. Kelly told me that Mrs. Jimenez lent her some Latin music CDs that inspired her to want to travel more in the future and to take salsa lessons. Mrs. Jimenez was also instrumental in planning the senior prom. Her presence was a joy because she was not one of the Jay Ellis naysayers. She believed in the students and loved the school. In fact, she always remarked how much she adored living in the countryside. Most important, she was an excellent, qualified science teacher. When she taught science, the students dissected frogs and pigs, participated in other types of labs, and received thorough lessons and well-structured tests.

Once Mrs. Jimenez left to move to Miami, where the rest of her extended family was living, the school system hastily replaced her with a teacher who did not have a teaching certificate and lacked experience in teaching science. On two different occasions, I observed Ms. Roberts's classes, and she taught virtually nothing at all. The day I attended the chemistry lab, her instruction was very confusing. She was making photocopies and setting the materials out while the students were waiting; and, of course, they found a way to entertain themselves, which happened to be by engaging in horseplay. When she finally started the lab, no one knew what to do, and at that point, there were only about fifteen minutes left in the class. It was a wasted period. When I asked one student, Letice, who her least favorite teacher was, she replied:

Ms. Roberts [the new science teacher]. *How come?* Cause we don't do nothing. *Did you used to like Ms. Jimenez?* We experimented in her class . . . dissected frogs, pigs. *Everybody says you don't do anything in Ms. Roberts's class, what does that mean?* No, we just sitting there. *You just sit there literally?* She sits at her desk and eat and talk about what need to be done at this school. That's why I think the ones that got to take this [statewide] science exam ain't gonna pass, cause she didn't teach them nothing.

Not all students completely disliked Ms. Roberts, though. To add further texture to the small school portrait, Ms. Roberts started a dance squad and a flag team when she came to the school. And that was the only physical activity available to the female students, aside from cheerleading and basketball. Despite bits of drama here and there, it was successful the first year for the dance and flag teams. The problem with Ms. Roberts was that she coached the flag team and did nothing else. As a result, when she was terminated at the end of the year, the dance and flag teams went with her. This is a perfect example of the trade-offs that often take place at a "too small school." Letting go of an unqualified science teacher unfortunately caused the discontinuation of an activity that many girls enjoyed.

Conclusion

This chapter has begun to lay the groundwork for what the reality of education at Jay Ellis is like, according to teachers, students, and my own observations. The history of the school has created what is visible today, from its beginnings as a family-oriented experience to the limited resources that the school's administrators must navigate. Through an exploration into the impact of school size, one can see that crafting a perfectly sized small school should be distinguished from having to "make do" with a "too small school," which is the predicament Jay Ellis suffers from presently. The adolescents, who remain at the center of my inquiry, flow through the school's structure daily, aware of the prominent features, yet largely oblivious to how acutely each feature of their school experience is molding their future. As will be seen in the coming chapters, they have much more to say about Jay Ellis's "Last Chance" caricature, which they cannot ignore because of their constant bombardment with these stereotypes.

Chapter 3
Educated at the Last Chance School

During my time in the field, Jay Ellis was engaged in an ongoing public relations war. When Kelly stated, "people say Jay Ellis is at the bottom and we don't learn nothing and we don't do nothing," she was not referring to a few people, she was referring to a widespread, accepted opinion, an ideology that permeates the school and community. Jay Ellis has been assigned a symbolic position at the bottom of every ladder, representing the poorest and worst-off among blacks, representing the worst school in the county system, representing the lesser of the two between the city and the county, even representing a "shame" to some alumni who now send their children to Carlyle schools.

My exploration into the social construction of Jay Ellis's Last Chance identity beckoned me, rather than the other way around. As I previously stated, I was interested in how Hamilton's youth were educated at a small school. But I was saddened to learn over time that the identity of Jay Ellis students was profoundly impacted by the constant struggle against simplistic, demeaning representations of their school, and by extension, negative stereotypes of themselves. The most frustrating element to observe was how battling for Jay Ellis at the level of caricature sidetracked those who could work to improve the school.

Unfortunately, education in Hamilton, while unique in its flavor, is utterly commonplace in its perpetuation of the socioeconomic hierarchy in the United States. Rather than minimizing the distance between the haves and the have-nots, schools, school systems, and the overall educational system in America often exacerbate them. Jonathan Kozol's widely read *Savage Inequalities* and Bowles and Ginits's pathbreaking *Schooling in Capitalist America* have demonstrated that profound inequities in resource allocation, geographic and environmental racism, resegregation, and so much more are verifiable realities. According to Bowles and Gintis, and other educational reformers influenced by Marxist theories, the problems with schools cannot be solved by placing band-aids on them, for they are intricately interwoven with our capitalist system.

Jay Ellis is also similar to many American schools in that the media and larger discourse surrounding educational institutions play a major role in upholding the system.[1] The average citizens do not know the details that undergird the political economic reality of the schools. What they know is what they view on television, read in newspapers, hear from friends, and absorb from the environment. Too often, what they absorb are messages about what schools, neighborhoods, and people to avoid for fear of contamination.[2] Whole public school systems, zip codes, and neighborhoods are demonized as a result. In my own hometown, Baltimore, Maryland, a brilliant and utterly nuanced television series, *The Wire*, has caused the whole city to be stereotyped as a toxic city that should be avoided.[3] Regarding educational discourse in particular, educational anthropologists Herve Varenne and Ray McDermott, in their work *Successful Failure: The School America Builds*, argue that in this country education—its purpose, outcomes, and culture—are interpreted through a very limited dichotomy of success or failure. The reliance on this hidden discourse disserves society broadly but especially limits those people and institutions that get labeled as failures.

In this chapter, I view the case of Jay Ellis's Last Chance identity primarily through a political economic lens.[4] Jay Ellis's characterization as a "Last Chance" school functions as an ideology that helps to maintain the current socioeconomic order and to ensure that a group of people are educated just enough to avoid hard-core criminal activity and, at the same time, do not constitute competition for the limited number of medium- to high-status jobs in a rural environment in which white citizens have historically been offered first rights of refusal.[5] When I asked Kelly if the public opinion about Jay Ellis was true, she had difficulty answering and tied the truth of the matter to "money supplies" and "more stuff." She was perceptive to link the two because lack of money not only limits Jay Ellis and creates some of its genuine problems, but also the desire to preserve money is what has allowed conversations about resources to degenerate into conversations about faulty values and deficient character.

Though ideology and identity are concepts to which many scholars stake claim, when I refer to "The Last Chance School" as an ideology and an identity in this chapter, I am primarily inspired by sociologists Peter L. Berger and Thomas Luckman's *The Social Construction of Reality: A Treatise in the Sociology of Knowledge*.[6] The chief concern of the sociology of knowledge is "the processes by which any body of knowledge comes to be established as reality."[7] In other words, the sociology of knowledge treats collective understandings of reality as social constructions that arise from within society.

Berger and Luckman define ideology as "ideas serving as weapons for social interests."[8] When I describe the Last Chance School as an ideology I am examining the way the caricature was used as a weapon against Hamilton, to maintain the political economic hierarchy. Berger and Luckman define identity as something "formed by social processes" that "once crystallized . . . is maintained, modified or even reshaped by social relations."[9] When I refer to the Jay Ellis's Last Chance identity, I am calling attention to the fact that this label has crystallized, taken root, and is reshaped by ongoing social relations. Ideology and identity are significant because they help scholars to examine "the role of knowledge in the dialectic of individual and society," and bridge "personal identity and social structure."[10]

Using Berger and Luckman's formulation of the sociology of knowledge does not preclude acknowledging the existence of an actual "reality," which they define as "a quality appertaining to phenomena that we recognize as having a being independent of our own volition."[11] In fact, concurrently analyzing social constructions of reality and some a priori "reality" is precisely what gives this theoretical tool its dynamism. In Hamilton, Jay Ellis's Last Chance identity is a social construction of reality, an ideological view of the school and all social actors associated with the school that is shared and constitutes a particular knowledge.

During the remainder of this chapter, then, I will compare the social construction of "The Last Chance School" with the political economic reality in Hamilton.[12] In doing so, I will show how this particular ideology distorts reality at the expense of Hamilton's youth. I will conclude by addressing some of the issues in the nearby Carlyle schools that render them to be an undesirable option for many Hamilton families. While the basic processes that lead to inequality in America's educational system are similar, there are some significant differences between the characteristics of rural, urban, and suburban educational shortfalls.[13] In this chapter, I will call attention to contemporary forms of educational inequality in a rural community.[14]

The Social Construction

One thing that disturbed me greatly when I interviewed students was their ability to describe what negative things people said about Jay Ellis more emphatically and proficiently than they could describe the history of the school, community, or their family, and often better than they could describe the school's reality from their own point of view. The language they used was strikingly similar. Words such as "nothing" and "the bottom" were voiced numerous times. While the uniformity of how the students presented others' opinions shocked me, the fact that those opinions were ever present did not. I designed my interview questions after having been in the field long enough to know that Jay Ellis was a contentious space with an image problem.

From my very first week at Jay Ellis, I grasped that there was internal discontent about everything from the effectiveness of the principal to county-level resource allocation. My part-time work as director of the local Sylvan Learning Center, however, provided me with some context on the outside "white" perspective about the school. When I first met the people with whom I worked at Sylvan, they were fascinated by my work at Jay Ellis, and they regularly reminded me how noble my work was, how those students *really* needed help. When the Jay Ellis football team tore down one of the spirit signs of a rival team after winning a big game, one would have thought a massive school shooting had occurred.[15] A story about this incident was featured in the local newspaper, and, as a result, what was "wrong with" Jay Ellis dominated the discussions that week between me and Jeff, the director of education at Sylvan. This particular incident ushered in conversations about disrespectful students, with their pants "sagging" and "their music," highlighting the power of the media in fostering critical gazes toward black youth.[16] As a part of this conversation, Jeff even managed to voice his disgust over how the NFL had declined since they let players do "their little dances" when they made a touchdown. Somehow this interlude was all sparked by Jay Ellis's disrespectful behavior: tearing down a paper banner. These banners were essentially disposable and rarely lasted beyond one game.

I tutored one Jay Ellis student at the local Sylvan Learning Center whose mother would often come into my office, close the door, and begin a sometimes hour-long conversation about the problems at Jay Ellis. She was on the board at Jay Ellis and was invested in its progress. However, even in her attempts to help Jay Ellis, she invoked the "Last Chance" caricature, in which teachers "don't teach nothing" and the principal "ain't about nothing." The student interviews provide the best evidence of what this socially constructed Last Chance identity entails. Reading their words renders an understanding of what the ideology is but, more importantly, signals which features are remembered, and I would argue, internalized by the students.

Missy:

Do you think you are mostly the same or mostly different from kids at Carlyle? I don't compare myself to them because kids at Carlyle have a way of thinking they're better than other people. They're always saying Jay Ellis this and Jay Ellis that and Jay Ellis ain't nothing. [They say] "the kids at Jay Ellis . . . there all they think about is sports."

That's not all they think about. *We don't even have that many sports. If that's all we had to think about, there wouldn't be much to think about.*

Sabrina (who used to attend Carlyle High):

So people talk about it a lot? Oh yes, down grade it a lot. *Even the kids or adults?* Kids and adults. *So what exactly do they say? I don't understand what's so bad about it. I'm fascinated.* You know we got—instead of having hard wood floors, you know we have like tile floors in the gym? *Right.* So they'll be like we got the kitchen floors in the gym, and the cafeteria in the gym. You know they just say little stuff and make little jokes.

Patrick and P.J. (two black students who attend Carlyle High):

So what do you hear about Jay Ellis? What do you think about Jay Ellis? What's the word on the street?

P.J.: They suck. That's it.

Patrick: That might be the student thing. But most of the problems I hear about Jay Ellis come from the parents of the students that go to Jay Ellis . . . [more here]. I don't know anything about it so I don't talk about it.

P.J.: Like you said, there are going to be rumors. That's life man. You might as well get used to it. People are never going to stop. That's how I look at it. So, I mean . . . but you don't have to believe them. Majority of the people, they're going to believe it and they're going to stick with it. It's going to be like a tradition. It's going to roll down, they're going to pass it down. And it's just going to be passed down. *What are the rumors?* "Man, don't go to Jay Ellis." "They don't do nothing down there, man. They don't teach you nothing. The teachers don't teach nothing, they just sit in class, play cards and stuff like that." You know. *Do you think Jay Ellis is a good school?* I really don't know.

The first three interview excerpts represent the full gamut of images that constitute Jay Ellis's caricature. They range from the absurd to the distorted. For example, Jay Ellis is not all about sports; most students don't play sports. The truth is that, unfortunately, there isn't money to support many activities at the school other than football and basketball, and by virtue of the fact that most students are related to other students, the whole school turns out to support their family members and friends at sporting events. Regarding the "card playing," on some Friday afternoons teachers gave free periods to the students after they had finished their work. Maybe one of these free periods involved playing cards, but that was not a central part of any teacher's classroom schedule. Furthermore, as was highlighted in the previous sections, teaching styles and proficiencies varied widely, as they do at any school. Finally, the comment about the kitchen floor was actually amusing although the history of the placement of the kitchen and the gym proves too complex to be included in the fantasy.[17]

Unfortunately, desperate attempts to combat the negative portrayal of Jay Ellis often precluded students' serious discussion of the school's composition. They sometimes fought fantasy with fantasy. Letice, who attended Carlyle public schools for a few years, states why she thinks Jay Ellis is a good school:

> *Do you think Jay Ellis is a good school?* Yeah [sigh and down tone]. *That didn't sound too convincing, Letice.* Yeah, I think it's a good school. *Why?* I knew you were going to ask me that. 'Cause it is a good school. *What about it is a good school? Like if you were going to send your child there, tell me the reasons why.* In the city school we had like two hundred people in one class. You can really get an education 'cause its less people in the classroom.

Although an entire grade level of students in the Carlyle school system may have numbered two hundred, I am fairly certain that individual classroom size was not significantly larger than it was at Jay Ellis. But, for Letice, school size was an easy answer, a supposed benefit that she had probably heard invoked many times before. She continued with a more realistic assessment of which people help perpetuate the stereotype.

> *Do people have a good opinion about Jay Ellis?* No, people always [speak] negative about it, call it a dumb school. And when it turn around they the ones ending up there. *Why do you think they have that opinion? Where did it come from?* It comes from Carlyle folks. Carlyle city schools. Probably cause they're like a 5A/4A school and we just a 1A. Somebody's always got to have something negative to say. *So compare it to A. J. Cobb to—what was it like for you when you first came to Jay Ellis, coming from the city school system. Did you want to come at first?* No. I wanted to stay at Carlyle. *But?* I ended up at Jay Ellis.

Janelle, who Ms. Smith described in chapter 1 as "crazy as a chestnut" but very smart, below acknowledges that Jay Ellis has a history as a prominent school. She, like Letice, also critiques those who perpetuate this socially constructed image. While Letice remarks that some of the Jay Ellis slanderers wind up sending their children to school there, Janelle insightfully points out that many naysayers are alumni of the school. She also provides us with one more ridiculous, exaggerated portrayal: students fighting and having sex in the school.

> When I came back to Jay Ellis, it was different from Carlyle, it was very different. Because like at Carlyle [you're] around more familiar people, not racist. *Do you think people have a good opinion about Jay Ellis?* [Shakes head no] *Why?* Cause Jay Ellis is not as—it's better than what it used to be. Cause people used to get caught having sex and all that in school. And it used to be a lot of fighting and stuff down there.
>
> Jay Ellis—it was a prominent school. People could only go to Jay Ellis, they couldn't go to Carlyle. *So you think people have negative opinion about Jay Ellis because?* I believe it's because it's an all-black school. *Do people from Carlyle talk about it, or?* All the time. But I don't get it because most of the people who attend Carlyle, the parents graduated at Jay Ellis. So I really didn't get that.

Evidence of an ongoing battle for Jay Ellis's public identity even can be found online. At a popular Web site that was founded by a former teacher in 1998, designed to catalyze nationwide parent involvement in education, and that boasted "25 million users in 2005," two Hamilton community members have left the mark of Jay Ellis's identity contestation. The Web site is designed to give basic statistics and information on schools in all fifty states. There is a section under each school's page entitled "parent reviews." Each of the five Carlyle High reviewers praise Carlyle for providing a good foundational education and for being the best "school and district around." The two alumni who comment on Jay Ellis first acknowledge that it is "put down," and then they differentiate between the city and county schools. These reviewers provide a segue into an examination of the reality of Jay Ellis's contested identity. They point out three relevant facts: the city school system is segregated, meaning that black children in the city school system are tracked; Jay Ellis does not get comparable funding to the city schools, so direct comparisons between them are arbitrary; and Jay Ellis offers a limited number of courses because of insufficient resources. Their perspectives illustrate the way Jay Ellis stakeholders feel pressured to "defend" the school. They also intimate that despite Jay Ellis's public reputation, its community consists of many successful graduates who are invested in its future success.

In sum, the social constructed "Last Chance" identity of Jay Ellis proffers as reality: a poor rural school, with dumb, violent, sex-crazed, sports-obsessed, backwards (e.g., kitchen floor in the gym), card-playing black people running it, teaching at it, and attending it. I have taken some creative license to string together the various features presented in this section. Although the synthesis of these elements may sound harsh, these images have been gradually engrained in people's minds. Even if one omits that particular crystallization, at the very least it is evident that people have stamped in their minds that folks at Jay Ellis don't do "nothing."

The Political Economic Reality

The current political economy of the school and community provides the best direct comparison between the social construction of reality and some form of "underlying" reality;[18] also, it provides an unambiguous explanation of who would stand to benefit from the existence of this negative portrayal. Historians have well documented that throughout Alabama's long history, including, slavery, Reconstruction, the Jim Crow era, and the civil rights era, its economic system has served to mainly benefit white citizens.[19] Sharecropping, convict leasing, peonage, "white flight," and separate and blatantly unequal policies created separate black and white communities, and control of labor power built the foundation for this racial system.[20]

In the South, especially, black subjugation stemmed from a desire to make capital interests as profitable as possible. In this context, racism has been a tool as well as an endpoint.[21] In his famous "Our God is Marching On" speech in Montgomery, March 25, 1965, Dr. Martin Luther King Jr. referred to the historian C. Vann Woodward's assessment of race relations in the South, stating, "The segregation of the races was really a political stratagem employed by the emerging Bourbon interests in the South to keep the Southern masses divided and Southern labor the cheapest in the land."[22] Ulrich B. Phillips, influential historian of the antebellum South, described the South as "'a people with a common resolve indomitably maintained—that it shall be and remain a white man's country.' That conviction, he observed, 'whether expressed with the frenzy of a demagogue or maintained with a patrician's quietude, is the cardinal test of a Southerner and the central theme of Southern history.'"[23]

Returning to the case of Jay Ellis School in 2003, I would argue that in the forty years since King's speech, the political economic motivations underlying the system have not changed, nor has the racial underpinning.[24] If one approaches Jay Ellis's negative portrayal as an ideology then the pertinent questions are (1) How can we delimit the socioeconomic reality that the ideology exists to maintain? and (2) What are the actual political and economic constraints that prohibit the "masses" from changing the system?

While many actors help to keep the ideology alive, and some of them will benefit at least indirectly from its existence, the primary stakeholders in the maintenance of the status quo have historically been determined and continue to be determined by the conflagration of race and class. According to the 2000 U.S. Census, 97 percent of Alabama's total state population could be characterized as either white or black alone, from single racial ancestry—white or black. Specifically, 71 percent of Alabama's over 4 million residents were reported to be white and 26 percent were reported to be black. In Alabama, then, a racially dichotomized demographic composition is still definitive.

This black/white racial binary, historically determined, yet contemporarily maintained, supports an equally polarized socioeconomic landscape. In 1999, the per capita income of whites in Alabama was almost twice that of blacks, with white per capita income reported to be $20,749 a year and black per capita income reported to be $11,665 a year. The difference in economic power that the racial groups experience is most pronounced when one combines the population figures with the income data. The aggregate white household income for the state of Alabama was almost $65 billion, four times the approximately $14 billion aggregate income of black households.[25]

In Hamilton, homeownership, income, and education patterns reveal that the socioeconomic landscape is markedly rural. Unlike in urban areas, where homeownersip might indicate who the chief stakeholders in the social order are, in rural Hamilton the data hide the full picture. According to the 2000 census, 92 percent of white homes were owner occupied while 87 percent of black homes were owner occupied. These numbers are astoundingly commensurate. From my purview, however, the seemingly positive reality that blacks and whites own their homes in nearly equal numbers contributes to black Hamiltonians' general lackluster efforts to fight "the system."[26] While poverty is real, neither homelessness, nor feelings of isolation, detachment, or meaninglessness seem to be major issues. Therefore, outrage at inequality is often overshadowed by a general sense of contentment.

Contentment aside, the median white family income in Hamilton, at $49,159, is nearly three times the median black income of $17,513. This disparity significantly contributes to Jay Ellis's real issues, which incense many community members. When I asked Kelly if she thought the negative opinions about Jay Ellis were true she said, "I can't put it into words. Like Carlyle, they have, they get more stuff than we do, because they have more money supplies, say, from the parents . . ." Why do they have more "money supplies" from the parents? one might ask. The answer is that they actually have money to give.

I interviewed the Attala County superintendent, Mr. Donaldson, to candidly ask him about what Jay Ellis's parents, students, and teachers reported to be some flagrant incongruities in the county system, especially between Jay Ellis and the county's "best school," Stark River, which maintains a majority white population. By the time I met with Mr. Donaldson in the fall of

2004, I was well aware of the fractured relationship between Jay Ellis and the superintendent from the perspective of the Jay Ellis community. Mr. Edwards attempted to help me understand how the warped relationship between the county board of education and Jay Ellis had developed over the years. Mr. Edwards explained:

> Well, let me say this. Several years ago, when a teacher from here presented a speech during black history month, and she said that, in the seventies when integration was on the verge of happening, that the superintendent at that time polled all staff members at the schools that were in the county system: TS Jackson, Jay Ellis, Attala, Stark River, Cock Seed High—that was a black school, I think. Anyway, all of the schools'. . . faculties and staffs were polled at that time to see whether they were for integration . . . When the polling took place, TS Jackson bowed to his persuasion and said no we don't want integration. *Cock seed?* Voted no, Start River voted no, Attala High voted no, and Jay Ellis staff voted yes. *Really?* And from that date to the present, over three different superintendents, Jay Ellis still continues, as far as I'm concerned, to be on the low end of the totem pole for that reason. I think it's been passed on, because the things that they do here, when they do them, they feel like we should be so appreciative.
>
> . . . We are all in the same school system. There should not be such a great deal of bias within the same system. Now I'm not comparing us to Carlyle city or Miller city, but we are—all four schools are in the same district.

There was no real way to prove or disprove Mr. Edwards's theory. But it represents the general distrust and dissatisfaction that parents and teachers had toward the county board of education.

The superintendent's office was also blamed for its role in handpicking Principal Moore, who was a controversial figure. If Jay Ellis was the public representation of Hamilton and its residents to the greater Carlyle and countywide community, then Principal Moore was the internal representation of Jay Ellis's issues to the teachers, students, and parents involved in the school. Since my first week at Jay Ellis, as I stated previously, I was made aware that Principal Moore was viewed negatively. As my fieldwork progressed, I witnessed and experienced many of the things about her that people judged to be problematic. Kelly's assessment of Jay Ellis presented at the outset of chapter 2 highlights most of the general accusations people held against her. There were namely five: that she shows "favoritism"; that she is "too nice" or lenient; that she lets too many "folks in the school"; that she'll want to put students out at the wrong times, or, in other words, is uneven in the enforcement of her rules; and that she is disingenuous. I particularly appreciate how Kelly expressed the last accusation: "She's a nice person I'll say. In a way." That was just how Ms. Moore was: mostly nice on the outside, but one could never be sure whether she was being sincere.

One major accusation about the principal that remained central in the discourse during my time at Jay Ellis was that Ms. Moore and her secretary were embezzling money from the school. Until this day, perhaps because of my own unending optimism and naïveté, I find it difficult to believe that Ms. Moore, who is an ordained minister, was stealing money from the school. I said that to residents in Hamilton many times, but was told each time "you can believe it or not"; "where is the money?" I never pursued the answer to that "question" because I felt uncomfortable to do so and my role at the school was not that of super sleuth or FBI investigator. The question of how these accusations fitted into the discourse was far more salient for my purposes.

The accusations of embezzlement ranged from cursory to venomous, but, more than anything, they were continuous. For example, I overheard several snide comments when Ms. Moore drove up with her new car. Her open discussion about the fact that it was paid for with "cash" did not help her case. Additionally, during a fundraiser for a bus trip to a football play-off game, in which buckets were being passed around the school and at the games for donations, people wanted to know if the principal and "that secretary" thought they (the parents) "were crazy." They said they weren't going to put money in a bucket that couldn't be accounted for when "everybody knows they're stealing money from the school." The accusations usually included humorous and detailed rationale for their skepticism. For example, "Why would you need money for a bus trip when you get all the admission money from the games? Where does all that money go? Where does all the concession stand money go? Isn't the athletic department given a budget each year?" All interesting questions, asked with little proof, however.

One teacher questioned what happened to the money and books that were supposedly received as a result of the major newspaper article that I discussed in the introduction to *Raised Up Down Yonder*:

> Nothing has been done with all that supposed money that has come to this school, that has made this school any better academically, physically, socially, there's nothing. There is nothing here to show why we belittled ourselves through that article, and we have nothing to show for it.

Ms. Moore's ineffectiveness as a principal was directly tied to the board of education's negligence or malice concerning the progress of Jay Ellis (depending on how one views it). While in Hamilton, I asked many people why the community did not attempt to have Ms. Moore removed since they were so unhappy with her performance. I was told over and over again that a principal cannot be removed easily. My next question, then, was how did Ms. Moore become principal in the first place?

According to one informant, after the previous principal resigned, no one applied for the position statewide. Therefore, the next logical step was to turn internally to promote one of Jay Ellis's teachers to the position of principal. I was told by many that the obvious choice would have been Ms. Smith, the guidance counselor, who was clearly interested in the position, had been working effectively at the school for over two decades, and lived only twenty minutes away. In addition, there were at least three other teachers who had been at the school nearly as long as Ms. Smith, and the majority of the teachers at Jay Ellis held master's degrees. However, the previous superintendent overlooked all of those candidates and selected Ms. Moore to be the principal. She had only been a teacher for five years, was teaching on the elementary hall, lived an hour away, and did not have her master's degree or her administrative certification. According to Mr. Edwards, such an "interesting" selection of a candidate was no accident:

> My personal opinion was that he [the superintendent] chose someone who he could tell what to do, when to do, how to do, and it would be no questions asked ... Because he knew that other people on the staff had been making independent decisions during their tenure here, and he knew that it would be hard to convince them to do some of the things that he wanted done personally, to the detriment of this school.

According to Mr. Edwards, while the predominantly white county school Stark River has never had an uncertified principal, the superintendent never even pushed for Ms. Moore to become certified.

After completing the following interview with Ms. Moore during my last few months at Jay Ellis, I began to view her somewhat as a victim of the county school system rather than as a villain.

Ms. Moore reveled in sharing with me her life story, one in which she was reared in an all-black community, participated in integrating a formerly all-white school and, unfortunately after having earned high marks and having so much promise, became pregnant in the tenth grade and earned her GED in 1972. She eventually went back to school after many years of hard work in a factory, as a hotel maid, and in a church daycare, and she became somewhat of a local celebrity success story. She said that she got motivated to go back to school in 1978 after she "got saved." When she finished her degree in 1993, she was offered the job at Jay Ellis that same year. She moved to Carlyle for her first two years and then moved back to Tuscaloosa when she married. In total, she taught on the elementary hall for five years.

The reason why I began to see Ms. Moore as a victim was that her eyes lit up in a way I had never seen when she described the experience of teaching reading and math. She recalled specific stories of students who experienced success with the Action Reading Program, which involved singing songs and playing games as part of the learning experience. Regarding one particular instance in which a student finally had a breakthrough she said, "When you see things like that happen to students it's so amazing; it's almost like getting the Holy Ghost." When she was teaching she also used to take some of her students to church on Sundays. I couldn't help feeling as if not only had the superintendent done the school a disservice by selecting her as principal, but he also removed her passion, classroom teaching, from her life.

According to Ms. Moore, the superintendent "called her out of the blue" and offered her the job. She said that she kept it in prayer, interviewed, and obtained the job. She also said that she was scared and didn't know what she was doing. Toward the end of our interview, she became reflective about how she was currently performing, stating things such as, "I don't feel like teachers know how much I appreciate them," "if you can't help me, move out of my way," and "there are things that make me angry . . . maybe I hold on to them too long or maybe express them at the wrong time." She also said students have "been coerced" to say that she has "pickers" and "choosers."

Some teachers told me that Ms. Moore did not accept input from them, was punitive, and nitpicked. What I observed was that she was not good at being an administrator and was specifically poor at earning the trust of parents, fostering effective communication in the school, evenly applying discipline, and setting a vision for the school's future. Ms. Smith's perspective concerning Principal Moore was:

> From what I can see, in Attala County—that's what they want. Somebody who will take orders from the superintendent's office and not buck the system. As long as you try to do what we want you to do, then hey, that's a good administrator.

Now, as I stated, by the time I was scheduled to visit Superintendent Donaldson, I had all of this institutional knowledge floating around in my head. Additionally, I had been to Stark River to observe, for myself, its brand-new technology center, and it did feel as if I was in a different school system. Thus, my meeting with him felt especially transgressive. Despite the fact that he had to sign off on my presence in the community and had allowed me to work with the cheerleaders, I was going to call forth my ethnographic chutzpah and force him to address these issues.

His office was generic and institutional; overall, it was underwhelming. When the secretary called me into his office for the interview, I took stock of this mythic character. He was tall and lean and looked like a politician. In contrast to my nervousness, he did not seem the least bit ruffled. As the interview got under way, he volunteered all the information that I thought I would have to "pull out of him." Donaldson unapologetically stated that incongruities in the county system are a perception only. He attributed visible differences to the enrollment numbers and the fact that the parents at Stark River support the school. Donaldson pontificated:

> You look at schools, you look at the community. It doesn't take money to make a school look nice. It takes support. What I see from some of our schools is people spend a lot of their energy and time looking at what somebody else has instead of what they have. And if somebody else has that, instead of coming up with some perception in their mind as to how they got it, they ought to say, "well let's all get together and let's work" . . . but they don't. You know, I don't hardly give Stark River anything. It's all community. I mean they've got a big PTA. They're the least funded school I have from here, from central office . . . What you have to look at is federal money and federal money is based off the number of students that have free and reduced lunch. Well, Jay Ellis's just about 100 percent. They get most of the federal money, per student wise. I mean they may not get the big pot, because they don't have the number of students, but as far as per student, they get the most.

Mr. Donaldson continued by inadvertently addressing one of the oft-invoked "Last Chance" portrayals: the kitchen in the gym. According to him, complaints about the kitchen were evidence of the ungrateful attitude characteristic of people at Jay Ellis:

> You know they've got a cafeteria? Well, they complain sometimes about the cafeteria—"It was built right next to the gym, they didn't even think about hygiene when they built it." Well instead of saying we really like this cafeteria and you know it's this or this . . . There are not many schools that are K–12 that are Jay Ellis's size that are even open. You know, most of them have closed. You know, Jay Ellis is the smallest school in the state that has a football program. They are the smallest. We give Jay Ellis what they earn, plus we give them some extra. I don't, you know—I have a conscience, and I'm not going to feel guilty about what I do for the schools. I'm at peace with what I do for Jay Ellis, just like I'm at peace with what I do for T. S. Jackson,

Attala, for Stark River. I mean, Jay Ellis football coach, he doesn't make less than what the other coaches make. He makes the same as the rest of them. The teachers, they're paid the same as the other teachers. So, equitably, we try to make things as fair as possible . . .

While the facts underlying Superintendent Donaldson's remarks were true, his cavalier attitude reflected his degree of interest in bettering the lives of Hamilton's youth. Rather than identifying with Hamilton community members, Donaldson criticized Jay Ellis for not being more grateful to the county school system: grateful to be open, grateful to have a football team, grateful to be "given" extra money, even grateful for equal teachers' salaries. Below, Donaldson does make an effort to "relate" to the plight of the average Jay Ellis student, but his identification with them morphs, midstream, into a lecture about people's ability to "better themselves":

> You know, the kids at Jay Ellis, I feel for them. Because I think one of the things that's helped me so much with this job is that I can look at kids at Jay Ellis and I can relate to them. Because I've been down that road before. We didn't have anything, I mean we didn't have—you know when your dad's unemployed, and your parents are divorced and your mother's only working and women weren't making a lot of money. You know, and we weren't subsidized by the government back then. I mean, we didn't have anything. So they can come up here and talk all this poor talk, but that's just an excuse, that's not a reason. If I can do it, you know I don't think when you get a superintendent's position it's because you're from Birmingham or from Mobile. I mean heck I grew up with nothing. We didn't grow up with a big old Christmas tree and presents everywhere. I've seen what it's like to be there. So, I understand, but I know that they can better themselves if they really want to.

As the superintendent, Donaldson never entered into a discussion about how the economic disparities were a shame or an outrage. He offered no plans to stimulate economic growth among black families or curb the negative effect that poverty is having on the school's progress. During our interview, he was far more interested in relaying the details of his self-characterized impoverished upbringing.

Juxtapose the superintendent's opinion with the educational attainment levels of blacks and whites in the community. Out of 575 white Hamiltonians who were at least twenty-five years of age or older, 90 percent had earned their high school diploma or equivalency, 55 percent had completed some college, and 21 percent had earned their bachelor's degree or higher. Out of 509 black Hamiltonians who were at least twenty-five years of age or older, 47 percent had earned their high school diploma or equivalency, only 12 percent completed some college, and a mere 1 percent completed a bachelor's degree or higher.[27] As was written in the chapter detailing the school's history, Jay Ellis has graduated many students who go on to be college educated and successful in their occupations. However, many of them have out-migrated to Carlyle, to counties and cities much farther away in the state, or moved out of state altogether, mostly in search of job opportunities.[28] The point is that such disparities in educational levels within the community exacerbate the existing economic inequities. Abundant human and social capital, which stem from advanced economic and educational levels together create a snowball effect; predominance of education leads to more human and social capital; they, in turn, lead to more education, which finally leads to the garnering of more economic resources.[29] Further, higher levels of education in families can be correlated with better performance within schools.

Through comparison of the data presented by the county board of education as part of the Nationwide Report Card System, one can view how race and economic factors play out directly in the school system. During the 2004–2005 school year, 97 percent of Jay Ellis's students were eligible for free or reduced meals, while only 68 percent of Stark River's student body and 52.8 percent of Carlyle High's student body were eligible. These data, once again, confirm that the economic disparities that influence the functioning and perception of the schools are linked to race.

What might the powerbrokers in this environment stand to benefit from maintaining the political and economic order? The answer is tied into the limitations of a local economy, which spurs competition for local jobs in an area where local residents want to stay. One thing that I took note of over the course of my fieldwork was Carlyle residents' love of their town. The literature on Carlyle that the chamber of commerce produces highlights many of its "charming" features, including a quaint downtown area, low crime rates, and great city schools, just to name a few. My cousin Tiffany was instrumental in educating me about the ongoing history of the local arenas, such as clubs, businesses, and private schools that have been closed to black people over the years. The local history of Carlyle written in a book published in 2000, in fact, pinpoints several prominent white families that have historically built and controlled the city, especially its chamber of commerce.

In addition, according to several informants, Carlyle takes pride in the fact that it has maintained control of the school system despite integration. When school integration was finally forced in the South, private academies were created for white students in integrated areas. Miller, the county seat, is an excellent example of a city school system that became all black as the white residents hurriedly transferred their children to the newly erected private academy. This was not the case in Carlyle. The local Carlyle private school, Carlyle Academy, which was renamed Mid Alabama Prep and admitted its first black students while I was in the field, is a small school, and a minority of the children from prominent Carlyle families attend it. The Carlyle school system might use that as a bragging point about their "progressive" track record. However, black community members argue that it was just a judicious move that enabled Carlyle, with its beautiful river and quaint business area, to remain a white-owned and -operated city. Instead of fleeing the city school system, white parents have kept their children in the Carlyle schools and maintained control through methods such as tracking and a "segregated" prom, which will be discussed further in the next section.

The point of that brief digression is that white stakeholders are invested in staying in the greater Carlyle area, including Hamilton, and involved in controlling the economy. Mrs. Scott, one of the white Jay Ellis teachers, expressed that her desire to stay close to home and to her family was her number-one priority when choosing where to work. Various social scientists who study rural communities have noted how the desire to stay close to family is often at odds with potential for upward mobility because the local economies provide few options.[30] In this community environment, not only is competition for jobs fierce, but producing residents with education and interest levels to match the local economic needs is a delicate balancing act.[31] With 55 percent of white Hamilton residents (this does not include Carlyle) having finished "some college," that number of matriculating students almost saturates that market. Table 1 (page 84) presents the scope of local occupations according to the 2000 census (including Hamilton and Carlyle). As one can see, professions range from farm managers to health-care support workers, to construction workers. By my own rough estimation, approximately 37 percent of those jobs are designed to be held by people with a college education, while the other 63 percent do not require a college education.

How do Jay Ellis graduates fare with respect to the occupation balancing act? They would be the ones to out-migrate, fill service-sector occupations, or participate in other occupations for which there is little competition.[32] There will always be room for an "exceptional few" students to stay and prosper, but widespread success and college degree attainment for Jay Ellis's students would benefit no one who currently wields power, only the students and their families.[33]

One final set of numbers that is presented on the Board of Education Report Card is the "results" of the technology program. According to board of education meeting minutes, the county board of education, in collaboration

Table 1. Occupations of Employed Civilians, Ages 16 and Older, in Hamilton and Greater Carlyle, According to the 2000 U.S. Census

Occupation	No.	of work Force %
Management professional, and related occupations	733	36%
Management, business, and financial operations	240	
Management occupations, except farmers and farm managers	166	
Farmers and farm managers	18	
Business and financial operations occupations	56	
Professional and related occupations	493	
Computer and mathematical occupations	4	
Architecture and engineering occupations	55	
Life, physical, and social science occupations	22	
Community and legal service occupations	43	
Legal occupations	21	
Education, training, and library occupations	206	
Arts, design, entertainment, sports, and media occupations	22	
Healthcare practitioners and technical occupations	120	
Service occupations	209	10%
Healthcare support occupations	63	
Protective service occupations	41	
Fire fighting, prevention, and law enforcement workers, including supervisors	34	
Other protective service occupations, including supervisors	7	
Food preparation and serving related occupations	45	
Building and grounds cleaning and maintenance occupations	23	
Personal care and service occupations	37	
Sales and office occupations	517	25%
Sales and related occupations	217	
Office and administrative support occupations	300	
Farming, fishing, and forestry occupations	25	1%
Construction, extraction, and maintenance occupations	181	9%
Construction and extraction occupations	82	
Supervisors, construction and extraction workers	27	
Construction trades workers	49	
Extraction workers	6	
Installation, maintenance, and repair occupations	99	
Production, transportation and material moving occupations	386	19%
Productions occupations	269	
Transportation and material moving occupations	117	
Supervisors, transportation, and material moving workers	7	
Aircraft and traffic control occupations	0	
Motor vehicle operators	39	
Rail, water and other transportation occupations	0	
Material moving workers	71	
Total Number of Employed Civilian population 16 years and over	**2,051**	**100%**

with the Miller city and Carlyle city school districts, agreed to establish an area vocational school in June 1976. The technology center was built to give the county students exposure to trades, such as welding or computers. Currently, each afternoon, a percentage of the junior and senior class from all four county schools are bused to this center where students work on various projects and assignments. I traveled to this center with Kelly one day and had a great time riding the bus, singing songs, and getting "crunk."[34] However, I didn't sense that any of the students from Jay Ellis took their particular trade that seriously. I never got a clear sense of how students were "chosen," "tracked," or "self-selected" to attend the technology center, other than to know that those who wanted to pursue "Advanced Diplomas" could not go.

In any event, the Board of Education Report Card reports that 75.4 percent of students in the county system are enrolled in career/tech classes, while only 56.4 percent of Carlyle city students are enrolled, and only 54.3 percent of the students in the state participate in a technology education program. The county system greatly exceeds both the city and the state in the percentage of students who receive career/technology education. For me, these statistics are troubling because I was able to witness the time that was wasted in the daily transit to the technology center, time during which students were not being educated. What was really jarring, however, was reading the report card's data on "Percent of Positive Placements in Career Tech." In the Carlyle city school system, 75 percent of the students who completed the career/tech program were placed in a related field or went to school. The data for Jay Ellis were not reported. How can a program to which so many resources are devoted not be followed up and evaluated to make sure that it is "working?" My answer is that the technology center exists primarily to baby-sit poor students rather than to provide them with opportunities. Even if these students actually adopted trades learned at the center, they probably would attain low-status, lower-paying, although technical jobs. Therefore, the existence of the technology center constitutes a "win-win" for those wishing to maintain the status quo.[35]

Thus far, I have linked the ruling class directly and indirectly to white residents of Hamilton and nearby communities, such as Carlyle. Historically and currently, they constitute the largest block of stakeholders. However, others perpetuate the Jay Ellis caricature and might think that they benefit from its persistent portrayal even if they actually do not. The people who benefit namely would be other black people who have graduated from Jay Ellis and feel that they have risen above it; black city residents who never attended Jay Ellis and prefer to identify with a "city breed" of Carlyle residents;[36] and blacks who attend other rural schools and who benefit from the idea that they are not "at the bottom." Whether one believes that any one of these groups is powerful enough to be a stakeholder or is used by those who truly constitute the ruling class to perpetuate their ideology is a moot point. According to ethnic studies professor George Lipsitz, "White supremacy is an equal opportunity employer; nonwhite people can become active agents of white supremacy as well as passive participants in its hierarchies and rewards."[37] Maintaining the caricature of Jay Ellis is effortless when so many residents aid in its persistence.

Of course, the Jay Ellis caricature does not operate to maintain the social order in isolation. It is just the feature that I purport has the greatest impact on young people's identity. Some of the other instruments of the system are a push toward more bureaucratic red tape, paperwork, and formal requirements in order to accomplish small tasks; the statewide Alabama High School Graduation Examination, which seniors must pass in order to earn their diplomas; the focus on meeting standards for the national No Child Left Behind policy; and the growth of the number of students at Jay Ellis who have been expelled from other schools. All of these obstacles, while emanating from disparate sources, move in the same direction: more hoops to jump through and intensified problems (e.g., expelled students sent to Jay Ellis) for a school with limited resources.

"Last Chance," not Worst Choice

After reading the presentation of the myriad issues at Jay Ellis, which are embedded in layers of history, structure, identity politics, racism, poverty, and individual motives, one might ask, why not just close the school and send the students to Carlyle? Jay Ellis senior Kelly Lawrence offered two key reasons why, when presented with the opportunity, she did not want to attend Carlyle schools. First, she feared being an outsider. Second, she worried that her grades would drop because of the level of difficulty of the classes. Indeed, trying to figure out how Jay Ellis "measures up," or actually prepares them for college, is something many Jay Ellis students privately consider. But both of Kelly's concerns can be placed under an inclusive umbrella: fear of what would happen in an environment in which the ability to manipulate cultural capital to the benefit of some and detriment of others is within arm's length. While the students at Jay Ellis may be the victims of systemic inequality because they are poor, rural, and black, they do enjoy some buffers from the daily reinforcement of these facts within their school. However, those qualities are starkly presented in Carlyle schools daily. They are not just presented in the form of teasing, taunting, or social exclusion; more significantly, they are imprinted in the school's formal structure.

The first day that I truly understood the limited options that Hamilton students face occurred one afternoon at Sylvan. I had already resided in the community for a year, but when our white Carlyle High intern, Jackie, flopped in the chair in my office and began to flippantly tell me all about some "drama" that happened at SFIO, I truly understood for the first time what "limited options" really meant. I knew off-handedly that some form of segregated prom at Carlyle High still existed, but I was so engrossed in Jay Ellis life that the segregated prom had disappeared from my radar. Jackie brought it back to the forefront for me. Once seated, she proceeded to tell me what drama had transpired at SFIO so candidly and matter-of-factly that I had to stop and ask her what SFIO was. She quickly blurted out, "Spring Formal Invitation Only," and then she followed it up with something like, "It's basically the prom for the white kids. The black kids aren't invited; they have it at the civic center. They've been doing it for years . . . I know it's stupid," and then she moved on with her story.

I cannot describe the anger that I felt when I realized that this white teenager had no problem explaining to me, her black supervisor, that there was a prom to which black students weren't invited. What further disturbed me was that the prom was not the point of her story. After conducting a bit of follow-up research, I discovered that Carlyle High no longer sanctioned a "white only" prom. Once the school board outlawed this form of discrimination, the white parents convened to create their own "formal" that would be held at the civic center. After the creation of SFIO, the overwhelming majority of the white students shunned the school-sanctioned prom, contrary to the school's efforts to provide a diversity of music and reach out to all students equally. Thus, a new form of segregated prom prevailed. Rules provide very little protection when financial and social capital can so easily be drawn upon.

SFIO is just one example of the blatant racism that persists in Carlyle until today. Living with my cousin Tiffany, who raised four sons in the Carlyle school system, I witnessed many other examples of racial discrimination in the schools. In fact, Tiffany's management of her sons' experiences in the Carlyle school system was like a full-time job; luckily, as someone who was educated and had worked with whites in Carlyle for years, she was among those parents best suited to take on this form of labor.[38]

One example of blatant discrimination that Tiffany had to combat took place when her youngest son, Jonathan, who was an eighth grader during my first year in Hamilton, won a school-wide "pi day" contest. This t-shirt design competition preceded a day's worth of events that celebrated the number pi. Jonathan put extra effort into the t-shirt design contest because he loved art.

Because he experienced a rocky year at the school, he was so proud to come home and report some good news: his design had won the "pi day" contest. Not only had he won, but also he was the first black student to ever win the contest. The week of hype and excitement leading up to pi day was matched only by Jonathan's big disappointment on pi day; when he arrived to school, there were no t-shirts.

The whole excitement of winning the competition was that everyone at the school would wear the t-shirt Jonathan had designed. I can remember seeing him at home the night after pi day. He was totally crestfallen. When Tiffany found out what had happened, she "hit the roof" and told Jonathan to give his poster design to her, so that she could have her own shirts made up. He then reported that the teacher who was in charge of the contest said she had "misplaced" his poster. He also said that the teacher gave him no real reason why the school didn't print the shirts. Tiffany instantly orchestrated a meeting with the teacher. At that meeting the teacher explained to Tiffany that they just "couldn't get it together this year." After sharply reprimanding the teacher, Tiffany threatened to go to the newspaper. In the end, she decided that "going public" would damage Jonathan more than it would help him. Unfortunately, Jonathan never received his design. Continued prejudicial treatment was one of the reasons why Tiffany's next eldest son, after eleven years in the same school system, decided to complete his senior year in the first integrated class at Mid Alabama Prep.

Endless are the examples of discriminatory behavior of faculty, staff, and administrators who have a modicum of power and influence in the Carlyle school system. The level of success that Tiffany was able to accomplish in the school system was, in large part, because her work schedule enabled her to take time off for these regular school "meetings" and interruptions. Most parents of black students are not so fortunate. In addition, Tiffany and her family were firmly ensconced within the middle class and were accustomed to interacting with white people. For those Hamilton students whose families fall in that $17,000 per year income category, racial discrimination is compounded by class discrimination.

Sabrina and Janelle, both of whom attended Carlyle High before transferring to Jay Ellis, reported frustration with race and class discrimination. Below, Sabrina describes how and why she came to the decision to attend Jay Ellis.

Do you like [Jay Ellis]? Yes, I actually like it better than I liked Carlyle, mainly because it's more of a family environment. In Carlyle, I felt more like I was just a number up there. And if you don't play sports in Carlyle . . . let me see how to say this . . . you're not like a person who the principal and counselor would know your name. And see down there [at Jay Ellis], everybody knows your name. *How did that start? What gave you the idea in the first place to go to Jay Ellis?* Shanice, my baby sister, she had to go to preschool at Jay Ellis cause they let her in. *Head Start?* Yeah, Head Start. So, since she, Johnny, and them [her brother] been going down there, and I just decided to go down there to see how it was since everybody was going down there except for me. *And what was your first impression when you got there? Like, before you got there what had you heard about it?* AHHH! The cafeteria and the gym [laughter]. It's so many stories. We used to actually stay down at school and discuss Jay Ellis sometimes in Carlyle. And I got down there, and I was like "it's not as bad as we thought it was." It actually turned out to be real nice.

So people *talk about it a lot?* Oh yes . . . *But you decided to go anyway?* 'Cause I didn't like how Carlyle was. See I got to the high school my ninth-grade year, and when I got there, it's like mass majority of white. I don't have a problem with white people or whatever but it was like up there they give whites more advantages than they will give a black. See, by me being black, down there [at Jay Ellis] I'm the valedictorian of the class, hopefully. But up there, I would probably be liked ranked number 17 or something, because even though I'm taking advanced classes up there, the white kids would get a better grade than I would get. *Why is that?* Mainly because half of them know each other . . . It was—his name is Coach Deer. They had his son in our class, and he was teaching us. And you know I thought that was very unfair . . . and he missed days and he would miss a test and his average turned out to be a 99 and I had like a 95. And you know I'm up in there every day writing down notes and stuff. And he missed class. So how did he make a 99?

So who did you talk about these things to? I never talked about them. I just, like, I'll see it. I never talked about them. I'll just sit and watch. And then, I was like, I'm tired of it. And I left like October of my freshman year and went to Jay Ellis. *What did your parents say?* Oh they didn't say nothing. They was like, I think they asked me why I wanted to change. And I just told them I wanted to see how it was. I didn't tell them like the real reason why I really wanted to change.

Sabrina's narrative reveals which students might not consider Jay Ellis to be the worst choice. Not only is it a viable option for "troublesome" youth, but also it constitutes a good option for those who feel stifled by racial and class discrimination. Over the course of my time at Jay Ellis, I watched Sabrina thrive in an environment where instead of "half of them" knowing each other and benefiting from social capital networks, "everybody knows your name." I found it telling that Sabrina never shared with any adults what she had observed.

While Sabrina describes the social capital that operated at Carlyle, Janelle focuses more on the financial and cultural capital from which she saw white students benefit:

> Well, actually I started off at Jay Ellis. And then kindergarten I came up here [Carlyle]. And I went from kindergarten to the tenth grade. *When you started kindergarten, it's 'cause you moved here [to Carlyle]?* It was my mother's side. My father didn't want me to leave. So, in the tenth grade, I—you know from kindergarten to like the eighth grade I got by. When I got to high school, it was so racist. All of them, you know. And it's just, if you don't have—it's all about who has money and who doesn't. If you're not "well off," you don't know [anything]. *Mmm hmm.* If you don't give money to the school, then you're not respected. So, I wanted to go back [to Jay Ellis].
>
> My mother wanted me to go back to Carlyle, but I didn't want to 'cause I was so used to being down there already. *When you say that they were racist, what kind of things would go on?* Per se, a black girl and a white girl got into a fight. Standard pro-cedure is that you have to spend twenty-four hours in detention, and you get three days at home, and you get five days in school suspension . . . if it's two black people fighting they get the same thing. But if it's a black and white fighting, just 'cause the other one of them is white, they don't have to go through all that. They just get three days at home and they get to make up their work. *Wow. Everybody knows that it hap-pens?* Everybody, everybody. It happens all the time.

When I asked my two black informants who still attended Carlyle High what they thought about the school system, they revealed a slightly different perspective. They focused on self-imposed racial boundaries in addition to class and money barriers.

> *So how do you like the Carlyle school system?*
> P.J.: To be honest, everybody [black students] looks at it like it's trash. They look at the principal like they can't stand him . . . but to be honest, it's really a good school. I mean, as far as the dress code and the rules and regulations, if you follow them everything'll be good. It will run smooth. But we have a problem with everybody not wanting to follow the rules. So, that's why they have to take action where as it will result in them getting suspended or . . . that's why when they get suspended or what-ever. They look at it like "he wanted to suspend me, I don't like this school." But, you have to look at what you did. You broke the rules, so they had to do what they had to do. So, it's a real good school.
> Patrick: Yeah, see I like school, but the thing I don't like about the school system is they don't have a lot of extracurricular activities, like certain schools have . . .
> *So, now I've heard that Carlyle High is very racist and very segregated. Like you were saying about the golf club, that black people don't do most of—they have all these things*

but most black people aren't . . . I don't know whether it's [blacks] aren't welcome, or . . . ? I don't know. What do you think? Is that true?

Patrick: I mean it's not really true because you have the opportunities where you can go out and be a part of the golf team, but then you have to buy your own stuff. If you can't afford the stuff, then you can't do it.

P.J.: You're right, I see what you're saying because like, you will have the opportunity to try out or whatever. It's just like, you're looking at it like, "man, that's white folks' stuff, I don't wanna get out there and do that." So, that's what they have in mind, so they're not going out.

When I asked them specifically about the rumor that there is a "two black member cap" on the cheerleading squad, Patrick said that some of the blame must go to black students for not trying out for more of these things. According to him, "You can't just sit back and expect things to go your way without taking actions." P.J. goes on to call the black cheerleader quota a rumor:

P.J.: It's black people that's doing that really. I'ma just say, straight up, it's black people. Bowling: black people. Cheerleading: black people. Golf: black people. *When you say it's black people that's doing it, you mean it's black people that are participating or that are spreading the rumors?* Spreading the rumors. *Do you get along with white people at Carlyle.* Oh, yeah, I have no problem with them. They're cool. *Do you think ya'll are on the level of acquaintances or friends, or . . . ?* We'll associate or whatever. We'll hang out sometimes, you know.

Are the classes mixed up pretty evenly, or is there any tracking where the upper classes are white people and the lower-level classes are black people?[39] Or they're all mixed up together?

Patrick: We can talk about that part 'cause they have—the class rankings are designed where white people take 04 [highest level], and it's mixed up in 03 and 02, where its supposed to be for black people. But, I mean it's set up now where mostly everything—except for 04—everything is pretty evenly mixed . . .

What do you think?

P.J.: That's what I was about to say.

Do ya'll think you're pretty much like the typical black students at Carlyle High or do you think you're different from most?

PJ: Oh, no. *You say, "no, no." Why?* Well, I'm not going to say . . . As far as acting civilized, you know, you can see them in the hallways doing things that's not even necessary. Like they're out of control . . . Just stuff like they have no home training. That's what it seems like. [They] walk through the hall, try to trip folks up or something like that. Hitting me upside the head, going all, just doing all. And you're sitting there like . . . ?

Do you agree with that? [Patrick shakes head yes]. *Why do you think that you're different? What made the difference for you?*

P.J.: I mean there comes a time to play and a time to get serious. You know you could play every now and then, but when you're in school and stuff . . . Like when I said you tripped somebody. You could've tripped him up, he could've fell and hurt himself, and then he'd have to take it to the school. And then they go again, "I don't like this school, man, they're trying to suspend me." But you gotta look at what you did.

P.J. said that he "gets along fine" with white people at school, but that he's not like the typical black people at Carlyle who "play too much" and "act like they don't have home training."[40] What I find interesting is that while Patrick and P.J. indirectly point out some of the same variables as do Sabrina and Janelle, their tone is far more critical toward black students. They see the cultural divide as a two-sided problem. What is significant for this analysis is that whether or not black students "contribute" to the present situation, even these two black students acknowledge that, in general, black students are seen as a problem. The attitude that black students are problems to be dealt with is another major issue that most black students in Carlyle schools face.

Conclusion

The perpetuation of a socially constructed Jay Ellis caricature, in which it's a school at "the bottom" that "ain't about nothing," benefits the system and condemns the students to wrestle against the system. An entire body of literature has documented how minstrel shows, cartoons, and other derogatory portrayals of blacks in the South have helped to maintain the social order over the years.[41] While in-depth analyses of particular stereotypes and historical images of black people fall outside of the scope of this chapter, some of the images marshaled in the Jay Ellis stereotype are eerily reminiscent of the well-documented archetypal portrayals of lazy, stupid, gap-toothed, watermelon-eating, shuckin' 'n jivin' mammies, pickaninnies, coons, bucks, and toms.[42] Of concern is not only that these students may be knowingly combating Jay Ellis's stereotypes, but also they are unknowingly combating a larger system of historically embedded representations of black people. Moreover, the degree to which these representations are internalized is difficult to measure, but is of central importance, especially since these stereotypes are invoked by so many Jay Ellis parents and Hamilton community members.

I have tried to demonstrate that Kelly's linkage of these destructive images with "money supplies" is pithy. An examination of the political economy of the community pinpoints race as a weighty variable. Historically and presently, white community members have maintained the upper hand in education and employment. In the greater Carlyle area, this has equaled control of the school system and the chamber of commerce. Simultaneously, black Hamiltonians, who are on the other side of this political-economic dichotomy, wade upstream in a muddy river of standardized tests, questionably effective technology education programs, and general lack of money in order to educate their children.

In the midst of this complex set of variables, an untrue, socially constructed portrayal of Jay Ellis advances an ideology that helps maintain the current political economy. In *The Possessive Investment in Whiteness: How White People Profit from Identity Politics*, George Lipsitz argues that "both public policy and private prejudice have created a 'possessive investment in whiteness' that is responsible for the racialized hierarchies of our society."[43] The hierarchies to which Lipsitz refers are maintained in large part through the manipulation of identity politics, such as the stereotypical representation of Jay Ellis. Lipsitz also provides a paradigm that helps explain how systemic problems are perpetuated by benign agents like Ms. Scott, the white math teacher. Mrs. Scott is not racist, and she, in fact, loves teaching at Jay Ellis. However, she factors into this possessive investment in whiteness by just wanting to get a good job close to home. This is a desire that many residents have, but by virtue of the privilege that she has inherited based on her socioeconomic standing and race, her dream is more likely to come true than the average Jay Ellis student's dream.

Moreover, whether it is a "white only" formal, individual teachers' discriminatory practices, unfair advantages based on unequal access to social, cultural, and financial capital, or just a general attitude that black students are problems, the Carlyle school system is as problematic an option for black Hamilton students as Jay Ellis School is. While some may consider the education in Carlyle to be superb, the level of agility and skill that a black parent or student must exercise in order to capitalize on the educational benefits make Carlyle an arduous choice.

Black students all around the United States face similar dilemmas. Many predominantly black primary and secondary schools are not reaching their full potential based upon a number of complex internal and external issues. In contrast, in many predominantly white schools, or schools in which educating white students is a priority, the cultural, financial, and social capital divides leave black students alienated, isolated, or even tracked. These issues are more pronounced in Hamilton because of the close proximity between poverty and comfort, the living history of more blatant forms of southern racism, and the "in-bred" nature of the major educational stakeholders—

teachers, administrators, parents, and students—who were raised in this system and for whom this labyrinth is normative.

In sum, Hamilton's youth are educated at Jay Ellis School, one part First Choice, and one part "Last Chance" School. This chapter has highlighted many of the challenges that frame students' education and social location. However, one must remember that Hamilton's youth are also dynamic and creative. Chapters 4, 5, and 6, will highlight the agency and identity of Hamilton's youth, even as they wrestle with a broken system.

Chapter 4
Reproducing Misfortune through Mess

A good ethnography must accomplish several goals. It should critically address important thematic issues. It should situate these issues within larger historical, political, and economic circumstances. It should ground these issues in the everyday affairs of life. Over and above all else, it should give readers the feeling that they know "this place and these people." They recognize what makes it distinct. They get the flavor. They can breathe it in. That's the ice cream. If an ethnographer is really fortunate, perhaps something actually *happened* when he or she was in the field. And as a result, above all, readers might get "a story." That's the cherry on top. This chapter is the cherries jubilee of *Down Yonder.*[1]

After reading this chapter one may never want to hear the word mess again. Or, perhaps, it will be added to one's lexicon. But there is no better way to give readers a sense of what *Down Yonder* was like for the young people in Hamilton than to explore the metaphor of mess. Mess is an umbrella term that actually merges many things that include gossip, poor intentions, favoritism, troublemaking, fighting, janking (another local concept), among other things. It was a word that was invoked nearly every day of my life in Hamilton. Over the course of my fieldwork, however, I learned that mess and messy were more than just novel indigenous terms. They were powerful cultural metaphors that helped to maintain the social structure and to form the axis of adolescents' emergent identities. Fashioned into an oppositional culture of overcoming negativity, mess served as an explanatory tool and a lens through which young people viewed their lives.

Consider the Jay Ellis football team. While mess is quintessentially Hamiltonian, perhaps nothing is more American than football. Thanks to the *New York Times* bestseller-turned-television-series, *Friday Night Lights,*[2] high school football culture has become a mainstream trope, an easy way to memorialize the larger-than-life feeling of high school drama, when in reality high school years quickly fade into the distant past. During my year in the field, I was fortunate that something did happen; it was a year-long saga involving the Jay Ellis football team, the Jay Ellis principal, parents, the Marengo County superintendent, and Hamilton's adolescents. While many social situations have been referenced throughout *Raised Up Down Yonder*, and one young lady's personal drama will be examined in the next chapter, this chapter will focus on the community drama that provided the backdrop of the whole 2003–2004 time period.

The Jay Ellis football saga, viewed through the lens of "mess," actually serves a critical purpose in the metanarrative of *Raised Up Down Yonder*. It helps explain why, despite the blatant inequality in the school system described in the last chapter, that no cohesive plan of action, protest, campaign, or movement was launched while I was in Hamilton. In this chapter, then, I examine the reproductive quality of mess. In so doing, I invoke cultural production theory. The French sociologist Pierre Bourdieu spent a lifetime theorizing the ways in which privilege gets transferred from one generation to the next, thus ensuring the perpetuation of systemic inequalities.[3] Cultural production theory is one outgrowth of Bourdieu's work. It seeks to explain how individual actions, carried out by the oppressed, and sometimes in direct response to an unjust system, can actually benefit the maintenance of the system.[4]

I find the way Phillipe Bourgois describes and uses this theory in *In Search of Respect: Selling Crack in El Barrio* to be particularly clear in its applicability to Hamilton. In describing New York's gritty street culture, Bourgois points out the conundrum fundamental to cultural production theory: "although street culture emerges out of a personal search for dignity and a rejection of racism and subjugation, it ultimately becomes an active agent in personal degradation and community ruin."[5] Most of Jay Ellis's chief actors are fighting for their dignity and a rejection of racism. Yet, as an intervening cultural unit, mess reproduces rather than combats misfortune.

To add one additional layer to this already heaping ice-cream sundae, I will use pioneering anthropologist Victor Turner's stages of social drama to tell the story of the football team. In doing so, I will point to the intersection of Turner's theory with theories of cultural production. Whatever theoretical contributions this chapter purports to make, however, it is, once again, the vivid description of mess and Hamilton that makes the enterprise worthwhile. Therefore, do not let this be the chapter that readers skim for "the bottom line"; if so, they'll miss the "down yonder" in *Down Yonder.*

The remainder of this chapter will explore the metaphor of mess. First, mess and "messy," two words that are familiar in the English language, will be redefined in accordance with the meanings assigned to them in Hamilton and specifically by Hamilton's adolescents. By featuring how and when the young people invoke these concepts, sometimes on their own, and sometimes in response to my probing, one gets the sense of how these words are creatively used and to what end. Second, I will examine some "mess," the year-long social drama that unfolded while I was in Hamilton. I will use this particular social drama as an example of the reproductive quality of mess. Finally, I will conclude with a brief examination of the intersection of social dramas, metaphor, and cultural production.

Defining Mess

I had only arrived in the community a few days prior, when I realized that the term messy was being used in ways that were novel to me. One day I was having a conversation with my cousin Tiffany and her niece, in my cousin's atypically large and modern kitchen, one that seemed more characteristic of *Southern Living* magazine than that of Hamilton's cultural milieu. We were chatting about the local Walmart where I had applied for a job. They told me that I should be grateful if I didn't get the job because folks down there were messy. "It's so much 'mess' at Walmart," they exclaimed. As Tiffany and Sarah described several fights that had occurred among the employees there, we laughed and "hollered," slapping the counter intermittently. This joviality became a regular feature in our communication. They further reported that one of the employees at Walmart drew a crowd because of her small waist and extra large rear-end. Tiffany exclaimed, "Baby, you really have to see that 'dute!'[6] And she be flaunting it, girl . . . she keeps that waist cinched in." Her son Jonathan recalled his friend's attempt to see the spectacle on a recent trip to Walmart. When Jonathan got all wound up you could hardly understand what he said between his laughter and screams. Tiffany's sons often inserted themselves in the conversation just as it was getting juicy.

At that point mess seemed benign and almost fun to me. However, as I heard the word invoked again and again—more than once every day—I began to realize that it was usually used to refer to malicious intentions and negative circumstances. I had gleaned that "mess," at least, was similar to the standard English definition. But, messy still baffled me. After a few more days, when Tiffany used the term messy again, I finally asked her what it meant. She defined it in relation to the context of our conversation saying something like, "when people are just jealous, haters . . . and don't have nothing to do but stir up mess." Tiffany lovingly warned me and consoled me on more than one occasion by saying that I would learn that "Carlyle folks are just messy." Sometimes she would tell me "these people in Hamilton are messy. They have nothing else to do but get involved in somebody else's business." As an ethnographer, I had crafted the first draft of my primary interview instrument around generic modes of inquiry, such as household composition and social networks. After a while, my interviews became more tailored to my particular field situation. Before long, engaging students about mess became central to my inquiries both formally and informally.

The *American Heritage Dictionary* defines mess and messy in this way:

mess n.
A disorderly or dirty accumulation, heap, or jumble: *left a mess in the yard.* A cluttered, untidy, usually dirty condition: *The kitchen was a mess.* A confused, troubling, or embarrassing condition; a muddle: *With divorce and bankruptcy proceedings pending, his personal life was in a mess.*

messy adj.
Disorderly and dirty: *a messy bedroom.* Exhibiting or demonstrating carelessness: *messy reasoning.* Unpleasantly difficult to settle or resolve: *a messy court case.*[7]

Looking at the above definitions of mess and messy one can see the foundation of this metaphor that is used so creatively in Hamilton.[8] Upon hearing the word "mess," one might imagine a kitchen or a personal life that is in disarray. But in Hamilton, situations aren't "messy," people and sometimes locations are messy. Further, most of the people are judged to be consciously, rather than carelessly, messy.

The *American Heritage Dictionary* definition also is limited in that it leaves out the flavor and spunk that have been attributed to African American vernacular English. John R. Rickford and Russell J. Rickford describe the essence of what they call "Spoken Soul,"[9] in this manner:

It marks black identity; it is the symbol of a culture and a life-style that have had and continue to have a profound impact on American popular life; it retains the associations of warmth and closeness for many blacks who first learn it from their mothers and fathers and other family members; it expresses camaraderie and solidarity among friends; it establishes rapport among blacks; and it serves as a creative and expressive instrument in the present and as a vibrant link with this nations' past.[10]

The invocation of mess in Hamilton, as just one Spoken Soul expression, fits that description well.

In 1994, Geneva Smitherman published a dictionary of African American vernacular expressions that spans ages, regions, and interests. In *Black Talk: Words and Phrases from the Hood to the Amen Corner*, Smitherman "takes you beyond a word list. [The dictionary] is a cultural map that charts word meanings along the highways and byways of African American life."[11] I was pleased to discover "mess" and "mess with" included in her cultural map. Her definitions are as follows:

> **mess:** nonsense; bunch of crap; bullshit

> **mess with:** to bother someone; to hassle or irritate a person. Crossover expression.[12]

These definitions come closer to evoking the feelings that accompany the term mess. However, I approach mess as a metaphor and a "cultural unit [that] has a reality of its own."[13] I learned many regional/cultural terms when I was in Hamilton, such as "womanish" and "biggity," and expressions like "don't it?" and "what you say!" But mess stood out as a fully developed cultural unit, an entity in and of itself. It influenced what people did and how they interpreted the world when the actual term was being used, and when it was not. Pioneering social anthropologist Victor Turner popularized Max Black's notion of a root metaphor. His concept of root metaphor also emphasizes the generative nature of metaphors that are quietly interwoven into speech and thought. Because these metaphors exist as organizing principles in people's heads prior to them being spoken, they help shape the nature of social dramas.[14] I will proceed, then, by exploring mess, "mess with," and messy as three variants of a root metaphor by examining the definitions and categorizations of mess provided by Hamilton's adolescents.

Mess: Nonsense; Bunch of Crap; Bullshit

Smitherman's definition summarizes the essence of what mess means in Hamilton: nonsense, a bunch of crap, and bullshit. I became accustomed to describing people as messy while I was in Hamilton. But mess was typically called upon in a broad, general sense, like "it's so much mess up there"—referring, for example, to Jay Ellis, Carlyle, or "the projects." People and situations were not called *a mess*, as they might be in standard English. The term mess was usually used without an article as if it described a general state of affairs. In the following excerpt, Sabrina replied to my question, why does mess exist:

> **It's** [existence of mess] because the financial situation that half the people are in that they feel the need to talk about other people to bring their self up. That's all it really is. Mostly people who grow up—like Janelle, for example, and Tara was the

same way—people who love to talk about other people . . . I realize it's because their self-esteem is low. And to try to bring their self up they feel like they have to bring somebody down to feel good. Is it hard for you to stay out of it? It's easy for me to stay out of **mess**, *because I don't pay them no attention. Like, Janelle, for example, she always have a little thing to talk about me or something. But, you know what? She been doing OK this week. I don't know why she didn't start talking to me this week. This week? I thought you were going to say this year [laughter]! Uh, uh. This week, this week . . .* **Mess is around us.**

Sabrina's usage showcases the ubiquity of mess. Rather than mess describing a particular situation, it describes a state of affairs, as in the way some English speakers refer to "drama." Not *a drama*, but *drama*. I found it intriguing that when I mistakenly thought Janelle had stopped bothering Sabrina for a whole month, she corrected me and then followed up with the statement "mess is around us." According to the verbal description of mess and the way situations actually transpired in Hamilton, mess was always lurking and within arm's reach.

Sabrina was not alone in her belief that having a long break from mess was an unrealistic expectation. Mess represents a trap that most young people said they tried hard to avoid. I usually asked interviewees if they saw themselves as mostly the same or mostly different from other students at Jay Ellis. Shanika, a very shy junior, quickly answered that she was different. When I asked her why, she linked her shyness to avoidance of mess.

Why do you see yourself as different? Because I'm quiet and I do not talk to nobody. How come you're quiet and don't talk to nobody? 'Cause I don't want no **mess**. *Have you always been quiet since you were little or you just got quiet? They tell me I always been quiet. My mom's quiet too.*

Shanika went on to say she's quiet on purpose. She said she likes to sit back and get information by observing.

While interviewing Janelle, the two of us briefly dialogued about the quality of her neighborhood. Because she, like Shanika, brought up mess on her own, this excerpt provides an example of how mess is used in casual conversation.

What is it like living around here, in this area, in this neighborhood? Do you know all of your neighbors? This is a quiet neighborhood. You know, it's not a lot of **mess** *and stuff. Carlyle is very* **messy**. *What does that mean? 'Cause people think—if they don't know your business, they want to think they know your business. And then it's just—*

But this neighborhood is not like that? Uh uh. *Where are the* **messy** *neighborhoods?* Uhh
. . . the projects is so **messy.** And Crossgates apartment like over by Piggly Wiggly,
those apartments. **Mess.** Those two.

Our dialogue portrays the way mess was used to describe and explain things on a regular basis in Hamilton. Janelle used the terms mess and messy to convey the idea that mess is the opposite of quiet, private living. When mess is around, people "want to think they know your business." The perpetual presence of mess can cause certain areas, such as apartments and neighborhoods, to become messy.

While an event wouldn't be referred to as *a mess*, an event could have been riddled with mess, and therefore be messy and include messy people. One example of a messy situation happened one morning at cheerleading practice the week before school opened for the new school year. The cheerleaders were a small squad of only eight plus the two coaches (including me), and we had been practicing and fundraising over the summer. By that time I viewed our group as a small family. I had no idea that there was mess brewing just under the surface until two of the girls on the squad got into a seemingly sudden verbal and almost physical fight in the middle of practice. The tears, rage, and anger that erupted startled me. When one of the girls involved yelled out, "You are a dirty, low-down snake. Lower than the snakes in the grass," I knew there had to be much more to the story. Although I have no record of this, when I got home that afternoon and Tiffany asked me how things went that day, an appropriate response would have been: "Mess."

Kelly, who was at practice that day and knows both of the girls, described what happened:

I didn't know what was going on at first 'til Trice told me. And she said that her boy friend's brother—well, her boyfriend and his brother got in to it and so her boyfriend's brother sent her friend Janice, who is on the cheerleading squad, a text message saying that he wanted to have sex with her. And she thought it was her friend's boyfriend sending her the message. Janice went around showing everybody this saying, "Oooh he want to do this and he want to do that. I knew he wasn't no good." Then she went and showed Trice. Trice went and asked the boyfriend did he do it. He said no, it was his brother. *****His brother did say he did it, but Janice kept saying it was the boyfriend who did it.** Then the friend brought in the other friend. And the other friend brought in the other friend. Which they should've been out of because it wasn't none of they business. But, uhh, they came up to the school wanting to fight Trice. It was stupid to me. *Well, why would they want to fight her?* That's what I don't even understand. I don't even know. I don't know . . .

This is an authentic recollection of a prototypically messy situation, as it includes confusion, hearsay, and betrayal, three central components of mess. Most important, the story involves intentional troublemaking. The part of the situation that is emphasized reveals that not only was there mess at cheerleading practice, but that Janice was being messy. One key element of the narrative, indicated with an asterisk, was that she found out the story was "mixed up" but intentionally continued to spread it.

Mess With: To Bother Someone; to Hassle or Irritate a Person. Crossover Expression

Smitherman defines "mess with," as "to bother someone, hassle or irritate a person." The way Sabrina described Janelle as "always hav[ing] a little thing to talk about me or something" is an example of someone messing with someone else. However, I never recorded the use of the actual expression "mess with." This might be because, as Smitherman states, "mess with" is a crossover expression, or has been adopted into standard English. Often times, if a Spoken Soul expression has been adopted by the mainstream, it will lose its credibility or appeal in the African American community. Although the expression "mess with" is not used in Hamilton, the concept is still a component of the cultural unit of mess.

Part of what distinguishes "messing with" someone from someone being messy and mess, in general, is that mess and messy situations are polysemic and often include a back story. However, to be "messed with" is casual. If a person is messy, his or her friends should never trust him or her because he could stab them in the back and stir up mess. But, even a messy person wouldn't "mess with" his or her own friends. The manner in which the Bailey sisters describe messy "kids" in Hamilton provides an excellent example of how "messing with" factors into the overall metaphor of mess:

> What's the major difference between living here and living in Ohio, in Cleveland? One: nothing really to do. Two: the kids are a lot more messier down here, too. Mmm hmm. It's a lot more mess. What do you mean by mess? The kids, they'll start with you because they're jealous or you have something that they don't. And they just pick at you cause from where you from.

What the Bailey sisters describe should be placed under the category of "messing with" because they are talking more about being "bothered," "hassled," or "irritated" than about a grander plot. In any event, according to the Bailey sisters constant hassles contribute to the overall presence of nonsense, crap, and bullshit in Hamilton.

Messy

The last component of this cultural unit is "messy," an adjective that typically describes people. The inclusion of this derivation of mess in the vernacular is one thing that distinguishes Hamilton. While mess conveys the image of a generally contaminated area, messy ascribes that contamination to the malice of individuals. Imagine yellow police tape that reads "do not cross" dividing the landscape. Usually this tape indicates that a police investigation is taking place. Crossing into the area marked off by the yellow tape might cause one to disturb the evidence and leave fingerprints or hair in that area. In other words, it's dangerous to cross the tape, and someone might wind up implicating himself and further muddling the situation. Crossing the yellow tape might be akin to getting in mess. That's why most of the adolescents I interviewed said they try to stay out of mess, a task that is difficult when "mess is all around."

Oftentimes in real life, yellow police tape does not necessarily mean that there was foul play. But as popular television shows such as *CSI* and *Law and Order* have made common knowledge, there is a point when the area marked off by yellow tape officially becomes a crime scene, indicating that an actual crime was committed and someone is to blame. The translation of mess from an unfortunate situation to something started with malicious intent, carried out by actual people, marks the use of the term messy. Below, when I ask Sam Miller what the term messy means, he immediately associates it with a person's character:

> What does the term messy mean? **Somebody** that keeps up a lot of stuff and keeps up a lot of "he say, she say" going on and like just get, just like to generate, just like to get messy, just like to get stuff started.

According to Sam, then, there are people who "like to generate" mess and "get stuff started." Returning to the crime analogy, to declare that someone is messy and should be assigned blame for some mess is like finding someone guilty of a crime. The use of the term messy in Hamilton goes one step further. People are not usually declared messy in association with one situation; instead, messiness is a long-term, enduring character trait. It is similar to a belief that people who commit crimes *are criminals*—they have a criminal quality that will cause them to continue to commit crimes.

At one point, Kelly told me that her social circle remains small because of the prevalence of "messy girls" at Jay Ellis:

> *Is there anybody at Jay Ellis that you're [close with]?* Mmm, hmm [laughter]. I don't talk

to too many girls cause they're too messy. *What does messy mean?* They want to talk about everybody. Wanna gossip. Wanna fight . . . Wanna talk about everybody [laughter]. And they sit around and you think that's your friend and they talking about you to somebody else and come back and tell you one thing.

Kelly describes messy people as people who "wanna" gossip, fight, and talk about everybody. Again, intention is key to accusing people of being messy. It's not just that they get caught up in situations that have spun out of control, but they seek out those situations; in other words, messy people love mess. According to Missy, not only do messy people love mess, but they hang around other messy people. Missy, therefore, classifies Jay Ellis students into groups, one of which is the "messy group":

What are some important issues at Jay Ellis? Some changes you would like to see made? I would like to see the students work together more. It's a lot of students grouped off to themselves. Like, we have the messy group, the group that talk about people all the time, even if they don't know you. Like people say I think I'm better than everybody. I don't think like that. And we have some people that . . . we have a group that like to stay off by themselves. *This is in your class or in the school in general?* School in general.

One central quality of mess is that it is always projected outward. In other words, no one would ever describe themselves as messy, although other people might describe them as such. To my understanding, most people might have cause to be judged messy at one point or another. I was curious, then, to see who this "fixed" group of messy people was. I continued to probe Missy about who was in these groups.

OK, so can you tell me who's in the groups? Who's in the messy group? Diamond King, Brittany Rone, Janelle Washington, Keya James, Janice Beasley. They just always talking about people. It's blah, blah, blah, this. Blah, blah, blah, that. "Oh, she's with so and so, and we saw her at so and so's house, at so and so time." And I'm like how does that concern you? I just don't understand it. And, like me, when I see something like that happening, I try to like get away from it. I'll be like, "Trice don't hang around that because they going to be saying you said it or something like that." I just tell her, "Next thing you know you going to be done said something that you really didn't say."

Missy was able to identify a group of people who are messy. As she continues, however, she confirms my hunch that because people pronounce other people to be messy everyday, all day, messy people cannot be limited to a small group.

> *You said there's a group that stands off by themselves?* Umm, they kinda messy too, because I'm a tell you what they did last week. Sabrina, Kevin, Cara Daniel, Isham Bentley, Kelly Lawrence. They were saying some students was picking on them. And I was with them students then, because it wasn't nothing really going on. So I talked with them. Talked about school and stuff and about their kids, 'cause Diamond and John got kids. *Mmm hmm.* And they said we was talking about them. I wouldn't waste my time talking about you when I know I got problems of my own. So, they went to the office and Ms. Moore was like she was going to suspend us. I was like, "For what?" I was like you don't even know if that happened for real. She didn't even get our opinion on it. *Mmm hmm.* She just assumed that—yeah. And they always sitting back thinking, "Oh, they talking about me, they saying this and that about me." I ain't got time to be talking about you. *So it sounds to me like you're kind of in between all the different groups.* Yeah, I mean, I'll try to talk to more people because they like she this and she that. They even call you stuck up. Because you hang with a certain person. So i try to talk to everybody. I don't be trying to make people think I don't like them.

With the addition of the group that stands off by themselves, Missy has called half of the senior class messy. In fact, although she would not declare herself to be messy, her above anecdote implies that other students would call her messy, too. She ended her classification with two other groups: the quiet group, and the boys, who mostly talk about national sports. Missy said she likes hanging around the boys' group. They seem to be least prone to mess.

Messy People Speak

By way of summary, mess is a general state of affairs that surrounds young people in Hamilton. They feel as if they have to regularly deal with "crap, nonsense, and bullshit," three components of mess according to Smitherman's definition. In Hamilton, this nonsense usually takes the form of rumors, fighting, and betrayal. Not only do young people in Hamilton feel that they have to combat mess, but they have to avoid stepping over the "yellow tape" into mess. Mess looms as a trap for everyone who is not careful who their friends are, what they say, and sometimes even where they physically stand.

Mess is purportedly carried out by messy people, or people who love to stir up trouble. Further, the prevalence of mess is regularly attributed to these messy people. One of the most fascinating aspects of the application of this cultural metaphor is that most people are judged to be messy, but no one ever sees themselves as messy. In fact, the pronouncement that people were messy was so cursory and frequent that I often feared I was one question away from being labeled messy myself.

Although everyone was subject to this sort of scrutiny, at one point or another, there were a few people who actually did like to "stir up trouble" and were unanimously described as messy. I was interested in whether they thought they were "messy," and how they saw themselves. Janelle, for example, may have been the messiest person in the senior class. She enjoyed everything from "messing with" people like Sabrina to participating in the rumor mill. When I interviewed her she admitted that throughout her life she has been a fighter. She told me even her mom knows she doesn't "back down to nobody." Still, I think Janelle's own self-image was far more benign than others would have portrayed her:

> *Describe yourself for me.* I am nice when I want to be and just easy going . . . very kind [laughter]. *What are your favorite parts about yourself?* Ummm . . . let me see [long pause] . . . my ability to come back with a smart comment no matter what is being said. *You are very good at that, I must say [laughter]. Where did you get that from? Did you get it from your mom, or . . . ?* [shakes head yes] *She has the same ability?* Yes, she does the same thing. And she's better than me at it. She does it way better than I do. *What's your least favorite part about yourself?* Umm . . . I used to have a negative attitude all the time. But I've kind've changed that because life is too short to walk around with a negative attitude all the time . . . and my hair. *That's your least favorite part? Why?!?* Because . . . you have to wash it every week. And it takes so long for it to dry—two and a half to three hours under the dryer . . .
>
> *How do you think other people see you?* I guess sometimes they think, 'cause I say whatever . . . In a situation, if I have something to say to you I'm going to say it to your face. If someone tells you I said something about you and you come ask me, I'll tell you. I guess that's why. You know I always been like that. Most people [think I'm] funny, and just the clown.

One truth that was rarely espoused was that most messy people had fun, and Janelle was a funny person. Working with her on the cheerleading squad was a frustrating experience, but interviewing her was another story. I wish this project had space to share all of the tales she told me during our interview. Yet, the "fun" that accompanied mess was usually at the expense of others. For example, my cousin Lewis said Janelle made his job as girls' basketball coach truly unbearable. Her irascible attitude, including the instance in which she cursed out the principal, contributed to his leaving the team.

Below, I ask Janelle about the fighting that had taken place on the girls' basketball team during the previous school year. Once we started talking about the locker-room fight, there was level of excitement in her voice, as if she was narrating a heavyweight title match. You can see that what was a nightmare for others was entertainment for her:

Why were ya'll fighting so much last year during basketball season? Were you one of the ones who was fighting? [quiet] *Don't look at me like that.* Oh you talking about in the locker room? *Just in general.* Oh, . . . yeah . . . Me and Trice, everybody. It was like everybody was hitting everybody. *Fist fighting?* Yes! *What?!? What were ya'll fighting over?* I don't know! *Why do ya'll fight?* I don't know! We just came in there. And first me and Trice was fighting. *About what?* I don't know! [chuckle]. And then everybody else started fighting. And it was just everybody. Everybody was in there fighting together. It was just everybody! It was the whole—we was just in there fighting . . . *I like how ya'll get over it though. That's nice that you're friendly now.* It was just—it was so funny. Then after it we were back talking like the next week.

But who was it last year that I remember hearing cursed out Ms. Moore? Who did that? Umm . . . after they got into a fight? *Mmm hmm, I think she tried to stop the fight or something like that.* [quiet]. Umm, was it boys fighting? Oh! Jeremy . . . He said some mean things to her . . . Awful.

When I asked Janelle about the fighting on the team I used my signature playful, yet judgmental tone. As her cheerleading coach, she knew that I didn't find fighting or mess to be acceptable. Nevertheless, she cleverly shifted the tone of our dialogue and proceeded to describe what was, to her, "a funny situation." She further dodged blame and judgment when I asked about an incident that she had been involved in. Instead of admitting blame, she described a different incident involving a student named Jeremy. By the time she finished narrating the details of what happened with Jeremy, I moved on to another topic. And she had successfully dodged "the heat."

James, like Janelle, described himself as "a nice, easy-going person." He was not such a clear case of a messy person because he did not enjoy fighting like Janelle did. In fact, he got along with everyone. He was also a classic instigator. Many of the young men in the school seemed to fill this role. Instead of directly fighting, they would encourage the girls to fight and then sit back and enjoy the mess that unfolded as a result. For example, I was observing a twelfth-grade English class taught by an elderly substitute teacher one day when one of the senior boys, Reggie, pulled out a one-dollar bill and offered the dollar to see Janelle and Keya fight. Everyone was aware that mess between them had been brewing and a fight was pending. Keya responded to

Reggie's goading by saying, "I don't need a dollar, I'll slap her for free," and threw the dollar on the floor. Janelle retorted, "Well, come over here and do it then." Although I halted the fight by returning the dollar to Reggie and calming everyone down, I secretly wanted to see the fight. Mess is seductive; Janelle was being a complete nuisance on the cheerleading squad, and they had been "talking" about wanting to fight for so long that I was ready for them to fight. Reggie concluded the incident by comedically announcing that he had a "dream" that there was a huge brawl at Jay Ellis in which all the girls were fighting.[15] Missy placed James in this category of a messy person—one who doesn't mind instigating some quality mess:

> *Is James quiet?* James is not quiet. James is with the messy group [laughter]. He be pushing people up, "Oh you gonna let her talk about you?" . . . The only teachers that really know him is Ms. Hall and Ms. Scott . . . James, he be telling little silly stories like "look at Reverend Butts, he just fell." And then we look over at Reverend Butts and he just walking to his car [laughter]. He real silly. James—the only time he's quiet is when he knows he's behind on his work. He be like, "Nah, I ain't gonna be the dummy and not get my work." He all business sometimes. But James is real cool. He's an all-around person, though. He talk to everybody.

When I asked James how he thought other people saw him, he explained why people might see him as messy.

> *How do you think other people see you?* As James. I told you, "only one like it!" . . . As a nice, easy-going person . . . See some people view me as being messy, 'cause I get along with everybody. You know folks . . . Say there's [person] A right here, and [person] B right here. I get along with A and B, but A and B don't like each other. So I talk to A, and I talk to B. And I go tell B what A says . . . *That is messy!* That's why they don't like me. [laughter]. That ain't being messy. That's just getting along with everybody. *That's not getting along with everybody. So, A being your friend, and B being your friend, if A asks you what B says, you wouldn't tell?* No! I'd say go ask A. I'm not going to tattle tell. *That's mess! That's messy!*
>
> *What does messy mean?* Messy is just when . . . you know, I don't know what messy is 'cause I ain't never been a messy person. You got to be about it to tell what it is. *You said you've never been a messy person, but you go back and tell A what B said voluntarily.* [laughter and protest] I didn't say that! I didn't say that! *Yes you did!* O.K, let's use real people as an example . . . Let's say me and Sabrina, we cool. But Sabrina and Janelle don't get along. *Right. Everybody knows that.* By Sabrina being my friend, Janelle's, you know, she's my friend, but she ain't as close to me as Sabrina. *Mmm hmm.* Janelle's going to tell me something. By Sabrina being my best friend—her and

Kevin—I'ma tell! I ain't going to keep it down, you know! *Well, that's not messy. But what about the other way around? If Janelle asks you something about Sabrina?* Oh no, no doubt. I wouldn't do that . . . *OK, well, that's not being messy, that's just like you're best friends.*

Once again, intention determines whether someone is messy. From Janelle's point of view, she was not messy because she was just being herself and having fun. According to James, overlapping social circles were the culprit behind his messy persona. Even Missy had to agree that James was "real cool," "an all-around person" who "talked to everybody." James's situation more than anything reveals that the prevalence of messy people may be a function of the small size of the Hamilton community, an environment in which social groups are bound to intersect.[16]

James was not always "trying" to be messy. Janelle, while not using the term messy, admitted to some of the behavior that is characteristic of mess: fighting, having something smart to say, and never backing down. Many of the adolescents I interviewed stated that messy behavior is learned from adults. Therefore, I was not surprised when one day in cheerleading practice, Janelle told me that she liked to hide in the closet and listen to her mom gossip on the phone. Indeed, one of the many interesting facets of young people's engagement with mess was that it was not confined to "youth culture" or created by young people. In other words, wrestling with mess was something that the young and old shared in common.

One Sunday in June a guest from California stood up to introduce herself during the welcoming of the visitors at Payne Memorial AME Zion Church. While she was standing, she took the opportunity to deliver an impromptu speech about "walking the walk." Pastor Duncan constantly encouraged his members to resist backbiting or talking about each other behind closed doors. Well, this day he enjoyed an assenting voice. In her short speech, the visitor emphasized that kids are hard to deal with because they are honest and they imitate and react to adults. She admonished everyone in the audience to tell the truth and "walk the walk" and not just "talk the talk." Kids, she said, "do as they see and not as they're told."

Missy shares this widespread belief that messy behavior comes from the environment. When she was categorizing the students at Jay Ellis, she put one student in the "messy" group, and she attributed his messy leanings toward the influence of his family:

Kevin with the messy group. I mean a lot of his family members are messy, so I see where he get it from. So, I try to ignore that . . .

Kelly attributed her ability to stay out of mess to her mom's warning. More than that, however, she said she decided not to be messy by observing others and "knowing for herself" that she should stay out of mess.

> *How would you say you escaped being messy?* Don't say nothing to them [people] at all, period. Just don't talk to them. *How do you think you became that way to not want to be messy?* Watching to see how the other ones are. How they be talking about each other and etc., etc., etc. *So you just always looked and saw and it always looked ugly to you.* Mmm hmm. *Did your mom ever talk to you about something like that?* She used to, but she ain't have to keep telling me over and over 'cause I already know for myself. So, that wasn't a big issue she had to talk to me about. She'd just say, "Mind your own business. If you tell your business, then your business going to be somebody else's. And then everybody's going to know about it. And they gonna add more on to it." [laughter] *Which they do.* They will tell what you said, twist it around, add more to it, take some off of it, and your story becomes a whole nother story.

To conclude, mess is not just defined by content but by context, as well. In order to understand mess as "nonsense, crap, and bullshit," and messy people as those who keep up the nonsense, one must examine what is judged to be mess, who is judged to be messy, and from where mess comes. Anthropologist David Schneider states it this way, "Words, as names for cultural units, is one of the best ways to begin to discover what the cultural units are. But they have one fundamental characteristic which must be taken into account. A word never has a single meaning except in one, limiting set of circumstances."[17] Through an examination of the various circumstances in which mess is called upon, I have attempted to present a textured definition of what mess in Hamilton actually entails.

From Misfortune to Mess: The Jay Ellis Football Drama

Up until this point, I have described mess based on my interactions and interviews with the young people in the study. By now, one can ascertain how thoroughly interconnected this metaphor is to the identity and everyday lives of the adolescents in Hamilton. Aside from being humorous, however, the principal activities and themes associated with mess have been negative—rumors, gossip, fighting, and betrayal, to name a few. In fact, staying out of mess and overcoming mess consume a great amount of young people's time and energy. Furthermore, discussing mess and discerning who is messy are definitive aspects of peer interactions.

If one of the basic tenets of cultural anthropology is that culture is adaptive, then one might wonder why mess, something so seemingly negative, survives and indeed thrives in Hamilton. Moreover, while some Hamiltonians might argue that young people learn messy behavior from adults, it must have deeper foundations. What, then, are the true roots of this metaphor that go beyond the mere sources of socialization? Below, I will present a narrative of several unfortunate events that transpired while I was in Hamilton. One would hope that any of these events had the possibility to fundamentally interrupt the flow of life in Hamilton, to disturb the social structure, and in doing so, disrupt some of the troubling long-term patterns of social inequality. Instead, the metaphor of mess provided a route through which these dramas could be processed and whatever actors involved in them could be reintegrated into the community fold.

I title this section "from misfortune to mess" because of the character of the predicaments that I will present. The manner in which some of these events transpired could be explained through logical connections among structural constraints, including racism and hegemony; others were simply the result of misfortune. One dictionary defines misfortune as "an unnecessary and unforeseen trouble resulting from an unfortunate event."[18] Oftentimes, while living in Hamilton I felt so amazed by the bizarre and disappointing series of events, which I classify as "misfortune," that I felt like I was living in a television miniseries. My appropriation of misfortune, then, hopefully characterizes the surreal, emotional quality that the events took on, in tandem. Without earnestly attempting to capture the feeling of the events, not only would the central importance of mess diminish, but I would do a disservice to the lived experiences of my young informants.[19]

I use Victor Turner's concept of "social dramas" to complement and elaborate upon Hamilton's particular year-long football drama.[20] Turner defines social dramas as "public episodes of tensional irruption."[21] In other words, social dramas are public community social situations that highlight underlying tensions. They are fascinating to study because these bouts of public disagreement illuminate the process of social change. According to Turner, these social dramas are not instinctual but are the product of "models and metaphors carried in the actors' heads."[22] Here Turner establishes the conceptual link between mess and misfortune by arguing that social dramas (misfortune) are generated by root metaphors (mess). He identifies four stages of social drama, and I will borrow these stages to frame the year-long drama at Jay Ellis.

The first stage of social drama is a breach of social relations signaled "by the public, overt breach or deliberate nonfulfillment of some crucial norm. The second stage is a phase of mounting crisis or escalation. During this phase the original breach becomes a public spectacle and "cannot be ignored or wished away." The third stage is redressive action, in which some sort of adjudication is attempted. During this phase, a "replication and critique of the events leading up to and composing the 'crisis'" may transpire. Finally the fourth stage consists of "either the reintegration of the disturbed social group or the social recognition and legitimization of irreparable schism between the contesting parties."[23]

As a whole, these stages are remarkably consistent with what I observed on the field. They not only frame the social drama that took place, but also they are explanatory, as well. Further, they generate new insights about the repro-duction process in Hamilton. I will revisit the theoretical musings at the end of the chapter. At present, it is time to discover what the social drama actually entailed.

Phase One: Breach

When I came to Jay Ellis at the beginning of the 2003–2004 school year, I had limited knowledge of its recent or long-term institutional history. Therefore, I didn't realize that the excitement and energy that I sensed was out of the ordinary. As each day passed, a spirit of pride and hopefulness became more pronounced, and that spirit quickly endeared me to the school. Of course, frustrations with Ms. Moore's leadership inspired a consistent amount of murmuring from parents, teachers, and students, drowning the attractive energy. Even the complaints did not detract from the overall positive vibes.

One of the regular Jay Ellis characters, Coach Saul Brighton, round and robust in physique as well as personality, told me that he was writing a book about the important history and heritage of Jay Ellis. He was a retired mem-ber of the Jay Ellis faculty, an avid Jay Ellis supporter, and a good friend of Ms. Smith, the guidance counselor. The football stadium was named after him because of the years of service he invested in the young people at Jay Ellis. He said that we should sit down at some point in the coming months and talk about that history. I was intrigued by his suggestion.

By October, I was able to pinpoint exactly what the booming excitement in the school was: a football team that had been losing for as long as anyone could remember was having a break-out, winning season. As a result, people were taking a second look at the "Last Chance School," and Jay Ellis students enjoyed a couple of months when they weren't at "the bottom." The catalyst behind this air of hope was the new Jay Ellis head football coach, John Re-marcke.

John Remarcke was a larger-than-life figure at Jay Ellis. Most likely, no one from outside of Alabama would know who he was. However, as part of the Remarcke family of football heroes from the University of Alabama, and a former pro-football player, he constituted a major presence in the community. In hindsight, his actual physical presence played a large role in the elevated atmosphere at the school. At over six feet tall, always well dressed, markedly laid back, and surprisingly gentle, he strolled the halls at Jay Ellis like a lion in control of his surroundings. Of all the people at Jay Ellis, it was apparent that Coach Remarcke *chose* to be there. The fact that someone with so many options and so much talent wanted to coach at Jay Ellis, loved the school, and respected the community had a subtle, yet significant impact on the positive self-identity of the students, especially the male students. Being at Remarcke's Jay Ellis I felt like I was somewhere special.

Remarcke seemed a natural fit for Jay Ellis. He grew up in a small town in north Alabama and attended a small rural school, similar to Jay Ellis, so he knew where the kids were coming from. He finished high school as the number-one tailback in Alabama, and from then on, sports became his gateway to the world. His vision, then, was to help students like himself make that leap. Coach Remarcke explained:

Coach Brighton had told me, my father had told me, the school has never really won. [They said] "Kids are not motivated to get into athletics. A lot of the parents don't want them to get out there and get hurt." And I accepted that as a challenge. I wanted them to see some of the things I had seen in my lifetime thus far. But it was just a challenge to see if I could get a program that never won, with kids that never had the opportunity, and a chance to try to get to college—see if I could make that happen. And . . . I think I did alright. It was a challenge. When we won on the field, a lot of the guys went to class. A lot of them started passing.

For Coach Remarcke, then, winning football was only a small part of his goal. Translating the winning attitude gained from being successful at football into a positive outlook on life was his broader goal. He would "peep in" on classes and let the students know that he was checking on their academics and that he cared. He said, "You have to let kids know that you really understand what they're feeling. If they're having problems at home and you don't recognize that, then you've lost them."

Even the local newspaper, the *Carlyle Times*, took an interest in the motivational style exhibited by Remarcke, who, by my first year in Hamilton, had already been there for one year. A September 3, 2003, article described the team's excellent showing. Jay Ellis decimated their county rival Attala High School in a game that they won 38–0. Yet, the newspaper picked up on the fact that there was a more significant story; Remarcke was careful how he spoke to his players after the game telling them that "there's a difference in playing a game and winning a game and being a champion." He, of course, was encouraging the latter. The paper continued with more effusive, detailed descriptions of the skill and acumen that the team demonstrated.

When I interviewed Coach Jones, the social studies teacher and assistant coach, he was enthusiastic about the team's recent successes. He was a wonderful complement to Coach Remarcke. If Remarcke was the gentle, loving, father, Jones was the trusted uncle, the warmhearted, boisterous relative who a child would go to when he was too embarrassed to share something with his father. Coach Jones taught all of the social studies classes from sixth through twelfth grade, so the bonds of trust between him and the students were long term and real. He used these bonds to talk straight and "jank" the kids, too. When I interviewed him, I asked him what his best moment was since teaching at Jay Ellis. He replied:

> It has to do with sports. Just to see our kids feel good about winning. Because to me for a long time they felt that they were not supposed to win. For us the last couple of years to have the seasons we've been having, just to beat people and see that look in their face, to go out and accomplish the goals that we set to accomplish . . . I mean that was good. That just felt good.

One article published by a local newspaper near Remarcke's hometown effectively merges the impressiveness of Remarcke's personal accomplishments with Jay Ellis's momentous football season and its effect. Entitled, *"Remarcke turns Jay Ellis into a winner,"* the article states that Jay Ellis had only won twenty-six games in the twenty-three years before Remarcke arrived. The first year the team went 4–6, but the next year, during the time that the article was written, they were 6–1. Not only does this article include more of Remarcke's inspirational quotes, which link athletic performance to classroom performance and encourage championship behavior, but it reveals that Remarcke invited former NFL players and Alabama players to come and talk to Jay Ellis's players about what it means to win in life. In the context of Jay Ellis, such displays of social capital truly were "remarckeable."

Shortly after that article was written, the feelings of hope the school had come to enjoy were abruptly truncated. I arrived at Jay Ellis one day in October only to hear that "they" were taking our games away. "Who is they?" I asked, genuinely confused. What's going on? The answers ranged from the state to the athletic department to "I don't know." Only the worst luck could make such a positive season go awry. A return to hopelessness seemed to have happened.

Unfortunately, the rumors were true. Somehow, the state department of education had received evidence that two of Jay Ellis's players were ineligible, because they had recently moved to the area. This caused the football team to forfeit all of the season's wins up until that point. With that, Jay Ellis was out of the play-offs and back at "the bottom." Immediately the mess started to circulate. Janelle voiced the most widely circulated opinion about what happened:

> You know [the secretary], she's the one who reported our football players. Her and
> . . . the librarian. *Why would they do that to our team? What did they have to gain from*
> *it?* Nothing. *And nothing happened to them after they did that?* No, there was no proof,
> but who else has access to those records but Ms. Moore and Ms. Smith? You know
> Ms. Moore and Ms. Smith didn't do it because Ms. Moore would have to pay out a fine
> if it happened. And Ms. Smith been at that school forever. So, it couldn't have been
> anybody but her.

This was some the messiest behavior someone was accused of in my experience at Jay Ellis. That a secretary and a librarian could seek to bring their own school down puzzled me. However, this was the same secretary who was often accused of embezzling money and was capable of giving people such harsh stares until they would try to avoid her altogether. According to the rumor mill, the secretary's boyfriend coached one of the schools that Jay Ellis had defeated. Jay Ellis had vexed a lot of people by temporarily stepping out from the bottom of the totem pole to take their symbolic rightful place. The secretary's boyfriend supposedly coaxed her into faxing materials that would implicate the school for violation of athletic rules.

The mess was not just that Jay Ellis got caught for intentionally doing wrong. According to various sources, it was that (1) the coaches were unaware of the player's ineligibility; (2) similar and worse infractions regularly take place on other area teams; (3) that this was done to intentionally stifle Jay Ellis's progress; and (4) that this was only one of the many methods used to that end. According to Remarcke, he found out about the forfeited games "on the street." After confirming what he had heard, he hated to have to tell the players what had happened. His account of the event was self-reflective and indicated that sore feelings in the football arena were partly to blame. He went on to tell me:

> My only regret is when I had Jeremy and Clyde. We had guys from Hamilton, Carlyle
> . . . Not knowing the zone, I fault myself for that . . . And they took four games from
> us, which knocked us out of the play-offs . . . Although they were good players, they
> really weren't deciding factors in the games.

He said that he found out that the state department of education had checked the grades on everybody first, and when it couldn't find any infractions in this area, they started checking names and addresses. He attributed some of what took place to his outspoken nature.

> The more and more I look and see the way things happen around here, it's still the good old boy thing ... People plotting up to do things against us ... Like I told the State Department, I said, "Go ahead and take the games from us, it's still not going to stop us from winning the rest of the games." And that's what happened.

The *Carlyle Times* broke the story on October 23, 2003, with a story entitled, "Ellis Must Forfeit Wins." Immediately, the first line of the article targets in on mess. "Rumors surrounding the Jay Ellis High School football team proved to be true this week . . ." The text proceeded to state that Ellis was reported to the Alabama High School Athletics Association by a team that lost to them earlier in the season. Rather than returning to hope and excitement, the rest of the year played out with dramatic highs and lows, punctuated by periods of extreme mess. As Remarcke told me, "We won games that people said we wasn't going to win, like the Miller and Stark River games." The wins further upset people. When Jay Ellis beat Stark River the week after the forfeiture was made public, Jay Ellis was vilified for tearing down the opponent's spirit sign in a show of emotion at the end of the game. The newspaper made it seem as if Remarcke had lost control of his team. Yet, when I interviewed Remarcke, he told me that following the next game, a local reporter came to him and said that he was sorry because he had been at that Stark River game and hadn't seen anything like what they published.

The team finished strong with a 4–2 record after the games were stripped, but the feeling that Jay Ellis did not have to be at the bottom deflated along with the team's pride. The promise of the next season still offered a glimmer of redemption. I wanted to be part of the next year's comeback and decided to take on the challenge of coaching the cheerleading team. In the meantime, other misfortune persisted and always unfolded in a similarly dramatic style.

I walked into the school one day in March, sensing that something was different, and I found that Principal Moore had suffered a stroke. True to her and Jay Ellis's style, it was never clear what happened, where get-well cards could be sent, how severe her health problems were, or if she was ever coming back. One day the school was just sent an interim principal, an agri-science teacher who had been filling in for his own principal while he was on military leave during the previous year. People simultaneously were concerned about Ms. Moore and strangely relieved that they were granted a break from one source of dissatisfaction. To make matters more emotionally draining and confusing, the entire school and community loved and embraced the interim principal.

I can recall the first day that I walked into the school after Mr. Gaines had taken over. The halls were sparkly clean, there were no students roaming around, and an aura of order reigned. According to Coach Jones, under the interim principal's leadership they even had positive faculty communication:

> How often do you all have faculty meetings? I hate to say this. When Mr. Gaines was there, we had faculty meetings every week. They were on Monday or Tuesday, like it should be. You could expect the faculty meetings. But now, uhh . . . at the beginning of the school year, we'll have faculty meetings regularly, but as the school year progresses or whatever, it gets slack . . .

One Thursday morning I was pleasantly surprised to see Mr. Gaines, who was slight of stature but commanding of presence, wearing a suit with suspenders, huddled with a group of students in Ms. Smith's office teaching them how to check the stock market in the *Wall Street Journal*. The more that students, parents, and faculty got a glimpse of what the school could be like with more effective leadership, the more mess started circulating. People "heard" Ms. Moore was never coming back. They thought that maybe she was going to retire at the end of the year and get a new job. But on April 29, that mess ended and reality set back in. Ms. Moore came back; she was greeted with mixed emotions.

Phase Two: Crisis

The last misfortune of the school year happened in such a way that the development of mess was inevitable. Like a snake in the night, someone, some force slithered in during the last week of school and terminated the glimmer of hope that still existed for the fall: Coach Remarcke was fired. This one act felt like a knife had been plunged into the heart of Jay Ellis. It was not that Jay Ellis couldn't find another coach, but Remarcke was more than just a coach. He was Jay Ellis's great symbol that it was not at the bottom. His termination seemed sadistic, mean spirited, and unfair. Parents, especially, had a hard time getting over his dismissal. Just a few weeks prior, Ms. Smith had announced that she was retiring. She told me that she couldn't endure any more of the ridiculous politics coming from the county level. Adding to the sadness of Ms. Smith's departure, the news about Remarcke felt nearly impossible to endure.

As usual, the news was more difficult to swallow because of the manner in which it was disseminated. I was holding cheerleading try-outs when I "heard" Coach Remarcke wasn't coming back. "Something about not completing his certificate," they said. After two wonderful years, Coach Remarcke didn't get a thank you, an assembly, or a good-bye hug from the Jay Ellis community. He described his reason for his termination and the manner in which he was "fired" this way:

> What I was used to, in a program when you're doing certifications, you have three years to do the program, and once your three years is up, you take the exam. What they came back and told me was you got two years to take the exam, but three years to finish the classes. Well, I finished with all of it in two years. So, I took the exam this summer, but "we're going to go ahead and hire somebody because we don't know if you're going to be here or not." That's what I was told.

He said he heard officially from the superintendent, but he didn't want to beg him. When he called Ms. Moore and said, "What's going on, Ms. Moore?" she said, "I don't know, Coach." But according to Remarcke:

> She already knew. She was like, "Uh, Coach, we're going to interview just in case." I said why are you interviewing when I'm not going anywhere? "We're just trying to make sure we're covered."

According to some of my messy sources, the new coach was being shown around the school before Remarcke even knew that he was fired. Once again, Ms. Moore's supposedly "nice" demeanor played out more like backstabbing.

When I interviewed the superintendent, Mr. Donaldson, he showed no regret or emotion about his decision to terminate Coach Remarcke.

> *What about the football coach situation? You know that was the big issue last year with Coach Remarcke.* You know, he didn't do what he had to do. You know, we don't hire really football coaches, we hire teachers. Football, basketball, they're what you call extracurricular. I mean as I mentioned earlier, Jay Ellis is the smallest school in the state with a football program. There are schools larger than Jay Ellis and there are still some smaller than Jay Ellis; they don't have football programs. Football is extracurricular. We hire teachers that can coach football, and they have to be certified. And Coach Remarcke didn't do his academic requirements that were needed, and he knew it. I mean it wasn't like he didn't know what he had to do. And I talked to him after his first year. And, he knew what he had to do.
>
> So, when he didn't have it done, I mean we had to move in another direction. It was a no brainer . . . You know, they give Coach Remarcke a lot of credit for this year's

team, for what Coach Remarcke did in two years, but they just need to go back a few more years before Coach Remarcke got there. Coach Fireman got that program turned around. Coach Remarcke inherited a good team and he had them for two years. And then, Coach Fireman came back. So, you know, I can say I don't have any bad feelings. And Coach Remarcke shouldn't either because we gave him the opportunity to get his degree or finish up the requirements that he had to keep his job. But he wouldn't do it. So, I have a job to do.

Mr. Donaldson's explanation was troubling for several reasons. First, as head basketball coach at Carlyle High for twelve years, he was all too aware that sports in the lives of young people should not be dismissed as just "extracurricular." He knew the transformative power of winning better than most. He spent the last twenty minutes of our interview regaling his own larger-than-life basketball coaching stories. Second, his comment, "You know, we don't hire really football coaches, we hire teachers," made it seem as if Remarcke was an uneducated jock. In addition to holding a bachelor's degree from the University of Alabama, Remarcke taught physical science and health in the Memphis schools for three years. Further, Remarcke argued that the time line for the required certification exam was not made clear (which was not difficult to imagine) and that he passed the exam over the summer. Finally, Donaldson's insistence that the missing certification was the plain and simple reason for Remarcke's termination was disingenuous. According to Coach Fireman, Remarcke's predecessor and replacement, Donaldson's reasons for terminating Remarcke went beyond that. According to Coach Fireman:

> Donaldson told me that he didn't get his paperwork in. And the ineligible players, and tearing down the signs at Stark River, that was just an embarrassment to the whole school and the school system. So him not having his paperwork in made it easier to let him go. *So, he did intend to let him go, that's what I thought.* Now, you cannot believe what the people tell you. *Who's "the people?"* The people around here. Like I just told you, that's what Donaldson told me when he interviewed me. He told me that's exactly why Remarcke got fired. I mean this is not the first time that a coach did something to embarrass the school and got fired behind that.

In other words, the messy people were at least partially right. Remarcke's termination had little to do with an incomplete certification. It had more to do with "the embarrassments" that Jay Ellis caused the county system. The "messiest" folks would probably say it had even more to do with Jay Ellis's unwanted success.

Not only did Remarcke's termination rip apart a positive role model from

Jay Ellis—a caliber of which doesn't voluntarily come to a remote rural location every day—but it firmly reestablished the almost-toppled "Last Chance" persona of this country school in the public eye. An article from the July 7, 2004, *Carlyle Times*, entitled "Remarcke-able Coach Gone," rehashes the Stark River incident with the same exaggerated language as it had before, calling it a "vicious scene" where the players "brazenly destroyed the paper" banner. It states that "Remarcke battled through the immature actions of his players," but also "built a strong program and sternly disciplined players for their poor behavior." Jay Ellis's inspiring, hard-fought, winning season was reduced, in the end, to the "immature actions" and "poor behavior" of its players. And Remarcke's legacy at Jay Ellis was that he knew how to "discipline" them.

Shortly after Remarcke got fired, Coach Saul Brighton dropped dead of a sudden heart attack before I ever got to interview him about his book plans or his time at Jay Ellis. The July 15 *Carlyle Times* published a beautiful article about his impact on Jay Ellis. The article said, "Brighton was Jay Ellis athletics. Coaching was his passion in life and the kids he coached were that passion's heartbeat." It went on to describe how in the thirty-four years at the school, he was everything from the school's bus driver to a dedicated and passionate coach, teaching every single aspect of football, as an art and science. One teacher said, "He loved coaching, he loved his players, he was their father and they were his children." Coach Brighton's funeral was packed with former students and colleagues, friends and families who came to pay honor to such a great man.

Phase Three: Redressive Action

Thus far mess has been portrayed as a silent partner to all of the misfortunate events that took place in this true-life story. In many instances, figuring out who was messy was critical in helping people to understand why so many negative things were happening. In other instances, lack of clear information required people to speculate about what was really going on. By the start of the 2004–2005 school year, mess had overshadowed misfortune as the dominant force at Jay Ellis.

Because of the manner in which Remarcke was let go, Fireman's return to the school was tough. First, Fireman had a history with Jay Ellis, as he had been the head coach at Jay Ellis for the three years immediately preceding Coach Remarcke. According to Coach Fireman, Mr. Donaldson, Ms. Moore, and some Hamilton community members and Jay Ellis students—when they weren't being messy—Fireman really should have been credited with building the foundation for the success of the Jay Ellis football team. To the average Hamiltonian, Fireman was someone who had abandoned the team after a better offer came. To them, rehiring Coach Fireman was not a stroke of good fortune or fate; it was evidence that they were going backward.

Second, Fireman's style was the polar opposite of Remarcke's. While Remarcke played the role of the firm, but level-headed, professional gentleman, Fireman saw Jay Ellis as his kingdom and liked to rule with discipline, humor, and brazen energy. He, as well, was at least six feet tall and brown skinned. However, if Remarcke embodied the traits of a lion, Fireman's persona was that of a tiger, muscular and lean, ready to pounce, dripping in youthful, aggressive energy. This kind of braggadocios banter was typical of Fireman:

> After everybody left [last night] I put a coat of wax on [the floor]. That's part of the reason I like small schools. I like it being mine—this mine. When you come in here, Ms. Moore's going to say, "That's Coach Fireman's." "Get out my gym!"—You never heard me say that? *Not to me* . . . . Athletics is mine. I like that about it.

While the community may have loved Fireman the first time around, after Coach Remarcke they had been exposed to a new way of handling situations . . . one that many preferred.

Finally, the unapologetically messy folks said that Fireman was really fired the first time. They talked about his anger issues, insinuated that he had acted improperly toward female students, and said that he offended a lot of people by the way he left with tasks like college scholarship applications unfinished.[24] Fireman described his own persona the first time around as "wild" and told me that he was "a ladies' man" back in those days before he was married. Besides these things, Fireman and Moore had a close relationship because he is one of her only "hires" in the school. Fireman said:

> Ms. Moore was probably the best thing for me coming out of college and having a principal—she was the best one for me. *Why do you say that?* 'Cause I was crazy. I was still young and wild. So anything those kids said, I would ball them up.

According to his recollection, Ms. Moore was patient and forgiving with him, recognizing his potential. He also said that he reminded Ms. Moore a lot of her late son, who was tragically killed since she had been principal at Jay Ellis. Overall, as far as mess management and moving the school forward, hiring Coach Fireman did not make for an easy transition.

When it came to football, Remarcke and Fireman had slightly different perspectives, as well. For example, the August 13, 2004, newspaper article that announced Fireman's return was entitled "Fireman's Goal: Win Football Games at Jay Ellis School." When Fireman was asked where he saw the football team on November 1, he replied, "Where every coach sees his team . . . getting ready for the play-offs." Coach Fireman's stated goal "just to win a game" contrasts with Remarcke's lofty mission presented earlier. One of the cheerleaders confided in me that before the ACP game, she overheard him tell the players that if they really wanted to win against the white boys at Alabama Christian Prep, they had to "know how to really say some dirty stuff to them when they get up close to throw them off." The students were very involved in the mess that this situation created, and they were constantly weighing in on it.

As the season progressed, the mess grew worse. There was misfortune, too; for example, there was a melee at an away game in which a parent from the opponent's team brandished a gun. Unfortunately, "nonsense, crap, and bullshit" reigned supreme. At one point, accusations of illicit affairs between some teachers and the coaches became the mess du jour. In general, throughout most of the season the wall that divided Fireman's and the parents' perspectives became more cemented. When I interviewed Fireman three days before I left in December, he oscillated between his characteristic cocky attitude and a very self-reflective hurt one:

And what did you think about last year, last season? I think that was Remarcke's fault and nobody's blaming him. *Why was it his fault?* 'Cause he knew them boys was ineligible. He knew that. But they're not blaming him. I was surprised at how much they loved him. They didn't love me like that.

Until the day that I left, he still never understood why Remarcke was so loved, and he resented it:

It was a big disappointment to me. The boys listened to the community. And uhh, they wanted Remarcke back. They was treating it like I got him fired. And the three games we lost, that's why we lost, 'cause they was pouting. And I told them, "I didn't get him fired, he got himself fired." But the irony is, I started every one of them that's playing football. Every one of them.

Telling the team that Remarcke "got himself fired" was not the way to win players over. In truth, however, he was speaking out of frustration. The community had become nasty and made it very difficult for the boys to play during the fall 2004 season. Players almost quitting, quitting, and returning were three nonstop features of the football season. And the effect trickled down to the cheerleading squad, as well. We started the season with seven girls and finished with only four. One of the low, messy, moments came during a game that we were losing. The crowd in the bleachers started a chant, "Bring back Remarcke, Bring back Remarcke!" Even Kelly, who typically stayed out of mess, was uncharacteristically harsh when it came to Coach Fireman:

> *How would you compare Coach Remarcke and Coach Fireman?* Oooh. Coach Remarcke was a good coach. He brought the team up from a long way. Coach Fireman calls the wrong plays. I can say that's clear. He calls the wrong plays. He thinks he callin the right plays, but he's calling the wrong plays [laughter]. *Ooohh.* He would say, "Man, I had the right play and everything." He did the same plays at that game over and over and over again. I think he loves football, but I don't think he's too good at it.

By the end of my interview with Coach Fireman, he actually voiced the full lack of trust that he had in the community:

> Do you know Tom Franklin? . . . Yeah. His son, Tony Franklin goes to Alabama A&M. Tony Franklin could not pass math to save his life. He was a senior. Everybody wanted him. He was an athlete, one of the best to come through. I tutored that boy in math every day. Every day I tutored him in math. Before practice, I tutored him in math. When that test came back and he passed math, that boy stood in the middle of that floor and hugged me, crying. Tom Franklin was leading the cheers against me, saying, "We want Remarcke back." Ain't that something? That's what I think of the community right there. Can't trust them. My coach in college calls them "stamp people." *What is "stamp people?"* You know, when they came out with those stamps for Martin Luther King and you looked at 'em, and you was like "man that's a nice stamp for Martin Luther King." But when you flipped it over what you did? *Lick it?* Spit on it. Stamp people. They praise you on this side and spit on you on that side . . . But that can't stop my work with these boys.

Phase Four: Reintegration

Ironically, despite his frustrations and his distrust of the community, Fireman got just what he wanted. And the end of the football season Jay Ellis had won more games than ever before and made it to the play-offs for the first time in school history. There was a slight joy in the team's "victory." But exhaustion and mess overshadowed the achievement, even for Coach Fireman:

> *How did you feel at the end of the football season?* I felt great. We made the play-offs for the first time . . . It wasn't as gratifying to tell you the truth, 'cause we could have did a whole lot better. If they would have listened to me from the beginning, instead of fighting . . .

By the time I left the field, I had discovered one hidden truth about how mess works, an explanation for why virtually everyone was messy: the only way to remain non-messy is to resist accusing others of mess. When I asked Darnel, who was at that point the football captain, and Mr. JEH about the mess, he proved that at least one non-messy person did exist:

> *What about Coach Fireman and Coach Remarcke? What are the differences between them?* There's not really a difference, but Remarcke was more experienced than Fireman was. You could learn more from him. But we also can learn from Fireman if we pay attention. But [there's] a little controversy between the team and the coach. *The team and Coach Fireman? Cause he left, or . . . ?* Some think it's because he left and came back. Say that he should respect us more. Some of the things he does just. It's not really a big difference. *Take me through—how did you feel as the season was going along? You were there when Coach Fireman was there the first time. Where was the team at that point?* The first year we was just . . . losing. The second year or two we was gradually going up, but we was going up. Pretty good, pretty good coach. *Why do you think the team was going up? What was changing?* Attitude. Being dedicated, taking responsibility for what they had to do . . . *So last year . . . the whole drama, the controversy with the games being taken away and stuff . . . what did you think when you heard about that?* Angry, mad. *Who do you blame for it?* No one. I blame no one for it. It just happened. Probably wasn't meant for us then. Things just happen. That's it.

The Reproduction of Misfortune through Mess

By examining the football saga through Turner's four phases of social drama, one can see how an initial breach, the football wins being taken away from the team, escalated into a crisis, which was generated by Remarcke's sudden termination. The redressive action to hire Fireman only further escalated the social drama. In fact, Turner states that "when redress fails there is usually a regression to crisis."[25] Another of Turner's theoretical insights rings especially true in the case of Jay Ellis:

> Where the disturbed community is small and relatively weak vis-à-vis the central authority . . . regression to crisis tends to become a matter of endemic, pervasive, smoldering factionalism, without sharp, overt confrontations between consistently distinct parties.[26]

"This endemic, pervasive, smoldering factionalism" was evident at Jay Ellis's football games, in which words such as "Bring back Remarcke" were chanted. Declaring people to be messy, wearing school colors, cheering for the team, and, at times, cheering against the team, all took the tone of smoldering, sometimes contradictory, factionalism. Indeed, the final reintegration of all the actors through a groundbreaking football season maintained the social structure, but did so in a most unsatisfying way.

All of the above actions, messy as they were, also functioned as powerful forms of resistance. According to Bourgois, a "culture of resistance is not a coherent, conscious universe of political opposition but, rather, a spontaneous set of rebellious practices that in the long term have emerged as an oppositional style."[27] Students at Jay Ellis do not compare notes about their individual practices; in fact, many are largely unaware that their invocation of mess significantly impacts Jay Ellis. Each is engaged in his or her own behaviors in their own contexts. Yet, mess has emerged as "an oppositional style." In his seminal text, *Weapons of the Weak*, James Scott argues that "as a form of resistance . . . gossip is a kind of democratic 'voice' in conditions where power and possible repression make open acts of disrespect dangerous."[28] In a small community dominated by racial inequality, open protest can and—in southern communities, especially—has been dangerous. Therefore, the metaphor of mess and the system of gossip that encompasses it have emerged as a style of resistance.

Yet, in the midst of misfortunate, conflict-laden situations, the metaphor of mess became the vehicle for the cultural production of misfortune. It helped to reproduce Hamilton's structure: those mechanisms that kept the school doors open, allowed the football program to continue, kept students engaged in school, prohibited out-and-out rebellion or anarchy, ensured that people had jobs and received checks . . . and termination notices, and set people's calendars according to a school year and a football season. Unfortunately, this basic structural maintenance also led to the continual perpetuation of Jay Ellis's "Last Chance" characterization in the press, and unchecked discrimination in the school system. In *Schism and Continuity in an African Society*, Victor Turner argues (quoting Carole Hill) "that conflict is inherent in any social structure, but that, with the exception of radical change, 'a set of mechanisms exists whereby conflict itself is pressed into the service of affirming group unity.'"[29] The metaphor of mess in Hamilton was the mechanism that helped to affirm group unity, in spite of the inherent structural conflicts.

Mess helped to reproduce the social structure in two specific ways. First, mess helped people to cope with devastating misfortunate events that were largely out of their control. By using a familiar language and set of symbols to discuss situations, people could move beyond and quickly accept even the most unexpected events; for instance, death and the loss of people with whom they had developed meaningful relationships, like Coach Fireman or

Coach Remarcke. Second, mess promoted social cohesion.[30] At all times, the culture of mess generated interaction. Stirring up mess, being messy, and calling people messy all involved other people. In misfortunate situations where people might have retreated into solitude or depression, mess deterred those options.

One captivating debate that the social drama presented in this chapter highlights is whether metaphors, such as mess, that work to maintain the social order actually promote a "false consciousness vis-à-vis social problems and social struggles."[31] Scholars of metaphor are keenly aware that in linking two new semantic domains, metaphor highlights certain properties of social existence and masks others.[32] By my estimation, in Hamilton, mess highlighted individual actors and motives while masking systemic, impersonal, forces of inequality. Did mess, then, do a good or bad thing by maintaining the social structure despite misfortunate events that took place in Hamilton? The ethnographic data presented here do little more than prove that there is no clear answer. On one hand, without the metaphor of mess, more students might have dropped out of school, or pent-up pessimism could have severely disrupted productivity. On the other hand, mess helped maintain the status quo. By focusing on who was messy instead of what plan of action could be taken, structural inequalities such as those discussed in the last chapter persisted. Without mess, Hamiltonians young and old might have been more forceful and effective advocates for social change.

Three closely related suppositions underlie the logic that determined how mess reproduced misfortune:

(1)**If:** Messy people exist
And: Messy people don't change
And: Messy people create mess
Then: Mess is inevitable.
(2) **If:** Mess is inevitable
And: I am not messy (people don't judge themselves to be messy)
Then: My actions won't impact anything.
(3) **If:** I underestimate the power of my actions.
And: I succumb to mess.
Then: I have the potential to create mess or cause unfortunate situations to occur.

Viewed in isolation, any of these suppositions can help explain people's beliefs, attitudes, or actions. As three parts of one whole, this logic explains how mess, itself, is created and perpetually regenerated by people who rarely believe that they are messy.

Looking at the case of the year and a half long social drama at Jay Ellis, one can see that responding to misfortune with mess eventually created misfortune. During the first school year, actual unforeseen events caused people to respond with gossip, speculation, fights, and so on. By the time the second school year began, however, the mess began regenerating itself. People believed that messy people had created and would continue to create a mess. So, parents criticized the coach and liberally speculated about his personal life. Students quit the football team and cheerleading squad, murmured and complained because they believed that their actions wouldn't really impact anything. In the end, everyone was active in making mess "king" over the football team and a long-awaited victory feel anticlimactic.

When examining the daily lives of the adolescents, one can see how larger social dramas help set the cultural tone for the enactment of day-to-day life. Consider, for example, one student Letice's evening phone-call ritual. The way she reportedly engaged life through the metaphor of mess resembles the way the larger community engaged misfortune through mess:

So you say you talk on the phone every night. What do you usually talk about? My relationship, how it's going . . . With my friends we talk about what we did at school today and what's the word on the street. What's going on and what are we going to do for our holiday . . . and just talk about regular stuff. When you say "what's the word on the street . . . ?" Like, who got beat up, "girl, who pregnant by who," stuff like that [laughter]. Do you consider that to be gossip? Yes. Do you like to gossip? I don't gossip about other folks, but I love to hear gossip from somebody.

And what about messy . . . do you consider yourself to be messy? No, if you listen to my voicemail on my cell phone I got, "You have reached the girl Letice at the right number, but at the wrong time. Sorry I'm not able to answer your call at this time, but if you would please leave your name, number, and a detailed message, I'll think about returning your call. For all the haters that have the nerve to call my phone about mess, I will appreciate it if you stop calling my phone. Because mess is not my specialty, and I don't consider myself messy." . . . And everywhere I go I hear mess and I will sit down and listen but I won't say anything about it. But who starts it? Where does it come from? Who keeps it up? Messy folks. It's certain people that keep it up.

What's the latest word on the street? What's going on now? It's settled down right about now. It's nothing going on . . . that I know of. It ain't got steamy yet [laughter]— Oh, oh, that my friend Latoya Daniels is pregnant and she's not! And Lena Jones. Why would somebody spread that? Hating. You have folks who just want to say something just to say something to somebody. *When you hear stuff like that [do] you know who started it or you just . . . by the time it gets to you, you don't know who said it in the first place?* By the time it gets to me I don't know who said it.

In Hamilton, large-scale collective misfortune was a partner to larger forces of oppression. Both were complemented by personal misfortune, such as teenage pregnancy. These misfortunes were all, in part, reproduced through the same metaphor of mess. Letice's voicemail message reveals the polyvalent, poetic quality of mess, which allowed her to at once poke fun at mess, express a belief that messy people were villainous, but welcome mess into her life. This excerpt also reinforces the understanding that creating minute categorical differences, for example, between gossip and mess, allows young people to benefit from the social cohesion associated with mess without feeling guilty.

Conclusion

In sum, I have argued that mess is a metaphor that impacts life in Hamilton on a daily basis. It is used to explain the nonsense that takes place in the Hamilton community. In addition to mess acting as a metaphor, attributing the existence of nonsense to mess and messy people is actually a ritual. On the individual level, mess functions differently for each adolescent. It determines some young people's social networks and behavior; it gives others a blueprint for acceptable values and qualities, and it allows others to dodge blame. On the group level, constant deliberation about who is messy provides social cohesion for the adolescents in Hamilton. Also, mess helps them to explain (and I would argue to cope with) why misfortunate events seem to always plague them. In a general sense, mess provides a symbol to the spirit of overcoming that is so much a part of their identity. Finally, on the broadest structural level, mess reproduces the social structure in Hamilton. Hamiltonians are united by this ever-present metaphor that is invoked before, during, and after any given social situation.

Chapter 5   Resistance and Spirituality

The past several chapters have situated the youth of Hamilton, Alabama, within the political economy of their everyday lives. Persistent racism and inequality, especially within the school system, undergird the minute social dramas that empirically ground daily life. In this way *Raised Up Down Yonder* has answered Kamari Maxine Clarke and Deborah Thomas's call for ethnographies that, in carefully examining ethnographic subjects within their particular historical and structural milieu, call attention to the processes that many black subjects throughout the Diaspora may share.[1]

The previous chapter, "Reproducing Misfortune through Mess," provided an analytical lens through which to understand how a creative metaphor perpetuates the status quo. However, one should not misinterpret *Raised Up Down Yonder*'s reliance on cultural production theory as "waving a white flag of surrender" in the face of inequality or as an acquiescence to the notion that all action gets subsumed under the process of reproduction. One of the strongest criticisms of social reproduction theory has been that it proscribes a narrow interpretive framework for understanding social action.

In his now-canonized phraseology, Gayatri Spivak asked, "can the Subaltern speak?"[2] Before and since Spivak raised that question, various scholars have maintained that they can. In 1968, Paolo Freire in his pathbreaking treatise, *Pedagogy of the Oppressed,* argued that adult literacy in Brazil could be marshaled as a tool to combat oppression, in effect using the oppressor's own weapons against him.[3] Sherry Ortner examined the debates over universal male dominance and concluded that male dominance may be a pervasive hegemony, but "there will always be (for better or worse) arenas of power and authority that lie outside the hegemony and may serve as both images of and points of leverage for the alternative arrangements."[4]

A number of powerful ethnographic studies have focused on the ways that the "subaltern" actually can speak. For example, in one recent ethnography, *She's Mad Real: Popular Culture and the West Indian Girls in Brooklyn*, Oneka LaBennett shows how her subjects employ popular culture to "resist class, racial, and gender inequality" in unpredictable ways.[5] In large part, focusing on resistance represents an orientational rather than a theoretical turn. It speaks to the kinds of questions researchers ask, especially of minority subjects. As I outlined in both the preface and the introduction to *Raised Up Down Yonder*, it is vitally important to find a balance between critically examining social inequality, and granting people, especially often misrepresented minority groups, agency. Not only minority groups, but also youth have been miscast as unable to exert agency. This misrepresentation has been based on a psychological and biological conceptualization of youth as incomplete adults, and many scholars are working to combat this issue.[6]

I define resistance as opposition to oppression in overt and subtle ways. Sometimes resistance is intentional, but sometimes it is purely embodied as a part of the general opposition to one's position in the social structure.[7] The ethnographic record is rich with examples of these forms of creative resistance within and outside of schools in the United States and abroad.[8] Most of these behaviors seem typical of teenagers; forms of joking and avoiding work, listening to and creating music, commandeering public space, or dressing in a certain manner are examples. However, in *Resistance and Rituals*, Stuart Hall and the subcultures group at the Birmingham Centre for Contemporary Cultural Studies (BCCCS) argue that these youthful displays of resistance are created by specific historical and structural circumstances. Any similarities between the styles of youth all over the globe, then, have to be linked first to processes in their own sphere of influence, both local and translocal, and then these contexts can be comparatively examined for similarity and/or difference.[9]

At Jay Ellis, the oppositional style of resistance ranges from janking, to "mess," to not doing homework assignments, to lingering in hallways and in the gym. Again, while there are threads of similarity in the ethnographic record, one must also refrain from overgeneralizing. For example, unlike the young people in Nikki Jones's recent work with young girls in California, young people in Hamilton aren't on the whole resisting violence as part of their everyday lives.[10] Unlike many of the fine ethnographies written about U.S. immigrants and social policy, they are not pushing back against assaults to their language or citizenship.[11]

What is the point? Resistance in Hamilton is subtle and playful. It is born out of the everyday character of young people's lives. When I was in the field, there were no social protests, no threats of violence in the schools, no rampant profanity in the schools. Yet, resistance was discernible, as evidenced by teachers and sometimes parents "observations," which are further addressed in the next chapter. Resistance was also identifiable because young people were often able to explain why they were behaving in ways that were judged to be problematic. Resistance in Hamilton, then, principally derives from five ongoing processes: constraints in the family, described in chapter 1; persistent racial and political economic inequality, highlighted in chapters 3 and 4; mischaracterization and racial bias in the local media, detailed in chapters 3 and 4; and a global political economy that provides narrow future options, which will be examined in the conclusion.

The fifth and final influential structural element that is greatly impacting the young people, and has thus far been left out of this picture, is the decreased significance of the church as a local institution. Elsewhere, I have written in detail about the major historical changes in Hamilton's African American churches, which were at one time the center of life but are now marginalized to a great extent.[12] Let me summarize the argument: as a result of out-migration, shifting labor patterns, school dislocation, recent complicated church history, and improved technology, the wedding of church and community has been dissolved. Consequently, young people have been greatly affected by these changes.

Most older black Hamiltonians grew up attending church every Sunday morning regardless of what they were doing Saturday night.[13] However, by the time of my research, although the students whom I interviewed all belonged to a church, their attendance and participation were irregular, and most reported that they were not very religious. When I asked James if he participated in activities with the young people in his church he said, "Naaaa. I listen to the preacher preach, that's it." Each Sunday morning in my cousin's household, Tiffany struggled to get Justin and Jonathan out of bed to prepare to attend church. Many Sundays she just left her sons asleep or playing Playstation in the living room. In sum, in approximately fifty years the black church has shifted from the centerpiece of the Hamilton community to its periphery.

This chapter, then, seeks to examine the resistance to social inequality that Hamilton youth deploy in response to diffuse structural constraints. I will examine one young lady's resistance within and outside of the school.[14] I choose to use Missy's biography to show the logic of resistance from the individual standpoint. Indeed, scholars from the BCCCS have identified biography as one understudied missing link in the investigation of styles of resistance.[15] However, Missy will stand in for all of Hamilton's youth and their forms of resistance that, while not identical to hers, have their own bases and particular logics. Missy's story, full of drama and poignancy, will be presented largely in her own words. The choice to present so much of her interview is intended to underscore the agency and subjectivity of *Down Yonder*. As Missy's voice emerges from the constraints of structure, history, culture, and other chains of abstraction, so, too, will spirituality emerge as one important component of creative agency.[16]

Resistance

Melissa Parker was a seventeen-year-old senior at Jay Ellis during the 2004–2005 school year. With her chocolate-brown skin and a healthy head of shoulder-length hair, she was quietly confident. Although she possessed a quintessentially high school physique (medium build, petite height, fit but not "worked out"), she was not a member of the cheerleading squad or the dance team. Instead, she preferred to be involved in school from a bit of distance, almost as if *she* were the participant-observer. Her sharp, witty tongue contrasted nicely with her luminous smile. In fact, her oscillation between straight faced and gleaming constituted a show of creative resistance in itself.

The first thing that set Missy apart from all of the other students I got to know was that she came looking for me. Missy was a victim of Mr. Buford, a controversial math teacher at Jay Ellis, who failed many of his math students during the 2003–2004 school year. Due to his erratic behavior and dubious teaching skills, most students in his math classes mentally and emotionally disconnected from the class, stopped doing work, and, as a result, earned poor grades. After realizing that she wasn't "vibing with" Mr. Buford, Missy decided to drop his class rather than earn an "F" and suffer any more "stress." She investigated and found out that she could take a geometry correspondence course through the University of Alabama that would count toward her high school graduation. The next year, that's exactly what she did.

Shortly after I started tutoring for the ACT course during the final period of the school day (September 2004), the students stopped attending, preferring to roam the halls or harass the guidance counselor about their transcripts and other college application details. Missy, in her understated yet forceful manner, wisely usurped this opportunity to get my help on her geometry work. I was glad that someone actually wanted my help, so we began to spend time together almost every day during the last period of school. The thing that surprised me most was that Missy was highly uninterested in my doing the work for her. In fact, she was highly uninterested in getting the right answers without understanding why or how. This was the first time that I had come across anyone in college, or in high school, who literally taught themselves a math course. She rewrote the textbook chapters in her own handwriting, attempted all of the practice questions, asked for help from the math teacher, Ms. Scott, on her lunch break, and worked with me every afternoon. This work was completed in addition to the assignments and exams that she was required to send to the University of Alabama each Friday to be graded. I was stunned by her resolve, especially in an environment where her tenacity (regarding math) was not the norm and for which there were almost no rewards.

When I attempted to share my delight about Missy's academic performance with a few of the "adults" at the school, they were unimpressed. Some were kind of cynical; they were glad that she "finally turned herself around." Others had commentary about her family situation or her attitude problem. Part of the faculty's ambivalence may have been caused by her particular brand of in-school resistance, which included behaviors such as tardiness.[17] Below she describes her occasional lateness, which was clearly a conscious form of resistance:

> *Who are your favorite teachers at Jay Ellis?* I try not to have favorites, I'll just say my favorite class: Ms. Scott [laughter] . . . I mean some teachers, like if you teach me, and you help me understand the best way you can, I'ma like your class anyway. Like Ms. Scott's class, like last week I had got to the point where, last week, I came to school two times at 11 o'clock. That's when Ms. Scott's class starts. Cause she teaches just about every day. Some days she say, "well, I'm going to give ya'll a small amount of work and you all do the work and you can have the rest of the period free."
>
> But she's like the only teacher that teach every day. Ms. Roberts, some days she get mad. I don't know what she be mad at, but she just . . . *What about Ms. Borland?* She try to teach, but the kids already know she let them run over her. So they gonna do what they wanna do as long as they can. And whenever she go get Ms. Moore, whoever the principal is, that's when they start doing their work. So, practically they just run over Ms. Borland. I know you hear her out in the hall hollering all the time.

Chronic tardiness and a general lackadaisical attitude about time were endemic at Jay Ellis. Missy discussed her lateness with me on other occasions in which she provided specific reasons for her lateness, such as family obligations or illness. Yet, I believe it is only in our conversation presented above that Missy truly discloses the real motive behind that behavior: rebellion against a structure in which she felt teachers often wasted her time. Missy "love[d] Jay Ellis," but her no-nonsense approach to her subjects meant that she expected to learn something new in each class every day. She exercised her agency by missing classes from time to time.

Once again, my interest in Missy's life was piqued when we were chatting in Coach Jones's classroom one afternoon and she expressed frustration over her mother's religious hypocrisy. She lamented her mom's inability to see that she can't profess to be so religious and "all into the church" and still yell at her all the time. This led to a discussion about Missy's spirituality, during which I found out that she attended a church in Mississippi, an hour away. Part of my befuddlement at Missy's willingness to share this part of herself was that she was the first adolescent who volunteered information about her spirituality. Moreover, Missy's physical presence did not insinuate her level of spiritual commitment—she always wore a pair of fitted jeans, a trendy shirt or pullover (usually in black or red, her favorite colors), her hair was always styled, and she had "edge." She was sweet, but she definitely showed attitude. One day, for example, she suggested that I try using baby oil on my heels to get rid of the "ashiness." "Ms. McMillan, you can't be all cute and then have ashy feet. It don't work that way."

When we finally talked in the formal interview situation, on the tranquil second floor of Hamilton's downtown library, I was overcome one final time by Missy's willingness to share, and her ability to tell her own story in a coherent way, as if she were penning an autobiography. There were few observations that I had made about her that she hadn't already made about herself . . . so much so that midway through the interview I told her, "You are a very self-actualized person. Do you know what self-actualized means?" She replied, "You mean I realize things about myself . . . yeah [laughter]."

Therefore, from this point forward I will include large portions of Missy's interview with very little of my own commentary. It is far more interesting to hear her voice the very things that I would have written. This interview was my longest—over two hours, so there is still much detail omitted. I have selected excerpts that highlight who she is and what aspects of her social location have become the seedbed for her creative resistance. Most important, however, one can observe how her spirituality has afforded her a creative space of her own.

By way of biographical introduction, Melissa was born in Carlyle but was raised with her mom, dad, and aunt in New York, Ohio, and Michigan until they moved back to Alabama when she began Head Start. From there, she lived with her mom in Deepwoods until the seventh grade, when she decided to move in with her grandmother, not very far away. She has an older brother and an older sister, both in college, one younger brother, who was in the tenth grade at that time, and one younger sister. Her father and mother split up when she was young and both remarried; Missy has six stepsiblings between both parents. In addition Missy told me, "my dad's got seventeen kids spread across the U.S. He finally admitted to it last year." I made sure to clarify this information by asking, "Really across the U.S.?" to which she replied, "Really across the U.S. I'm serious."

We begin Missy's voice with an explanation of her self-described "attitude problem" that she developed in the sixth grade:

Umm, like I said I had to try to show people that I was, I couldn't let them walk over me. *Did you feel like people walked all over you [I interrupted].* Yes, I did . . . And I was . . . let's just say me and Tasha James and this girl named Jessica, we was the outcasts. [laughter] No body wanted to hang with us or whatever so we was off by ourselves and if any body said any thing we just got an attitude with them, whatever. And people didn't like Tasha because she had short hair. Her hair was like that long [she snaps]. It never would grow. And, over the years I just stopped hanging with her . . . .

I had gotten it in my head that I needed to be bad 'cause I needed to show people that they couldn't walk over me[18] and I had took it a little too far and I got suspended three . . . I take it back . . . it was five times, to be honest. One day he [the principal] just sent me home and told me I needed to cool off. . . . It was a lot of stuff; I used to tell people to kiss my [pause]. *You Melissa?! You seem so sweet.* That was then, I'm TRYING to change. I had a SERIOUS attitude problem. I would always tell people how I feel, regardless of how you felt about it.

Missy transferred to another school that she liked even less and eventually came back to Jay Ellis for high school. By then she was tired of fighting, realized that she "wasn't getting no where by fighting," and began to mellow out. She had one boyfriend and one English teacher who helped her on her journey to "the new Melissa," but mostly her change was just a gradual process. She had to "space herself from negative people" and begin hanging out with older people. Below, Missy describes her mother as one of her problems rather than part of the solution. Missy's mom worked as a clerk at Walmart and ran her family store, a small general store, whose upkeep required a lot of energy. Through all of this turmoil, writing emerged as a form of Missy's therapy.

What did your parents have to say about all of this? Mmm, my mom, she would always try to talk to me, but . . . I don't think I would ever listen to her. (her voice gets real quiet) *Why?* I don't know. I don't like listening to her now. I just don't understand . . . . I guess 'cause she always yelling and stuff, I don't know. But, anyway . . .

What do you do with most of your free time? Write notes out of a book. *In your room? At the store?* At the store my momma always nagging me about I don't do this and do that, so I try to help her . . . as much as I can. And if she starts with me, I try to get away from her.

So, you write down notes in your free time? What else do you do? You go to the store *and help out your mom.* I used to write. I have . . . six tablets. It's probably more than that now, 'cause I started back writing last month. *That's wonderful.* I write, but I don't want anybody to see it. *Why?* It's just . . . *What kind of stuff do you write?* Everything. Poetry, short stories, umm, I'm working on a narrative . . .

What do you want your major to be in college? Umm, accounting. When I was in the ninth grade, I wanted to do, like, communications. Me and Jazz both of us wanted to do communications. She wanted to do journalism school and I just wanted to do general. I changed that to accounting and a minor in English. Then, I have an interest in pharmacy and marketing. I have to do more research on marketing, but I like, it's a lot of stuff. But I want to do all of it. I want to own my own hair salon. I want to be part owner of a pharmacy, I want to work as an accountant to know what it's like, and I want to do something with writing.

Where did you get all of these goals from? I mean they just came about, like I don't want to say this, but I'll go on and say it. I used to sit in my room and cry and be like I don't want to be like my mom 'cause my momma husband made her stop going to school. I said I would never let a man ruin my life.

Thus far, several of Missy's structural constraints and her responses to them are apparent. First, by linking the shortness of her friend Tasha's hair to her status as an "outcast," she is alluding to oppressive standards of beauty that signal African American women's position as marginalized, second-class citizens.[19] To borrow Zora Neale Hurston's insightful phrase, black women are "the mules of the world."[20] This metaphor describes black women's unrewarded hard work. Ironically, similar to Hurston's main character Janie, Missy's "mule" work was expended at a general store owned by her family. Missy also invokes Hurston's iconic character Janie Crawford, when she proclaims, "I said I would never let a man ruin my life." Much like Kelly's family, described in chapter 2, Missy's family situation provided a source of discomfort, while writing provided a means of escape. Amazingly, through all of these diffused forms of oppression, Missy has envisioned a life for herself that includes any number of career paths.

Spirituality

The remainder of Missy's narrative primarily centers on her budding spirituality. In *Between Sundays: Black Women and Everyday Struggles of Faith*, Marla Frederick explores spirituality among African American women in Halifax County, North Carolina.[21] In her work, she defines spirituality as the aspect of religion that is personal and processual. She argues that the prevailing examination of African American churches and their relationship to the reproduction of inequality through a dichotomy of "accommodation versus resistance" misses the mark. She concludes that spirituality is a much more powerful concept because it allows us to see how black women exercise creative agency around, through, and perhaps in spite of church structures.

In the case of Missy, I already mentioned that the church has undergone some significant changes that have impacted the youth of Jay Ellis. For many reasons, it seems that the church is not engaging youth in the way that it used to. Missy reminds us, however, that a process, like spirituality, cannot be defined by a formal structure such as a church. Missy's spirituality serves as a form of resistance to the local church structure and as an avenue of creativity in many other ways. When I asked her during our interview if she attended church, this question opened a floodgate of information about her identity and her path of resistance.

Do you attend church? Every Sunday. *And what's the name of your church?* Cathedral of Love. *Which is nondenominational?* Yes. *And before then you were attending . . . ?* Jericho Baptist. *And tell me again why you changed churches or how that came about.* Because it was based on religion and tradition, and my mother felt like we needed to get out of that, and then there was a lot of mess arousing in church, so . . . she just felt like we needed to be away from that. *And how long have you been at the Cathedral of Love?* Last September . . . September 6 was our first day going and I joined January 6 (laughter).

And how do you like it? I enjoy it. It's a whole new experience because I'm working with audiovisuals. *Mmm hmm.* Like, I got to show you the DVD. I taped the last play. I was on camera, the front camera, facing the play, so . . . I learned how to run the camera. I learned about recording tapes and DVDs and about shots, like a long shot, a close-up shot. I can look at the TV screen and be like that camera ain't sitting right. *Mmm hmm.* Or either, they have the top part of their head is cut off, it's not supposed to be like that. It's supposed to be a half inch of head room. So, I learned a lot about that.

And then, the lady, that's with audiovisuals, she actually majored in that. Umm, our pastor paid her way through school. She wants to start her own business with photography, audiovisuals. She's got this thing, she do computer photographs and stuff. Umm, she made some pretty copies of some pictures. I knew—I didn't think my prom pictures was cute. She was like well let me do some touch-ups on it. She went on the computer for like ten minutes, and she was like look at the printouts. It was so pretty. It's amazing.

Wow, that is cool. So, ummm . . . what about the experience of going to church? What is it like compared to [church in] Carlyle? It's a new atmosphere. Umm . . . like Jericho, some people will speak and some won't. Like, most older people will speak and hug and whatever. But at Cathedral, people greet you at the door—"hey, how you doing?"—they hug you. And, the ushers are real nice . . . I mean, some of the ushers at Jericho they, some of them are grouchy, be like no don't sit in the back, and you're like could you move. The ushers (at Cathedral) are like please this and please that. It makes you feel welcome. And I feel like Cathedral's a second home now. *That's great. Have you gotten to know a lot of people since you've been there?* YES. And then, it's like five churches so people from other churches be coming, and you be wanting to make them feel welcome, so . . . You meet new people. A lot of people be like, "oh you should come hang out with us one weekend."

Already, one gets the sense that Missy's new church nurtured a very active spirituality. Rather than sitting in the pews, she took an interest in video production. In addition, attitude is a huge theme in Missy's life so she is sensitive to positive and negative attitudes. And the change in attitude from Jericho to Cathedral validated spirituality as something real, as opposed to formularized "religion and tradition."[22] Finally, Cathedral of Love introduced Missy to networks of people she would not have met in the close-knit town of Hamilton. In the passage below, it becomes apparent that Cathedral of Love also entered Missy's life at the right time, a time in which she was focused on and ready to do what was necessary to stay on the right path. Spirituality, for Missy, solidified her life's transformation.

Do you think it's changed your life in any way, going to this different, going to a new church? Yes, I think it has. I'm . . . church has a positive impact because I feel like it's a lot of people there that understand me. And like I can talk to the lady in audiovisuals, because she's like "Missy you don't need to get in this and that, because it will lead to so and so." I've actually thought about the stuff she said leads to it. So . . . I kinda changed my path and I just like talking to her. *Ummm, what is the purpose of going to church?* Umm, so I won't stray away from . . . let's say so I won't get back on the . . . trying to prove things to people. 'Cause I had gotten to the point where I valued people's opinion more than I valued my own. I don't feel like somebody should value someone else's opinion over their own. I mean, if it's not family, you shouldn't care what they say. *Mmm hmm.* I had gotten to the point where I thought I was ugly because people said my nose was big. And then . . . after I got there (Cathedral) I was like I don't care. *Melissa you're so pretty.* I mean, people telling me that every day all day, I don't know, I get . . . I don't know.

What about, ummm, would you describe yourself as very religious? Not at all. *Why not?* Because in my free time my mother tells me to read the Bible. Her pastor has her reading one chapter a day. She like, "Missy, you need to read one chapter a day." "Momma, I'm not into reading the Bible." So, I'll read it like every so often. Like, I'm sitting there like I wish somebody would call me. I'll look over at the Bible—"oh I could read the Bible." After I read a couple of verses and try to get an understanding of the first or second verse, somebody will call . . .

What makes a person a good Christian? I never thought about that—what makes a person a good Christian—I think you are a good Christian. I mean you're so happy and so . . . you're just so happy all the time. You're always nice. *That's so nice of you to say, thank you.* I think you're a nice person because you're always motivating and . . . like I said I wanted to go to the navy, you was like that wasn't a good idea. You gave me some other thoughts to think about and I have thought about those. *I'm glad, I'm glad, that's good.* And I think you're a nice person and a good Christian.

What does it take "to be saved" in your mind, or what have you been taught it takes "to be saved?" Umm, [heavy breath] . . . you know how I told you Jazz think people don't like her . . . Umm, renewing your spirit is more [like] somebody that thinks something and actually asks them for forgiveness if they don't . . . even if you don't think like that. I mean, just correcting the wrong even if it's not wrong. That's how I feel . . . and like renewing your spirit.

Spirituality is clearly active in Missy's life. Her faith has allowed her to resist those oppressive beauty ideals discussed above and "kinda change her path." But even when she takes her own journey out of the equation, and analyzes the concepts of Christianity, salvation, and religiosity, she reveals an active view of faith as resistance. Missy doesn't consider herself to be religious because she does not read the Bible every day; this hesitation shows the value that she places on hard work and action. Just as being a devoted student requires hard work, to call herself religious Missy feels that she would have to have put in some hard work; in this case, the hard work is Bible reading—that's the positive spin. But, if one reads her comment about being religious as an implicit criticism, perhaps religiosity for her connotes tradition, which she escaped by leaving Jericho, whereas salvation and "being a good Christian" are arenas for a more sincere, active faith. For example, she said that I was a good Christian because I was nice and motivating (active) and that salvation is about "renewing your spirit," and "correcting the wrong even if it's not wrong" (also active).

In the final selections from Missy's narrative one can intuit how the Cathedral of Love, as an alternate space to the local church Jericho Baptist, has provided Missy with acceptance from her mother while also giving her the additional distance from her mother that she requires. Moreover, it is apparent just how close Missy is to her family, even though her relationship with her mother is still strained. Lastly, her references to drug abuse in the community and drug use even by her own brother highlight the seriousness of her walk with God. For Melissa and many of the other youth in the community, developing a spiritual relationship with a higher power and/or undergoing a transformation are serious issues; resolving these issues may literally make the difference between life and death.

> *So who goes to church with you . . . your brother, your mom?* NO, NO, NO (Melissa cuts me off). *Oh that's right, your mom goes to a different Cathedral of Love.* Yes. (Her mom goes with her husband) . . . That's why I say she's so all about her husband. They didn't even tell us they was changing churches. We heard the pastor mention it in church and I'm looking around like, "What?!"

Missy was attending church with her two sisters, brother, and two cousins every week. Her older sister came back from Alabama A&M University, four hours away in Huntsville, to attend church with them every other week. And her mom and stepdad attended another Cathedral of Love Church an hour away from Hamilton in the opposite direction of Missy's church.

> *Give an example, and I think you already gave me one, one day, but give an example of when something religious has come into conflict with another aspect of your life . . . or when, umm, something you have learned from religion has made you look at something differently, like you see a contradiction. Or it's helped you make a decision . . . I* used to drink and smoke. Umm, Pastor used to be like, he don't want his members to sneak a drink every so often, if he can't do it. He knows we will think he's wrong if he sneak and drink every so often. So, I'm like, if I expect him to live righteous and holy, why can't I? So, I stopped drinking and smoking. *Smoking weed?* Ummm, Black and Milds. I tried weed when I was like thirteen, fourteen but all it does is make you feel drowsy and . . . *Do a lot of people at Jay Ellis smoke weed?* Yes. *Really [me]?* Umm, cocaine is the thing now around here. [Gasp] . . . *Melissa, stop?* Yes . . .

To my dismay, Melissa went on to tell me that her brother Roger had started selling and trying cocaine over the summer. I could not believe I was hearing this. Roger was charming, bright, athletically gifted, and handsome; he was my "play boyfriend" at Jay Ellis. On the days when I really needed one, he would always find me and give me a big hug. Missy told me that the same uncle who had introduced her to weed was instrumental in getting Roger to stop doing cocaine. Also, when their dad found out about Roger's drug use, he "whooped his hands till they was bleeding." According to Missy, "He was like, he catch it in his hand again, he gonna try to hurt him. So, . . . everybody played a role in getting him away from that." When I asked Missy how this happened in the first place, she told me their "aunt sells it, so it was easy access."

Of course, I was curious about whether Roger was affected by the church.

Does Roger go to church with you guys? Yes. *Do you think he's paying attention to what is going on, do you think it's impacting him at all?* In a way, I think it is. I mean, as far as going up to the altar, after service . . . I think he's afraid of that. Because when I first started going I was like naaa, I ain't going up there. I used to count the people that used to fall out [laughter]. But then, I would be like, maybe it'll get me somewhere, maybe it'll help me change who I am . . . and then I'll think about what I do and stuff. So, I actually started going to the altar.

Then they had children's church, so I made my sister go to children's church, 'cause she's like "Missy, Missy Missy" and I be like naaw, don't be janking on me. Roger, he just sit in service just like this [staring intently], but then he be . . . I got [him recorded] on the play. He was sitting there just like this on the DVD, just looking around. I was like, "aww look at my brother . . ." *Well, that's good. Make sure he keeps going 'cause even if it doesn't seem like it's having an impact it is.* But you know, like how "young people be drinking like hatorade," Pastor said that one day. He [Roger] repeated everything Pastor said. I was so proud of him, I was surprised he was listening. That made me think he was listening.

At the end of the interview, I asked Melissa to fill in the blank:

The biggest block or challenge to my future success . . . would be keeping myself on a positive path. I mean, it's so much that can steer you away from what your mind is set on. I mean, you could start talking to a certain person and they talk negative about different things and you be like, you start to get that prescription in your head so that's why I try to . . . ummm . . . surround myself with positive people and positive things and like inspirational stuff.

Conclusion

Missy's story highlights the nearly insurmountable oppression of the local environment from her standpoint. Her family structure, school structure, and her former church structure worked together to prescribe for her a bleak future. Specifically, a poor math instructor, insincere friends who contributed to low self-esteem, a difficult blended family situation, easy access to drugs and alcohol, and a disengaged religious structure could have spelled disaster for Missy. Additionally, translocal influences, such as historically embedded negative opinions about black women's beauty, stifled her. Ironically, hers is also a story of agency. Missy was able to dramatically transform each of these situations into something beautiful. From taking a college-level distance math course, to expressing herself through writing, to taking her siblings and cousins to church, she has fought to change her negative circumstances. What is amazing is just how aware she is that she is in this fight to "keep herself on a positive path."

Rather than attribute her success to personal resolve alone (while that is a huge factor), scholars must continue to debunk the "pull yourself up by your own bootstrap" myth.[23] Although at the time of my fieldwork no one in Missy's immediate family had earned a college degree, her older brother and sister *were* pursuing bachelor's degrees, and her mother, while not finishing college, did come close to graduating. In addition, her family is tightly knit and supportive in many ways. She has gained strength, especially, from a loving aunt who "listens to her," and she has drawn valuable lessons from her grandparents with whom she has lived for most of her life. Finally, Melissa was exposed to varied environments at a young age. Not only did she spend the first five years of her life in New York, Ohio, and Michigan, but she visits Michigan every summer, and these distant locations remain a part of her identity. Therefore, Missy was not just floating downstream before trying to swim against it; she was more aptly caught in crosscurrents trying to navigate her path.

A biographical level of analysis has provided a window into forms of resistance that are not easily discernible through power-laden, institutional levels of analysis, such as analyses of schools. According to the Distinguished Professor of Political Science and Anthropology James Scott, "much of the ethnographic material supporting the notion of . . . 'ideological hegemony' is . . . simply the result of assuming that the transcript from power-laden situations is the full transcript."[24] Analyses of school resistance will often reveal behaviors that are visible in public spaces. Just scrutinizing Missy's chronic tardiness, for example, would have led to an analysis of the commonplace forms of resistance that young people deploy every day that are easily subsumed as culturally and structurally reproductive. Even examining resistance through the lens of "the church" might reveal sleeping, malingering, and other behaviors that I sometimes observed. Often, forms of resistance that are actively fighting hegemony will only get noticed when organized into social movements or organizations. In Hamilton there were no social change organizations or youth movements, but Missy's biography fills in the gap. An active concept such as spirituality enabled me to access forms of resistance that are slow processes rather than snapshot behaviors, a type that often gets overlooked. While Missy stands by herself in the particular path she travels, I could have chosen any number of youth biographies that would point to intersections of oppression and resistance in their lives.

Most fascinating, for me, is that Missy's narrative exposes the creative, generative power of spirituality. Before Melissa joined Cathedral of Love, her church life was on the list of negative influences in her life. It wasn't just that Jericho wasn't helping her on her mission, but Missy described it as a hindrance to her metamorphosis—the messy people, the poor attitudes, the stagnation. After she joined Cathedral of Love, her spirituality produced something positive in her life. It gave her improved self-esteem, tangible skills, expanded social networks, inspiration to renew her spirit and put down drugs and alcohol, and new spiritual experiences, like "going up to the altar." In short, Missy pushed beyond the local environment, finding inspiration to continue her personal transformation through a church in another city. She connected to a community of believers, who did not have to feel as if they were fighting the currents alone. The words on the home page of Cathedral of Love's Web site summarize their task best: "Breaking the Curse!"

A Three-Dimensional View of Resistance

After our interview, I drove Missy home. Her grandparents' trailer is located down a long road that then turns off a dirt road. It had rained pretty badly this day; the downpour created muddy craters that I had to maneuver around in order not to slide off of the road. Melissa apologetically said, "This road gets so bad after it rains." And I assured her that my cousin's dirt road was in as bad a shape, when in actuality it wasn't. I had pulled up to the trailer before when dropping her off after the Sunshine game. I was stunned when she asked me to come inside for a moment and meet her grandmother. Melissa seemed so shy and cautious when I drove her home before, almost as if she was ashamed for me to see her home and really understand her family situation. Today, she was beaming with pride. During the interview, she proudly reported that her grandparents have owned their trailer for twenty-six years, and that they owned three acres, but had just sold two. The land came from her grandfather's brother who lived in New York but had died two months ago. They own cows, two horses, and four dogs, but I saw the dogs only that night.

I entered into a small square room. The kitchen was right next to this room, and a bedroom was off to the right. Like many of the homes I had visited, hers seemed to have a brown cast over it, partially because of the wood panels. The floor was made of bare wood, and it was spotless. There was one floral couch near the wall where the front door was located and the matching loveseat was near the right wall facing the kitchen. Across from the large couch, two arms' lengths away, was another brown fabric-covered loveseat, on which I sat, and when it was all said and done, I was sitting about two feet off of the ground. I didn't notice how low the seat was until Melissa brought her grandmother in to meet me and she insisted that I sit on the other couch because that was there "just waiting to go out."

Her grandmother was a sweet-faced woman with honey skin; she apologized for her dress (a snap-up-the-front pastel house dress). Melissa smiled so big while I was there. I could just see the pride in her face when she introduced me to all the members of this household: one mentally challenged uncle; one uncle who was lost in New York for twenty-six years until he was miraculously found; her grandmother; her grandfather; her bouncy, coy little cousin, who was a toddler; her little cousin Jim, who was in elementary school; her middle-school-aged sister; and her brother Roger (he passed through a bit later).

The television was sandwiched in the corner of the room between the two loveseats so it's no wonder Melissa said that she didn't ever watch television. It's positioning just didn't seem "user friendly," and the living room space was clearly the center of activity. One of the Halloween movies was on TV while I was there; "the middle-schooler likes scary movies," Melissa said. Nicholas didn't want to sit on the loveseat next to the television because it was scary, so he was instructed to go sit on the nice high-back chair near the wall adjacent to the kitchen. Roger was in and out of the room talking on the phone. As I was getting ready to leave, he was shifting furniture and announcing that his game time was about to start; he was hooking up his Xbox decidedly and frantically.

I played with Melissa's cousin most of the time while I was there. She was so lively. Melissa kept saying that she loves to play, as I tickled her with her little bear. She had a lot of energy, running back and forth laughing and trying to entice people to play with her. Melissa said when her grandmother went to "whoop" her one day, she said, "Don't whoop me, I love you." She said her mother taught her how to say that. I could just imagine this darling toddler saying that so warmly and mischievously.

Before I got up to leave, Melissa announced that she was going to go finish copying her geometry notes so that we could work on her assignment to be submitted tomorrow. She also gave me a movie version of *I Know Why the Caged Bird Sings* and a copy of her church play to watch that night. I left feeling grateful.

Chapter 6   Not Just Down Yonder

At the outset of *Raised Up Down Yonder*, I revealed the origin of the book's title. It came from Sabrina's desire for readers to know "that we're not what people think we are, what city people think we are. We're not all country, can't talk, cannot pronounce words and you know talk like 'down yonder.'" In this book, I have taken Sabrina's challenge literally, attempting to reveal the complexities of life for the black youth growing up in twenty-first-century *Down Yonder*. My journey *Down Yonder* has taken me from history to structure, reproduction to resistance, and institution to biography. I hope that emotion, subjectivity, and drama have breathed life into this story.

Yet, two sets of questions remain unanswered. The first set of questions stems from Sabrina's own defensive stance against a "country" identity. Was Sabrina's sensitivity to a rural identity as pronounced among the other young people in Hamilton as it was for her? Further, what does this sensitivity connote, especially when one compares a rurality to other collective identities? The second set of unanswered questions stems from Sabrina's exhortation that speaking with a "down yonder" dialect is not a total relegation to *Down Yonder*. I surmised that Sabrina wanted to transcend more than just a portrayal of her as being linguistically stuck, but also she desired to transcend a portrayal of herself as physically and emotionally stuck *Down Yonder*, as well. In this chapter, then, I explore just how far down the metaphorical dirt road *Down Yonder* really is.

Three important conceptual lenses guide this chapter and link it to the overall narrative of the book. First, similar to each significant concept throughout the text, I treat identity as a process, a "'production' which is never complete," and "always constituted within, not outside, representation."[1] I view identity as a categorical abstraction that helps make sense out of the fragmentary bits of the social world. One can assemble these fragmentary bits as an abstraction of the self.[2] Or one can house them in a separate conceptual world, such as blackness or social class, which the self can access at will.[3] Some might label this distinction to be individual versus collective identity.[4] In either case, it is important to understand that I treat identity as "real." "It" erects boundaries—even if fluid—that can generate behavior in the social world. I reject the notion that social class identity is the only "real" identity because it arises from material, economic conditions. Rather, I recognize mental processes to be just as potent in their ability to generate both behavior and mental processes. Further, I reject just as heartily the notion that economic structure is more real than identity, for it, as well, is just an abstraction.[5]

Second, throughout this text, I have rarely referenced "youth," writ large, or "youth culture." This omission is not accidental. I view connections between the young people in Hamilton and young people who are undergoing similar processes all over the world to be vitally important; indeed, I have tried to provide the raw materials that would enable readers also to make those connections independently. However, "youth" and "youth culture" are fraught with conceptual "fuzzy math"[6] and weighted down by the politics of representation.[7] I have not wanted politics to overshadow the substantive description of Hamilton's youth and their subjective spotlight. During this chapter, however, by bringing local concerns about "youth" to the forefront, and linking these conversations to uses of popular culture, I am directly tackling the politics of representation.

Finally, in examining popular culture, I embrace a methodology that values textual analyses, verbal analyses, and behavioral analyses of particular ethnographic subjects, in tandem. Though there is a proliferation of work on youth and popular culture (hip-hop, especially), much of it only combines one or two of the aforementioned methods, thereby rendering an incomplete picture of how popular culture is creatively deployed.[8] Another type of this work focuses on the politics of representation and the larger sociopolitical context into which popular culture enters.[9] These contributions have been substantial, without a doubt. However, scholars of popular culture and youth culture must continue to ground theoretical insights in the careful study of the everyday lives of subjects. Textual analyses on their own may reveal a deep "psychostructural" level of analysis, but rarely do they provide data on the interpretation and reappropriation of the material. Likewise, we must talk to people, who are often candid about what they believe and do not believe, in order to make use of their categories of abstraction. Finally, observation of behavior is a must. And this is the greatest contribution of ethnography, for it is in behavior that we can glimpse the performance of absorbed symbols and ideas. There are a few notable exceptions to my general observation about the absence of this tripartite methodology, and it is my hope that more studies that use this methodology will follow.[10]

Ironically, my analysis of popular culture in this chapter is relatively brief. Even though I went into the field to study translocal influences on a rural community through the presence of popular culture, once I began the fieldwork process I discovered that the mess with the football team and the politics of family life were significantly more influential in the lives of young people in Hamilton than was popular culture. The disjuncture between my plans and the reality in the field was severe enough for me to change my topic (I am certainly only one on a long list of anthropologists who have done the same). In *Down Yonder*, then, there is a caution, an implicit charge that anthropologists not get so caught up in academic and popular trends that we fail to do the work of ethnography. While I acknowledge the fact that we are all "writing culture"[11] to some extent, I knew that to write a book about the importance of popular culture in Hamilton would have been, at that time, disingenuous. I suppose that I have left plenty of work for the next ethnographer who studies Hamilton to do.

For the rest of this chapter, I will provide some ethnographic meat for these theoretical bones. I will first explain the prominence of a rural, southern identity among Hamilton's adolescents, recasting ruralism according to the centrality of interpersonal relationships rather than geographic place. Then, in the second half of the chapter, I will examine the significance of popular culture, which simultaneously reinforces the young people's rural, southern identity and connects them to a broader youth identity. I will argue that dichotomies such as "good" versus "bad," or, in this case, "crunk" versus "lyrical" are more superficial than they are sound. In the final analysis, Sabrina should be pleased that Hamilton's youth are presented here as unequivocally "not just down yonder."

Defining Rural as Relational

During each of the interviews that I conducted with the adolescents who have been featured in this book, I asked a series of "mostly the same" or "mostly different" questions. These questions asked the respondents to say whether they thought they "were mostly the same as" or "mostly different from," for example, "black kids their age" or "white kids their age" or "kids from the North." I hoped that these questions could help me to ascertain how the adolescents identified with larger collectivities. I did not anticipate that the questions would be answered in a way that uniformly pointed toward a strong rural, southern identity.

As for racial identity, the responses I got varied somewhat. All of the respondents said that they were mostly the same as other black youth their age. The reasons varied, but generally pointed to shared race, similar backgrounds, and similar ways of speaking, dressing, and acting as reasons why they saw themselves as mostly the same as other black youth their age. This response did not surprise me. Yet, the responses regarding their similarity to white youth their age did surprise me. While a few respondents said that they were different because of speech or dress, the majority interpreted the question to ask whether or not there were differences that justified inequality or unfair treatment. Most respondents, therefore, said that they were equal to whites, that there was not any difference. One adolescent said that the difference was that white kids "have a way of thinking they are better than everyone," while most black kids don't. Racial identity for the young people in Hamilton, then, gained significance in its relation to the existence of social inequality and racism.[12]

Nevertheless, the young Hamiltonians unanimously and emphatically stated that they felt mostly different from people in the North and people in big cities. Considering their connection to popular culture, I was surprised by their insistence on clearly marking their own identity through these perceived differences. While most hesitated and thought about whether they were the same or different from young people at Jay Ellis, Carlyle, blacks, and whites, they interrupted me to eagerly point out the differences between the North and South and the differences between cities and rural areas. Among the differences that they listed were dressing differently, talking differently, having "different ways of doing things," differences in maturity, being more or less prone to gang violence, having more or fewer advantages, having "different things to do," being faster or slower, being "more strict" or more "laid back," and even different prices of items at stores. Janelle represents a typical response when she says that young people from up north or in big cities are different because "they're probably more mature . . . they have to adjust to city life faster, you know be an adult . . . they grow up faster than us down here in the South." When I asked her what gave her a rural identity she said, "I'm very country . . . Like when I come outside, I don't even like to wear shoes or anything."

While in Hamilton, I discovered one great misperception that teachers and other adults in the community held about young people in Hamilton. Most of them genuinely believed that the adolescents had been stuck in Hamilton their whole lives and had never traveled anywhere. This stereotype is likely imported from the popular media's cursory assessments about what it means to be poor, young, and black—to be stuck. On the contrary, every single adolescent I interviewed had traveled out of the state, and most had traveled out of the rural South.[13] Thus, many of the delineators of "rural" and "southern" identities were named as such based on experience. The first-person accounts in the responses of Sam, Letice, and James indicate that their own experiences helped inform their rural, southern identity.

Sam, who stayed a week in Chicago two summers ago and has visited Detroit, Florida, New Orleans, Ohio, and "some of everywhere," below describes why he sees himself as different from people in the North:

Do you see yourself as mostly the same or mostly different from people from bigger cities or the North? Like when you visited—Different, they WAY different. They are very different. They can like, when I go to Detroit to visit with my cousins, they can stand all this hot heat, but I can't. They don't even have—both my cousins don't even have air, and then when they come down here they can't stand for us to run the air conditioner for a very long time 'cause they get cold. *Right.* And the same thing when we go up there in the winter time. They like cold weather up there, but I don't. We wrapped up. But they up there every day. And the way they walk the street, they could walk right by some crime that's happening and keep on going, whereas if I walked by one: no. Like they walking by, somebody shootin', they can keep on going. But I can't.

Sam provides an example of the typical responses young Hamiltonians gave to me when I asked them about similarities and differences between people in the North and South. First, he mentions something that is seemingly trivial: reactions to heat. This symbolic difference inverts the predominant stereotypes of country, heat-loving Alabamans and cold-weather-tolerant northerners. According to Sam, the southerners need air-conditioners while the northerners can "stand all this hot heat." He goes on to isolate reactions to crime as another major difference between the North and the South.

Letice, who had spent the previous summer in Detroit with her uncle, thought that there were major differences between northerners and southerners, as well. She describes northerners as "high class":

[Kids who grow up in the North]—Waaaay different [laughter]. High class. They different. They just different really. They don't play the little games we play around here. They just different. *I don't know, Letice, I don't know if I agree. Which games?* I will say the main game that they don't play that we play is Baskin Robin. *Mmm hmm.* Two Square—I went up there, they don't know what Two Square was. They call it "Hit the Ball." I'm like it's two square. *I think they probably do everything else.* Hide and Go Seek—they didn't know what that was. *No!* They had a different name for it, but they didn't play it the same way.

When did you start going to Detroit for the summer? This summer was the first time, my first time. *How did you like it?* It was fun. *Really? Do you want to live in Detroit or something like that?* I said I wanna go back up there when I graduate. *To Detroit?* [shakes head] *What did you do this summer?* I went up there, shopped. Well, I went to the bar for the first time in my life. My cousin, she own a bar. And we had went up there—it was in the morning. It was like breakfast and stuff like that. We can't go at night time. *Good. OK, and what else?* We went to the movies up there. Mall, that's it.

Was it really the same or really different from down here? Different. *How come? What was different?* In the mall, it was huge. It was just a lot of people. Had store names that ain't even down here. They had brands that weren't down here, like if they hit up there first. *What else?* The movies. You have, it's like five or six entries they sell you different movies. And down here, you just go in the same little spot with each other and watch one movie.

Were people the same or were people different? Hmmm . . . from down here? Different. More nicer, stuff like that. Got friendly folks up there. *People say the South is more friendly than the North.* Well, the North more friendly to me . . . When I went up there, they had to pay me to talk, too. When I was in the bar, they was like, "talk." And I would talk and they would just laugh with it. . . . I had a friend up there—she was from Louisiana, her name was Peaches, and we would walk around, and we attracted so many people. And we talked, they were like ya'll ain't from around here. I was like no, we're from Carlyle. Not "here," I was like "her." And they would be like, "Man I'm going to the South just because y'alls' accents."

After spending a summer in Detroit, Letice pinpoints accents, big contemporary stores, and knowledge of games as three things that make her "way different" from people in the North. Interestingly, Letice, like Sam, inverts a popular stereotype when she states that northerners are friendlier than people in the South.

Finally, James, who has traveled to Michigan, New York, Illinois, Florida, Georgia, Tennessee, and "rode through" Rhode Island, compares regional and racial identity:

How would you compare Hamilton to most of these places? Hamilton is real slow compared to most of these places. *What do you do when you go?* Mostly just hang out with them [family]. *Do you think people from the North are different from people—* Real different. *Why?* They're more advanced and stuff, you know? From their language to the way they act and everything. But most, you know . . . let me think of a way to say that . . . a black person's going to be a black person. I'll say it that way, you know. You say what you want to say. A black person's going to be a black person.

Contrary to James's statement that people from the North are "real different" from people in the South, his experiences lead him to conclude that racial identity trumps regional identity in its salience. Even though he says people from the North are more advanced than he and his friends are, he concludes that "a black person's going to be a black person."[14]

Having identified that a distinct rural, southern identity was foremost in the minds of Hamilton's adolescents,[15] my next question was, what does it *really* mean for them to be rural? Their responses alerted me that they perceive of themselves as different, but I looked elsewhere in their interviews and checked other data to discover what aspect of their lives really set them apart as rural or southern. What stood out to me was an apparent focus on life as it is lived in relation to others. Sociologist William Falk, who traveled to a historically African American community in the South Carolina low country to collect "stories about their lives 'on the land,'" found that his informants' "linkage to the land and feeling for place [could not] be separated from their family ties." In other words, their apparent focus on and love of the land was defined by their family connections and connections to institutions, such as the local school.[16]

My own participant observation in Hamilton yielded data that highlight the significance of kinship in the lives of young people. Likewise, my interview data reveal that Hamilton adolescents see life as a shared, intimate experience. I posed many open-ended questions that were answered with responses that alluded to and included other people. What the young people did with their time, what they considered fun or meaningful, what made them happy or grateful, what disappointed them, or even how they saw themselves often centered on relationships with others.

In a series of oral fill-in-the-blank questions, I asked students to complete statements such as "I am happiest when I___." Over and over, students gave responses that related to spending time with others. For example, the following two responses were given to the question, "I am grateful because___":

Bailey Sisters

Grateful: Because I have a family that cares

Grateful: Because I have a great mother who loves us

Grateful: Because my mother loves us, and I have people who care about me.

Sabrina

Grateful: Because the Lord has blessed me with a big family, and he has blessed me with the knowledge of right and wrong and how to get stuff done.

Sabrina's remark is especially noteworthy when one considers that she was only seventeen years old at that time and shared a very small living space with her parents and three out of her five siblings. In spite of the lack of financial resources in her family, she considered a big family to be a blessing.

Furthermore, when I asked the young people to describe themselves, how they relate to others again occupied a chief place in their responses:

Sam
Describe yourself. Nice, easy going, very . . . I'm easy to get along with, just well mannered, one of a kind.

Darnel
Describe yourself. Fun, pretty nice to get along with, a great listener.

During James's interview he said that he thought others saw him as either "a nice, easy-going person" or messy. Additionally, he reported one central philosophy that directs his life: "In life you've got to get along with everybody. There's always going to be somebody you don't like, but I ain't met one yet." He also said that he was happiest around his peers and his family and did not plan to move anywhere in the future. Relationships with people were central to all of his statements.

Letice's interview provides one of the best examples of a narrative that has a relational focus throughout. From her description of Jay Ellis to the reason why she liked Sylvan, to what she liked to do with her free time, getting along with and interacting with others factored prominently into her worldview:

So let's talk about Jay Ellis. Do you like going to school there? Yeah, it's alright [down tone]. You can get along with everybody there. *What do you like and what don't you like about it?* What I don't like about it is they just letting anybody in from different schools. When students get kicked out from the city school, Jay Ellis accepts them right away. And what I do like about it is it's kinda organized a little bit. Everybody get along with everybody. Get along with all the teachers. No hatred towards teachers, no teachers hating children. *Mmm hmm. Even Mr. Washington?* Oh, that's hatred, that's pure hatred [laughter].

What about your teachers? Who's your favorite teacher? My favorite teacher has to be Mr. Edwards because he loves janking us. He stays janking us . . .

How did you like going to Sylvan? I— *Tell the truth! I don't work there anymore; it doesn't matter to me.* I liked it. *Why did you like it?* 'Cause you were there. *Aw, but you were going there before me?* Yeah. *How'd you like it before I got there?* I really didn't like it. I hated going. I would try to get my way out of going.

What do you do with most of your free time? Hang out. At TKs, Crossgates [apart-

ments], across from Waffle World. *What's so great about Crossgates?* They're crunk.
Everybody be out there. They be at the same house . . .

Letice liked and disliked Jay Ellis based on the quality of the people and relationships it fostered, not because of the facility, or the number of programs
offered, or the overall quality of education, or even the history of the school.
In addition, Mr. Edwards's continuous "janking" or poking fun at people set
him apart as one of her favorite teachers. Indeed, janking comprised one
of the key relational activities in which all young people in Hamilton participated. Moreover, according to Letice, the number of people at Crossgates
apartments made hanging out there so much fun. Interestingly, Letice stated
that her least favorite part about herself was her low self-esteem; she said,
"I'll let somebody pull me down in a minute." The idea that others opinions'
could "pull them down" is something that many of the female participants
mentioned.

Most activities that young people engaged in had a relational aspect to
them. Even watching television and playing video games were usually done
with others. This may have been partly the result of the way homes usually
are arranged, where items such as televisions, computers, and video games
are located in public spaces.[17] Still, adolescents reported enjoying these activities with others rather than complaining about them. In addition, out-of-
the-house activities usually involved going to people's homes and "hanging
out." I was told that "the only real hang-out spot was the movies and people's
houses." It was well known that an adult should not go to the movies on
Saturday night and expect to "see the movie." The movies were actually the
place where young people went to have fun together; they used the movie as
a mere social launching pad. They told jokes, walked up and down the aisles,
and imitated the people on screen, anything, as long as it constituted hanging
out and enjoying others.

Thus, for Hamilton's youth, a rural, southern identity centers on the pronounced role of other people in their choices, attitude, and behavior. This
is especially evident when one considers the example of mess and how it
operates. Certainly, this finding relates to Falk's conclusion that a focus on
family and belonging are part and parcel of what it means to be southern and
African American. However, Falk also cites the land, or the sense of place,
as inextricably linked to the centrality of relationships, and vice versa. This
ethnography signals a diminished importance of place. Only James reported
having a connection to the land. For all of the other adolescents, setting was
a minor detail that supported the cast of characters in any given situation.

A singular focus on people, and *not* place, may mark more broadly a significant shift in Hamilton's culture and perhaps rural communities. The history of Jay Ellis presented in chapter 3 reveals that relationships with people always have been central to life in Hamilton. In addition, however, connection to land used to form a dialectical relationship with a focus on people; that is, the people in Hamilton were tied to the land. Picking cotton, walking the roads, hunting, planting—these were all integral, enjoyable aspects of growing up together in Hamilton. Moreover, as the blacks in Hamilton strove to better themselves and break away from the weights of slavery, building institutional identity was key to creating and sustaining progress. The schools, churches, and community organizations were essential to the development of collective and personal uplift.[18]

When I interviewed Mr. Gaines, Jay Ellis's interim principal, he noted students' lack of focus on institutionally defined achievement. According to his theory, this shift might be explained by the relative comfort that this generation enjoys compared to what the previous generations strove to transcend:

> To me the kids used to be a lot more interested and saw the need and the interest in education, where as now it's kind've a lackadaisical approach to education. I sometimes talk with the other teachers. When we were coming along, you had to have education to do better. But now the kids, they're not doing quite so bad when you look at, you know, where they are and what they have access to versus what we had and what we wouldn't have had if we hadn't done anything.

Many from outside this rural community might be shocked by Mr. Gaines's belief that young people are "not doing quite so badly." Certainly, expensive cell phones, cars, designer clothes, fancy or oversized furniture, and organic foods were luxuries to which most people in Hamilton did not have access when I was there. However, young people generally had a bed to sleep in (even if shared), full stomachs, a place their family could call its own, and a relatively safe environment. Also, TVs, CD players, and Xboxes were toys that the young people did enjoy. Most importantly, however, since young people's primary focus was on people and not things, they only seemed to need a few material possessions and situations to help promote their enjoyment of family and friends.

While not defining it as such, the growing disconnection from land and institutions frustrated many of the adults whom I interviewed. Coach Jones decried what he viewed to be the rampant laziness of this generation:

> When I was in school, kids cared about people and school work, but right now, kids

don't care about nothing . . . I don't think we're putting enough responsibility on them; that's why they try to sham and be lazy because we're not expecting anything from them. Give you an example: Justin Allen, he's in the twelfth grade. I saw his grandfather cutting grass . . . There ain't no way in the world I'd have a big joker—you know Justin Allen in the twelfth grade—ain't no way in the world he'd be laying up in my house eating my food, and I'm out there cutting grass. And he's in the house watching TV, eating. There's just no way, no way. But I mean that's just the type of things we're dealing with now. They're so into TV and these games and music or whatever that it's got their mind blown.

Coach Jones espoused one popular point of view: that increased engagement with popular culture was to blame for the changes evident in young people's attitudes and lifestyles. Sergeant Daniels, who provided much of the history of education in Hamilton in chapter 3, expressed frustration with a young boy who stopped by his house during our interview. While not directly connecting youth behavior with popular culture, his manner of addressing this young man reveals his genuine disdain and disgust about the attitude and trajectory of the "X Generation":

Why you put your?—sit your butt down! Don't you move—why you put your?—your shoes are not strung up. Your shirt's on backwards, on the outside, wrong side. Why? *'Cause I didn't want to get grass stains on it.* See, that's, that's the X Generation. No ambition, no nothing, he just reached and put it on, don't care how he looks, what he looks like or nothing. And then comes stepping out . . .

Sergeant Daniels, who has spent his life investing in institutional development, was disturbed by the disheveled appearance of this boy. From Sergeant Daniels's perspective, if he walks around with his shirt on backward, how can he build an institution?[19] My conclusion is that the young people in Hamilton are not interested in building institutions. The institutions in which they participate, primarily the school and the church, are only significant in so much as they involve others.

While having the same critical tone as Coach Jones and Sergeant Daniels, Mr. Edwards, the English teacher, came closer to pinpointing what the "problem" with the young people is. For Mr. Edwards, more than being "lazy" or "having no ambition," the root of the observed trends in behavior is a preclusive focus on others:

If you could say what you think are the biggest influences on the young people that go to

school here, the biggest influences on their lives in terms of the decisions they make, the
way they see themselves, what would those things be? Well, to me, when you talk about
influences, they influence one another more than anyone else. Plus, the other influence is . . . A lot of times, they influence each other greatly because they don't want
to do right, so they look at other people and imitate them. They imitate a lot—you
talked about movies and music—and they want to imitate a lot of what they see on
television and what they hear in music and stuff. They want to imitate that, you know,
because they just want to do things that they see other people doing, whether it's
right or wrong. They just want to imitate it. And that's a lot of it. They want to imitate
others to the point that they lose their own individuality, and that's why a lot of them
won't do things that they really want to do. But a lot of them are so worried about
what their classmates are going to say or other students are going to say . . . .

That the young people in Hamilton view their lives in terms of others and feel
largely disconnected from land or institutions explains many of the "problems" that adults in the community often bring up, including why the young
people participate in long-term relationships from an early age; why Jay Ellis
students cease activities when they are no longer fun or their friends stop;
why young people who say they want to move away often don't; and why Jay
Ellis valedictorians and salutatorians sometimes don't finish college.

A focus on relationships does not explain the presence of these phenomena in isolation, but this explanation is equal to, or outweighs, the oft-blamed
twin culprits of popular culture or Generation X laziness. Adults in the community also attribute "problematic" adolescent behavior to lack of exposure
and proper guidance. What makes the centrality of relationships so important is that this pattern stems from the local environment. Unfortunately, the
same people who are dissatisfied with the effects of this cultural focus often
unknowingly encourage this outlook on life.

In brief, young people in Hamilton see themselves as markedly rural and
southern. But, being young and rural in Hamilton is not primarily about roll-
ing hills, outdoor activities, or preserving the community's institutions. To
be young and rural in Hamilton is to go from place to place in search of people. Meaningful relationships might be cultivated in the church, at school,
outdoors, inside, in front of the television, or at the movies. However, these
are all places where people can "bring you down," relationships must be mediated, and mess looms large.

Popular Culture: Both "Crunk" and Lyrical

Thus far, I have demonstrated that southern and rural identities are pronounced among the young people in Hamilton. I have argued that some of

the complaints that older Hamilton community members have about young people's attitudes, behaviors, and choices can be linked to the adolescents' focus on relationships. Some older adult community members, however, would prefer to blame changes in youth behavior and aspirations on the impact of popular culture, especially hip-hop. The so-called pervasive influence of popular culture has stimulated global "moral panics" about the social and moral demise of society. According to scholars at Birmingham Centre for Contemporary Cultural Studies, a moral panic is "a spiral in which the social groups who perceive their world and position as threatened, identify a 'responsible enemy,' and emerge as the vociferous guardians of traditional values."[20] Indeed, in Hamilton, the United States, and around the world, black youth, especially, have become a scapegoat in the policing of the political-economic status quo (masked as the "moral order"). They have become a symbol of unwanted social change.

For the remainder of this chapter, I will use existing moral panics about youth in Hamilton as a segue to present a more nuanced understanding of how young people actually do interact with popular culture. By exploring popular culture practices among rural African American youth, I will debunk some assumptions about the flow of ideas from city to country and how a literal focus on "objects" and "texts" can distract one from the more important question of context and style. In doing so, popular culture will be shown to simultaneously reaffirm a rural identity and connect the young people to a collective youth identity. Without a doubt, popular culture adds a significant dimension to the portrayal of the youth *Down Yonder*.

In the passage below, Coach Jones voices a perspective of young people and popular culture that is shared by many from within the Hamilton community and the United States more broadly:

Tell me what you think about young people and popular culture, how it impacts their life and work. To be honest with you, I think like rap became popular when I was in high school. But in high school, I understood that rap was just entertainment. I listed to the words, I listened to the lyrics, I watched the movies on TV, I saw the violence on TV, but I knew even in high school that it was just entertainment to me. Our kids now, they can't decipher the difference between the two. They don't realize that these guys who are on TV shooting up everybody and these guys who are rapping about this lifestyle, they're not actually living that type of lifestyle. They are saying all this stuff to simply get your money, to entertain you. Like, so what our kids are trying do, they're trying to imitate that behavior, which is unreal. It's unreal. So, I mean until they realize that it's just entertainment, I don't have to walk around with my pants sagging down, I don't have to talk this way, I don't have to call this girl this and that, I don't have to do all this stuff they talk about in this right here. Until they realize that this right here's just entertainment, we ain't going to get no better. So, I think they are heavily impacted by music and by television. So they are trying to emulate that right there, which just don't go along with the environment they're in.

I would like to use two of the central arguments that Coach Jones makes above to structure a discussion about how young people use and are affected by popular culture, especially hip-hop music. First, Coach Jones argues that young people cannot decipher between entertainment and reality.[21] Second, he argues that the lifestyle promoted in rap music doesn't "go along with" the local environment in which young people live.[22]

One of the issues that I have with hip-hop, in particular, is the derogatory, misogynistic way that women are often portrayed. As a result, one of my latent research goals was to contend that bright young people have profound thoughts about the representation of women, in music videos, especially. Thus, I became like a broken record, asking students about the portrayal of women in hip-hop. During my first school year, the guidance counselor asked me to lead a "girls' talk" with the junior- and senior-class girls during seventh period. Among the topics that I presented for discussion was popular hip-hop artist Nelly's "Tip Drill" video. At the time, he was involved in a big controversy because he was scheduled to sponsor a bone-marrow registration drive at Spelman College in 2003 for the foundation that honors his sister, and the college uninvited him after this video was released. The video in question featured women simulating sex with other women and one man sliding a credit card between the cheeks of a woman's buttocks.

During my "girls' talk," I expected that I would at least hear from the young ladies a couple of different perspectives on this issue. Eventually, the discussion turned, and I was simply browbeating the students to view the "Tip Drill" video from my viewpoint. To sum up their point of view, the young women in the class argued that the women in that video and similar videos were representing themselves and no one else. They neither saw themselves as being represented by those risqué images, nor did they accede to my point that the images, if not representing them, at least influenced other young women to imitate the women in the videos or influenced young men to treat women as sexual objects. They stood firm in their collective belief that people have the right to "express" themselves whether their particular form of expression is judged to be positive or negative.[23] The idea that individuals should be granted an unadulterated right to "express themselves" was voiced to me again and again by the participants in this discussion. I was thoroughly disturbed and disappointed. Consequently, for the next year, I had my antennae up, chasing signs of young female Hamiltonians being disrespected by their male counterparts and looking for issues of low self-esteem being funneled through their sexuality.

At the end of my next year in Hamilton, Kelly hosted a "hip-hop" music video party for me. A small group of us sat around Kelly's living room watching videos, talking about the images we were seeing, gossiping about the behind-the-scenes stories, sharing what we were and weren't "feeling," and occasionally rapping and singing along to the music. I was in a completely different place than I had been the year prior, but I still pressed my "lines of inquiry." When I asked how the guys and the girls felt about the gyrating "naked" women in the videos, they corrected me with "they're not naked!" and sort of laughed. Both guys and girls repeated their mantra, "It's just entertainment." Unlike the year prior, however, I accepted the answers I received and moved on. By that time, popular culture, especially music, had provided the soundtrack to my field experience. During the football/cheerleading season we continuously choreographed dances, got hyped for the games, celebrated victories, and lamented misfortune; and music—sometimes hip-hop and sometimes not—was our partner.

I had to examine my field notes to discover whether or not I had gotten "soft." Had spending time with young people dulled my senses to the point where I lost my discernment, judgment, and feminist integrity?[24] The answer was both yes and no. Lived experience is far different from judgment from a distance. Therefore, after one year, the images and issues that had once stood out to me as central paled in comparison to questions of self-expression and creativity—precisely what the young women in my class had been trying to tell me the year before. If I had the girls' talk to do over, I would skip the "Tip Drill" representation issues and directly approach some of the issues in which I was interested, such as self-esteem. Moreso, I would approach them through their own favorite artists, such as R&B artists Aaliyah and Christina Aguilerra.

Now, to address Coach Jones's observations. Were young people in Hamilton able to decipher between entertainment and reality in popular culture, specifically music? Yes, for the most part.[25] As I stated earlier, part of the young people's bemusement at my obsession with representation issues was that to them certain music was just "entertainment." I found it interesting how much energy they invested in actually figuring out which artists were more and less "real." Finding out who was posing, who exaggerated, and who kept it real were important questions to them. During the hip-hop party, some of the guys got very "hyped up" when Atlanta rapper T.I.'s song, "You Don't Know Me," came on. When I asked why, they explained that it's "his beats," and "he's real with it. He's just straight out real, no lies. A lot of folks lie with their lyrics." This blanket approval of T.I. and the young men's declaration that he was real comprised a rare level of affirmation. I also found it interesting how the lyrics to "You Don't Know Me" relate to the concept of staying away from messy people: "Save all that hatin and that poppin pimpin / Quit tellin people I'm yo partner listen / you don't know me." T.I. was judged to be real not only because of his personal track record, but also because his lyrics made sense according to the local paradigm of mess. Still, I sensed that young people took even the "realest" artists with a grain of salt.[26]

Regarding male/female relationships, the young men at Jay Ellis were respectful of me at all times. In general, they were respectful of their female peers, and their family members, as well. Perhaps the reason why the images of half-naked women were so easily dismissed by the young women in Hamilton is that they were seen as being very distinct from reality. Accusations of promiscuity among the young people at Jay Ellis were strangely nonexistent. In general, the girls did not dress in what might be judged to be revealing clothes, and even with all the mess that circulated, I never heard a young person accused of being "hoish" or having multiple sexual partners. The pattern among Hamilton youth was to develop and maintain long-term relationships rather than casually date.[27]

Now, I did state that they could *mostly* discern entertainment from reality. I added this qualifier for a couple of reasons. First, the manner in which the guys instigated fights between the girls at Jay Ellis smacked of the type of female commodification that is exalted in hip-hop culture.[28] Also, over time, I developed a concern that the students took entertainment *too much* at face value. Disrespectfulness was not an issue I encountered or noticed among Hamilton's youth—aside from the regular biochemical moodiness associated with adolescence in this country. However, small four- to seven-year-old boys and girls were constantly being told they were "so grown" and "too grown." Many of the adolescents remarked that their elementary-aged brothers and sisters could recite the lyrics to some music better than they could and they saw this as a problem. Recognizing that something is "entertainment" for elementary schoolchildren has its limits.

Coach Jones's second observation is that the lifestyle promoted in rap music doesn't "go along with" the local environment that young people experience. What he really was referring to is the "hard life" that some of the young people associated with a northern, urban identity. Most young people in Hamilton recognized that an urban "lifestyle" should and could not be imported into their rural community. However, if one reads the lyrics to much of hip-hop as metaphorical and the *style* as definitive, then one can see how these elements of hip-hop do fit the lifestyle of the country. In fact, in *Resistance through Rituals*, Stuart Hall and his colleagues demonstrated how British youth subcultures purchased raw materials through youth industries, but transformed these things from their original use and context to create new styles. The objects are less significant than the process of stylization. Remove the element of hard-core violence, and a lot of the other themes found in the lyrics address what the young people in Hamilton experience. Substance abuse, strained relationships, "hating," systemic rage, gossip and mess, creative use of language, and disappointment are all found in hip-hop and in the local environment. Additionally, southern rappers have put those elements together in a way that comprises a unique style.

One of the chief elements that is missing from the local environment, but that factors heavily into a wide range of hip-hop music, is the culture of "bling" or material possessions. During our hip-hop session, I asked the young people what was the difference between "Dirty South" and other forms of hip-hop. Dirty South is a subgenre of hip-hop birthed in the early to mid-1990s in southern communities and made popular by artists like the Geto Boys and UGK. One of the guys answered that Dirty South is more "crunk" music. He continued to say, "everybody else just talking about money and cars, we just talking about having a good time." Once again, rural identity is separated from the tangible, such as possessions or place, and linked to the intangible, such as having a good time and developing relationships. One Web site entitled "Urban Definition," from which people upload their own definitions of various slang terms, defined "crunk" in this way[29]:

1. To get crunk is to have a good time.
2. Crunk is also thought to be derived from a combination or a portmanteau of the words "crazy" and "drunk," or a combination of "chronic" and "drunk," referring to the state of being both drunk from alcohol and high on marijuana, at the same time.
3. A style of music most commonly made by rap artists from the southern states, aka the Dirty South. Some crunk artists (or groups) are Lil' Jon, Pitbull, Lil' Scrappy, Trillville, and David Banner.
4. Something at a high level, as in volume.

In Hamilton, many of the young men, especially, related to Down South or Dirty South rap more than to other kinds of hip-hop. Getting "crunk" was a big part of the allure. The way the term getting "crunk" was used in Hamilton connoted getting hyped-up or excited, as in a party mode. I had the privilege to get "crunk" the day I rode the school bus with Kelly to the technology center. A couple of the guys had headphones that they passed around to share with everyone. As the bus bounced down the road, and we bobbed our heads and bodies up and down, the bus literally threw us from seat to seat. I have no idea what the lyrics were about, but that was one of my most surprising, memorable experiences in Hamilton. It certainly transported me temporarily out of whatever had taken place at Jay Ellis that day.

I would like to expound on one other reality that addresses Coach Jones's viewpoint presented at the beginning of this section. Based on my observations and the student interviews, I realized that the young people used different genres of music toward different ends. Often, rationality and logic get overshadowed in conversations about young people and popular culture, especially hip-hop. However, I discovered that hip-hop was not in the average Jay Ellis student's CD player at all times. Certain artists were used to get "crunk" for games, certain music was described as thinking music, other music as riding music, and yet other music as unwinding music. For example, on the cheerleading squad, we had to use certain music for our dances and watch certain music videos to "steal" dance moves. In these contexts, offenses get quickly ignored and videos are seen as entertainment, which allows "goals" to be accomplished such as choreographing a "cool" routine.[30]

One of the songs that was popular during the second football season was rapper Lil' Flip's "Game Over." During that year, I saw so many spirit signs with "Game Over" written on them that I decided to investigate what the saying was all about. Only then did I discover that "Game Over" was a hip-hop song. While the title's application to football culture is obvious, the lyrics, themselves, like those in a lot of "crunk" music, only relate to particular situations in the most general sense or not at all. The chorus simply repeats, "Game over, Flip, Flip, Flip, Flip, Flip, Flip, Flip, Flip" four times. The verses have little to do with football, but as with a lot of "crunk" music there was a general spirit that was appropriated—in this case the spirit of domination.[31] Also, the lyrics include several allusions to sports, such as "my crib big like a football field," "I make 'em bounce all across the globe," and "a franchise like a Houston Rocket." The lyrics are peppered with references to "gats" and "pimps" and include plenty of expletives, but I was surprised by how many times young people confessed that they really didn't know the words to music they listened to, but just liked the beat and recited the "hook" or chorus. I was further shocked to learn that "Game Over" was created, or at least marketed, to be used for sports games:

> Lil Flip says this about "Game Over": "I'm a big fan of sports; football, basketball . . . I wanted the song to have the energy of the Compaq Center after the Rockets wins, like how I feel during a show. This is the type of

track where the crowd really gets involved. We're excited that people are lovin' this single the way that they do, and all the support we're getting during the Super Bowl."[32]

"Game Over," then, reveals that "crunk" is one part emotion and one part calculation from the perspective of the producers and consumers.[33]

The title of this section, "Both 'Crunk' and Lyrical," alludes to the simultaneous appreciation that individual young people have for many different styles of music. Discussions about adolescents and hip-hop culture often dichotomize their musical appreciation; that is, they must love hip-hop to the exclusion of all other genres or despise hip-hop and prefer something else. On the contrary, young Hamiltonians imaginatively integrated different genres of music into their cadre.[34] At Kelly's hip-hop party, I posed the question: "what artists would people be surprised to know you listen to?" One of the Dirty South fans replied, "Dolly Parton," and another said he liked pop chanteuse Avril Lavigne; both responses were outside of my own preconceived notions.

A desire for self-expression unifies the adolescents' various musical tastes. The way self-expression becomes manifest in musical choice is frequently separated along gender lines.[35] For the young men, it seems that a desire to express rage, thoughtfulness, and tenderness are central to their patterns of musical choice. These somewhat complementary and somewhat contradictory desires demand that "crunk" energy and lyrical quality be combined. Darnel provides the best example of how the desire for self-expression creates interesting juxtapositions in his musical choice.

Darnel was uniformly described to me as a kind, fun, good-hearted, and well-mannered person by his peers and older community members. He has been featured in many chapters throughout this project. By way of summary, his parents' relationship dissolved early in his life, so his mom and grandmother raised him by themselves, a fact he was proud to report during our interview. As captain of the football team, Darnel exerted a lot of physical energy, and, in his own words, did not have much "free time." He said he didn't watch much television, unless it was sports. According to his account, he was usually at school, at practice, sleeping, or hanging out with family or friends. To get "crunk," he said he listened to rappers DMX, Lil Wayne, or Juvenile—this also doubled as his "riding music." R&B crooners like Marvin Gaye, Al Greene, and newcomer Anthony Hamilton sang him through his thinking moods. Other musical genres such as reggae also had guest spots in his CD player.

Darnel was light-hearted and, as he said, "easy going," but when I interviewed him I sensed some feelings of hurt or bitterness. For example, he was my only interviewee who declined to answer the question "describe one thing that someone did to really hurt you or break your trust." At the end of our interview, I asked him to play for me some music with which he really identified. One of the songs he played was "Warrior" by rapper Lloyd Banks. At various points it proclaims: "I'm a grown man dog I ain't no bitch (A warrior!)" . . . "Before I shit on my family I lie in a ditch" . . . "Uh, You heard right motherfucker—My grandmama' daughter ain't raised no sucker." What is interesting about this song choice is that the defensive, aggressive tone of the song contrasts so distinctly with Darnel's persona. While his identification with this song may seem to be a non sequitur, a song like this one may have allowed Darnel to express tender emotions such as family loyalty and, at the same time, convey more rage or toughness than he ever would express when not in his "crunk" alter ego. On the football field, in his family, and with his friends, Darnel was a "warrior."

Another one of the rap groups that Darnel appreciated was Pastor Troy and the Congregation. Perhaps he and Pastor Troy share some of the same juxtapositions. This is a description of Pastor Troy presented on his Web site:

> Born Micah Levar Troy in College Park, GA, Troy, 24, is the son of a drill sergeant-turned-pastor who laid down strict household rules and made sure his son was introduced to the church at an early age. But like most kids on his block, the young Troy was also exposed to street life. It is that dichotomy, that contradiction of influences that continues to be reflected in his music today: the respectful preacher's kid who knows better but can't resist indulging his naughty side; the gentlemanly boy next door who seems oblivious to the wiles of his street corner friends but, in actuality, is far craftier than they could ever be.

Many of the other "nice" young men in Hamilton enjoyed nurturing a somewhat "naughty side," too. For Darnel this theme carried over to his taste in movies. He reported that his favorite movies are gangster-themed movies such as *Harlem Nights* and *Scarface*. Darnel appreciates *Scarface* because the central character "came from nothing to something. It was in a bad way, but he did it. Showed that anything is possible."

Many young people in Hamilton have a secret hobby of writing poetry. Darnel shared two of his poems with me:

The Ladies Man
The Ladies Man is such a gentle man
He's always respectful and never harmful

But can deliver words that are painful
He can look in a woman's eyes and say they are beautiful as the sky
And if there's one thing he desires, it's being with a woman he admires
That's a ladies man

Shine

Shine when it's your time
But always keep it in your mind
When it's your time,
You'll feel like you're on Cloud Nine

These poems, when compared to Darnel's pop-cultural preferences, high-light young people's ability to consume and produce seemingly divergent methods of self-expression in such a way that musical tastes, life histories, and perhaps even psychological needs are quite well integrated and are not the least bit nonsensical. Transcending stylistic differences, "Ladies Man," "Shine," and "Warrior" all address similar themes. Indeed, Iain Chambers has emphatically argued that "from plantation to ghetto, black culture, and especially black music, has provided one of the strongest means of survival—a secret language of solidarity, a way of articulating oppression, a means of cultural resistance, a cry of hope."[36]

Self-expression also drove the musical choices of the young ladies I inter-viewed, as well. The themes that their preferred musical selections repeated-ly focused on were interpersonal relationships and self-esteem.[37] While they appreciated R&B and hip-hop, the female's brand of self-expression often led them to embrace a variety of musical genres such as pop and country music. According to Letice, who said hip-hop and R&B were her favorite musical genres, she also really loved R&B singers Aaliyah and Maya. She said, "They express themselves, and say what's on their mind. Like Aaliyah, she express herself to a male in a song." Letice, who had been dating the same Jay Ellis student for two years, told me about some of their high and low points. I was not surprised, then, that "We Need a Resolution" by Aaliyah was a song to which she said she could really relate. The chorus asks, "Am I supposed to change? Are you supposed to change? Who should be hurt? Who should be blamed?" and she goes on after several more questions to arrive at the con-clusion that they need a resolution.

Self-expression for most ladies included "crunk" music, too. The way they usually expressed themselves through "crunk" music was by dancing to it and enjoying the beat, not through a connection to the lyrics. Letice said that she appreciates a "crunk" beat:

What do you look for in music? Beat and lyrics. *When do you listen to music?* Every time I jump in the car. Like Usher's "Confessions," I listen to when I'm on the phone with TJ. In the car, I just play straight up hip-hop. Not regular hip-hop, but the gangster one [laughter]. *Why do you say that?* 'Cause it be crunk. Have the base up loud. It sound good.

More than one young lady distinguished between songs for dancing and songs for listening.

All of my female interviewees referred to some particular musical ballads that focused on self-esteem and interpersonal issues. Kelly's family narrative was featured in chapter 2 of this project. In it, she described how painful her parents' divorce has been. She said her love of music was a constant comfort and source of inspiration:

What do you do with most of your free time? In my room with my radio and writing poems. And, well, I ain't wrote a story in a while—but poems and song lyrics . . . with my radio. *What's in your CD player right now?* Christina Aguilera, Alicia Keys, Michael McDonald [laughter]—that was my momma's CD but I took it. I got the Motown CD, Fighting Temptations Soundtrack, Justin Timberlake. *Do you have a lot of CDs?* A lot. *Give me a number.* More than fifty, more than seventy—it's a bunch of them. *What makes you pick a CD to buy?* The person and the lyrics and the beat. I don't care if they're white, black, pink, purple, it depends on what they're singing about. And if the beat sounds good, it's alright with me. 'Cause I got Selena. And it's another Spanish group called Saloona. Then I got from the Temptations to the Jackson Five, on up. *Who put you on to that old stuff?* My momma. She had Jackson Five and Diana Ross on eight track.

The artist that Kelly identifies with most is Christina Aguilera. "I'm Okay" and "Sing My Song" are two songs that she said could have been written about her. The first one expresses a young lady's resentment at having grown up in an abusive home. Kelly's father was not physically abusive, but she might argue that her mother suffered emotional abuse and that she was caught in the middle of the situation. The second song is about self-empowerment. In Kelly's words, the song is about how "some folks say all the negative stuff about you but you just say, I'ma move on. I'm going to keep on doing what I'm doing. I ain't studying you and stuff like that."

While general patterns, such as the gendered ones presented above do exist, the range of diversity within Hamilton's adolescents should not be ignored. For example, two students, eleventh-grade Sam and eighth-grade Darius, told me that they don't really listen to hip-hop at all. Darius said:

I stay in gospel. What influenced you to like gospel music? I listen to it, 'cause it's good for you. Like I said, back in my old days, I listened to rap, but it wasn't that much. *Why do you think rap is not good for you?* Because they have bad words like killing somebody, killing a nigger, or sniffing on that dope or some things like that [laughter]. *That's not good. Do all your friends believe that, too, or you're the only one?* That's my belief.

Darius shares his musical tastes with his parents, who both listen to gospel. Sam also shares his musical tastes with his older family members:

I don't listen to all rap. I listen to like the blues, or slow songs, and at least some rap. SOME, not all. Some of it's OK and then some of it's just awful. *Which rap do you like?* I don't know the names because I mostly just hear it on the radio.

Sam's own music collection is comprised of blues and "slow songs."

While I have mostly focused on music, thus far, before concluding this section, I want to briefly highlight young Hamiltonians' connection to broader youth culture through video games, movies, and television. Most of the young people reported playing video games on game systems like Xbox or on computers. They also said they rented movies and went to the movie theater relatively frequently. Favorite movies ranged from Tyler Perry's Madea plays to movie blockbusters such as *Titanic, Drumline, Ace Ventura, A Time to Kill,* and *Steel Magnolias.*

Young people in Hamilton spend at least as much time sitting in front of the "tube" as they do listening to music. Therefore, their tastes in television must be taken seriously as entities that both shape their identity and reveal something about their identities.[38] During our interviews, I was reminded how young the Hamiltonians in my study really were, as each of them told me they liked the Cartoon Network, Nickelodian, and ABC Family. Other popular stations were Lifetime, ESPN, all of the premium movie channels, and all of the music video channels.

From time to time, one of the young people would surprise me by telling me they watched something off the beaten path and seemingly out of the ordinary.[39] James, for example, was unique in his appreciation of the Outdoor channels and the Speed channels. He also humorously reported that he likes to watch "those birthing shows" so he can know how not to get "trapped." Similarly, in the middle of Sabrina's going down her usual list—TNT, MTV— she interrupted herself, remembering the Food Network, which she described as "off the chain!—Emeril Lagasse is off the chain!" I could hardly contain my laughter imagining Sabrina sitting in front of the television captivated by the Food Network and HGTV (Home and Garden Television). When I asked her if she cooked, she said:

Oh, I don't cook, I just watch Emeril cook. That's what *I* do. *Do you want to cook in the future or just watch?* Yeah, I'ma cook. See, if I ever get married and have kids, I can cook for them by watching Emeril cook, and I'll know what to use and stuff.

Sabrina told me that her mom, dad, brother, and sister did the cooking at her house. I still find it entertaining that a black woman growing up in the rural South reported learning how to cook from celebrity chef Emeril Lagasse, a native of Fall River, Massachusetts, who has become most famous for his New Orleans cuisine. Not only does Sabrina's love of Chef Emeril challenge stereotypes about southern black women, but it also made me feel better about my own lacking culinary skills (at that time).

Whenever the young people were rattling off a list of shows and they stopped and added an exclamation, I knew that a program was particularly enjoyable. For example, Kelly exclaimed "*Charmed*—That's my show!" Similarly, *Family Guy*, a cartoon that features a dysfunctional family and an obnoxious baby named Stewie who talks like an adult, frequently engendered that type of reaction from the young people. Sabrina told me, "Stewie, That's my buddy!" Family Guy fit in well with the culture of mess, which may be why so many young people loved it. Stewie is the "messiest" baby on television, always stirring up trouble and having something obnoxious to say. Sabrina told me that Stewie represented her dark side.

One television show represents the manner in which popular culture can at once connect young Hamiltonians to a broader youth culture and, at the same time, fit within their existing local paradigms: *Saved by the Bell*. Of all the shows that could have been salient among the young people in Hamilton, I did not expect it to be *Saved by the Bell*. This situation comedy centers on the life and experiences of relatively affluent American teens and their school "Bayside High." It aired between 1989 and 1993, nearly two decades ago. But more than one young person told me that they got up in the morning to watch this comedy series about six friends, with distinct personalities, and their misadventures. When I interviewed Sam and asked him what fictional character he most identified with, he chose Zack Morris from *Saved by the Bell*:

I would have to say Zack off of *Saved by the Bell*. *Why is that?* Because he does a lot of, you know—he's like the leader of his class and he do, he get them into a lot of stuff. And most of it be bad and . . . stuff they shouldn't do, and . . . funny person. So I would have to compare—me and him would be just like brothers.

Zack Morris was the consummate class clown, and he would have fit in well at Jay Ellis, janking and being messy. In addition, I think the limited number of characters on the show resonated with Hamilton's youth. The only recurring characters were the six friends and the principal, who always was frustrated with their shenanigans. Like Jay Ellis students, the characters never tire of one another or present a boring episode, though the size of the cast, school, and community is small.

I would like to conclude this chapter by presenting an extensive series of excerpts from my interview with James. Our discussion about his consumption of popular culture brings together many of the themes addressed in this chapter: how music, specifically hip-hop, operates among the youth in Hamilton; how self-expression figures prominently into musical choice; and how popular culture connects Hamilton's young people to one another, their parents, a rural identity, and even a broader youth identity.

Although I have quoted James throughout the book, let me briefly recap the central parts of his biography. I became acquainted with James at Jay Ellis School. He, like many of the seniors, had a "free period" during the seventh and last period of the day. My interactions with James usually stemmed from trying to convince him to come to ACT prep instead of roaming the halls; he indirectly and amusingly intimated that he was neither pressed nor impressed. He was tall, chocolate brown, and broad, laid back, cool, and stubborn. He didn't look "country," per se, but something about him could not have been mistaken for city. Beyond his accent, he just seemed comfortable in his own space.

When I interviewed James on the second floor of the public library, I found out how close he was to his mom, dad, and extended family, and I discovered how much he loved history. He was also one of the only young people who, when I asked, actually said he had talked about "the old days" with his grandparents, former sharecroppers who picked cotton. James remained consistently hilarious throughout the interview. He often derived joy by making me beg for more of his wits and information and by forcing me to dig deeper. This dynamic of prodding for and revealing information led me to discover his intentional boundary pushing at Jay Ellis and the "love ethic" that he learned from his parents and his church. As we continued, I was struck and amused that he—even if only temporarily—forgot the name of the church that he's attended every second and fourth Sunday of his entire life.

In the chapter on mess James was shown to be passive in his participation in the networks of gossip. If something came across to him that needed to be passed on, he most certainly would, but he wasn't going to seek out drama. In short, James was a laid-back guy. As he told me, he "ain't no gettin' out person." He loved to be outdoors and go fishing, fix cars and hunt, but he was not looking for the next party or where he could drive on Saturday. With his already multifaceted back story, we get to learn about James's pop-culture preferences:

What kind of music do you listen to? Rap, R&B, blues . . . little bit of jazz. I don't know nothing about it, but I hear it. *Alright, who are your favorite artists? Rap? Yeah, any.* Rap—I like, I like that Down South stuff. *Aww that stuff I can't stand . . . 95.7? Yeah. Every time I hear 95.7, all I hear is [I mock beats, laughter].* Yeah. Blues— You know, I like that old stuff . . . you know, like people like Al Green and Johnny Taylor. I like that. You know I grew up in it.

In just a few short lines, one can already see that James is connected to the South. He "grew up in" blues, which is quintessentially southern, black, and rural. And he alerts us that a new southern, black, rural genre has taken center stage: "that Down South stuff."

What kind of music do your parents listen to? 1400—that's all they listen to. My dad, he listens to 92.9. You know, the blues, stuff like that. I get him to listen to some rap every now and then. I know what I want my mama to hear that I listen to, and what I wouldn't want her to hear. *Ohh so you censor?!?* Yeah. *What artists would you let her hear that you listen to?* Little soft stuff, like, you know, Usher, R. Kelly . . . I'll let her listen to that. *And what don't you let her listen to?* When it comes to like Tupac—you know, stuff like that. You know, because music like that . . . they put the black woman down! *No, you don't say!?!* Yeah they do! But you know, it's entertainment. I don't believe in that stuff. *OK, so explain to me this: What is entertaining about listening to things you don't believe [laughter]?* I just like to hear it, but I don't— *Is it the beat? Is it the lyrics?* Yeah. *It's the lyrics and the beat?* Yeah. *It's all of it?* They know how to put it together.

James adds three layers of dimension to his identity and to his musical choices. First, he makes a distinction between that "little soft stuff" that he would let his mother listen to and other music that is more appropriate for him, which distinction alludes to a masculine gender identity that is "hard." Additionally, by admitting that he censors his mother's music, he shows a dimension of his gender identity that positions him as her protector. And third, he volunteers that some of the music he listens to "puts the black woman down," but defends his choice as just entertainment. He demonstrates the complex and contradictory negotiations that go into people's choice to listen to certain styles of music. Paradoxically, the intense love that he has for his mom (which we talked about during the interview) manifests itself through a masculine gender identity that protects her from certain music while, at the same time, he craves that same "hard" music (that "puts the black woman down"). He goes on to elaborate more about soft music:

As far as hip-hop, right now, I like Kanye West. I don't like that dude. Why? He sings that little soft stuff. He ain't hard. It's not soft. He ain't hard. It's intelligent. If you'd listen to his lyrics, he's a thinker. Like "Jesus Walks With Me," yo, it's tight enough but . . . [laughter] you know. *No, but I mean his CD has a lot of other singles on it, too. His lyrics are insight-ful. You know how Ludacris has a lot of catchy—* Yeah, you mean like "Move, Get Out the Way?" I would let my momma listen to something like that.

Before I could make my point about Ludacris, James cut me off—just in case I missed the extremely clear distinction between hard and soft music—to make sure that I knew Ludacris's song was soft. I continued to further probe him about music videos with themes central to moral panics about hip-hop.

Do you watch music videos? No, that ain't never entertained me. *You don't like the na-ked chicks in the bikinis?* It ain't never entertained me. It ain't never excited me. I hear a lot of people talking about it—*But it's never excited you?* No. *What about lyrics that are demeaning to women, like calling them bitches and hos and stuff?* Yeah. Let's see. Me, personally, some of the women, they fit it. The truth is that. I'll leave it like that.[40] *And what about the women who don't "fit it?" What about your mother? She doesn't "fit it?"* I know she don't fit it . . . *What about singing songs about women like your mother?* I ain't never heard one. Maybe like the old stuff, like the old . . . *Maybe like India Arie?* I don't listen to her. She ain't hard enough.

For James, contrary to the predominant stereotype, music videos with scant-ily clad women were not his preference. He echoed one of the main argu-ments in defense of hip-hop, according to pioneering hip-hop and cultural studies scholar Tricia Rose,[41] that some women "fit" the demeaning lyrics; just not his mother, about whom no worthy lyrics have been written, at least recently. Below I try to figure out who, besides Tupac, passes his "hardness" test.

So tell me who these artists are that are so hard. Pastor Troy, TI, Lil Wayne—he getting a little soft himself [laughter], Master P. *Why do you like hard? What's the emphasis on hard? Why don't you like "soft" music?* I like it, but I don't like to listen to it. *Well, why do you like to listen to hard music?* 'Cause it's what everybody's listening to. *So if everybody wasn't listening to hard music, you'd listen to something else?* Yeah. You know, James is James. He's going to listen to what he want to. *Do you listen to Lloyd Banks?* Who? *Lloyd Banks.* That's that city stuff. They soft. They ain't like that Down South stuff. *So when did you start listening, 'cause Down South is new? What did you listen to before?* You know, that whole west coast thing. Tupac, Biggie—*Biggie is east, watch it.* You know the whole east coast / west coast thing. That's all we had to listen to back then. *And when did "Dirty South" become big?* That was sixth or seventh grade.

To round out James's musical tastes, he identifies a few hard artists, but says that even they are in danger of becoming soft. He reveals a decidedly performative and mutable kind of masculinity, in which people can become soft. I would argue that James, himself, could become soft if he started listening to soft music, which is why he "likes" soft music but doesn't "listen" to it. Finally, he reaffirms his belief that city is soft and "Down South" is hard. Ironically, after all of these very idiosyncratic opinions, he admits that he listens to hard music because everyone is listening to that right now; this admission connects him to a broader youth identity. Just for the sake of comparison and contrast, I will conclude by highlighting one of his favorite television shows:

> *Can you give me an example of a television show that represents reality?* Saved by the Bell. *Ahh!* [laughter] *You took it back old school. Why Saved by the Bell?* I watch it every morning before I go to school. I have to watch it [laughter]. You know, there are always going to be these students in class. You're going to have your little group. You always going to have a slug you're going to use—not use, but you know he gonna look out for you, like Skreech, you know. *What TV character do you identify with most? I know what you're going to say: Zack Morris.* AC Slater! *Ahhh, OK. For real, Zack.* He's straight.

I didn't expect James, who during the course of our interview told me that none of the popular music I appreciated was "hard enough," to say that *Saved by the Bell* was a show that reflected reality. His comments about *Saved by the Bell*, in their full context, reveal the complexity of popular culture in its ability to instigate and sustain many forms of identity. For James, hard Down South music was just entertainment, while *Saved by the Bell* represented reality.

Conclusion

This chapter has explored the collective identities of Hamilton's adolescents, specifically focusing on rural identity, youth identity, and their relationship. Contrary to popular stereotypes, many young Hamiltonians have traveled outside of Alabama more than once, and these trips have highlighted their distinction from northerners in everything from clothing to accents. While these border crossings help sustain feelings of difference, young Hamiltonians' rural identity actually centers on the pronounced role of other people in their choices, attitudes, and behaviors. In fact, a singular focus on people, and *not* place, may mark a significant shift in Hamilton's culture and perhaps a change in rural communities, more broadly.

I have also demonstrated how popular culture simultaneously reaffirms a rural identity and connects the young people to a collective youth identity.

Coach Jones's criticism of his students' consumption of popular culture provided an entry point into an analysis of moral panics about young people and hip-hop culture in particular. While my informants' critical engagement with issues such as misogyny fell short of my own hopes, over time I more clearly understood the complexity of their musical tastes, especially when viewed within the context of self-expression. The terms "crunk" and "lyrical" symbolize the appreciation that young Hamiltonians' have for many different styles of music.

In the final analysis, whether through family vacations, hip-hop music, or television programs, adolescents in Hamilton draw from diverse translocal sources in the creation of their identities. Rather than destroying "the local," imported images and ideas create interesting hybridities, such as Dirty South hip-hop; sustain local paradigms, like mess; and export their own refashionings of music concepts such as "crunk."[42]

Conclusion

The last few words of this manuscript were penned in Raleigh, North Carolina, where I was visiting family in the summer of 2012. Almost eight years had passed since I completed my ethnographic research. Though Raleigh is on the surface very different from Hamilton and Carlyle, Alabama, everywhere I visited I observed the themes of *Raised Up Down Yonder*. As a professor at a Historically Black University (HBCU), I find HBCUs to be fascinating repositories of history and possibility. One day, I went to Shaw University to work on this manuscript. Shaw University is a small private HBCU situated in downtown Raleigh. On the Friday that I paid my surprise visit, the campus was quiet, as summer school had just ended. When I found my way to the library, I couldn't help but imagine that if the same national newspaper reporter who wrote about Jay Ellis School traveled to this library, he might also describe it as a "trip back in time," but he would have missed the mark, once again.

Certainly compared to the behemoth North Carolina State Library where I had worked the day before, the Shaw Library paled in comparison. With a student body of only twenty-five hundred students, this library cannot support hundreds of thousands of titles and two coffee bars. Yet, any characterization of the library as a trip back in time would miss three essential points. First, the library is at least partially an intentional trip back in time. Everywhere I looked, I saw references to the history of the school and to the history of African Americans, generally. In the lobby there is a tribute to Ella Baker, the valedictorian of the Class of 1927, who returned to her alma mater in 1960 to found the Student Non-Violent Coordinating Committee and was a leader in the civil rights movement throughout her life. On one wall of the first floor, there is a mural that celebrates the legacy of African Americans such as Fannie Lou Hamer, Dr. Charles Drew, and the Reverend Absalom Jones. The university, then, uses history to mark its space and link the space to the processes that have helped to create it. The Jay Ellis placard on the outside of the building, which bears the name of George Wallace, similarly grounds the school in an all-too-recent history that many would like to forget.

Second, calling the library a trip back in time might imply that the political economic milieu in which Shaw University is situated is somehow out of the ordinary when, in fact, it is unfortunately very common in the present time. Many Historically Black Universities have closed or are in danger of closing because of a complex set of political and economic processes.[1] Since the mid-twentieth century, after a series of Supreme Court decisions, a greater number of Traditionally White Institutions began to admit African Americans. As a result, the middle-class blacks who supported divinity schools and medical schools at institutions like Shaw left HBCUs "behind" for the resources and the prestige that accompany whiteness. Labeling HBCUs as "out of step," irrelevant, and dated helps sustain the political, economic hierarchy of elite education in America; false ideologies about predominantly black schools and their supposed miseducation, in the long run, attract more of the "kinds" of students that elite universities desire to them, while they lock poor and working-class students out of the system of higher education altogether.

I have shown that in Hamilton, this marginalization is about more than just race, although racism plays its part. It is also part of an objectification of rural places and people. In *Knowing Your Place: Rural Identity and Cultural Hierarchy*, Barbara Ching and Gerald Creed argue that "the cultural devaluation of rural and rustic people may be grounded in economic marginalization."[2] The phenomena mentioned above are strikingly similar to the processes described in *Raised Up Down Yonder* that have created the history and current state of Jay Ellis School. Once a small African American school, created by the community to educate its children, Jay Ellis has become a "Last Chance School," an untrue caricature that uses blackness and rurality to sustain the local hierarchy. The reality is that without Jay Ellis, African American children in Hamilton would be forced to attend Carlyle High, with its minefield of racist, elitist practices.

Finally, calling the Jay Ellis library or the Shaw library a trip back in time would miss the dynamic and amazing juxtapositions found in the local context. Simply judging the library based on the brown wood aesthetic, the small space, the traditional bookshelves, and the limited collection ignores the state of the art computers, the flat-screen television in the lobby, and the e-book collection. Similarly, Jay Ellis's youth bisect these dichotomies all of the time. The students have cell phones and CD players, connect with friends and family through Facebook, travel to many regions in the United States, and still choose to come home to live with their families, sometimes on the family "compound" itself. Further, and this is an important point in this work, if scholars leave the young people, themselves, out of the equation, we cannot adequately answer any of the questions that we have about the culture and the institutions that surround them. I was disappointed that the Shaw students were not on campus. I would loved to have interacted with them to find out about their backgrounds, what they think of the education they are receiving, and how their education fits in with the rest of their lives.

Throughout *Raised Up Down Yonder*, I have tried to let the young people speak with me and to you: to engage with my opinions, to allow them to speak about how they fight the oppressions in their everyday lives, and to reveal what is meaningful to them. Sometimes they agreed with me, as in the case of Jay Ellis's "Last Chance" characterization. Other times, they disagreed with me—for example, they did not agree with my problem with misogyny in hip-hop music. Other times, we learned from one another. Missy taught me how to put baby oil on my ashy feet, and I shared with her my opinion that entering the navy may not have been her best option.

Why draw comparisons between a university located in a major city in North Carolina and my field site in rural Hamilton, Alabama? I am trying to demonstrate that even with all of the idiosyncrasies of everyday life Hamilton is connected to other towns and cities across America, especially in the South, in significant ways. Small communities and rural areas often are depicted as invisible and backward. Schools that are compared to some imaginary mainstream educational institution must justify why their doors should remain open. Young people are defined more by moral panics that are generated about them and their social locations as youth, or black youth, than they are by any real knowledge about their everyday lives. These missteps are made by academics and nonacademics alike.

As Sunaina Maira and Elisabeth Soep advocate in *Youthscapes*, I believe that scholars need to advance a research agenda that examines the everyday lives of young people, situating them in their historical, political, economic, and meaningful contexts. Too many young people are shuffled around American school systems like chattel, but similar to the young people attending Jay Ellis, children's families and identities are tied up in these institutions in essential ways. Before making major educational decisions based on institutional trends and quantitative data, policy makers must contextualize these institutions and ground the quantitative data by examining the needs and desires of the students. It is imperative that ethnographers continue to collect this qualitative data to find out what happens if these institutions close their doors. One simple, powerful photo among several in a photo gallery in the Shaw University Gallery depicted two children, hair and clothes disheveled, standing in front of a shotgun shack in "anytown" USA. Most American citizens make unconscious assumptions about who can and should be educated, even as we proclaim to believe in the American Dream. We don't really know who those children are, but we need ethnographers to help us find out.

Most important, *Raised Up Down Yonder* calls attention to the importance of meaning in social analysis. The young people in Hamilton had a strong rural identity, even if what that rural identity is comprised of has changed. They saw themselves as rural because of the slow pace of life, their small school, how close they were to their families, and because of the kinds of music they enjoyed: country, blues, and "crunk" hip-hop, among others. I determined that their rurality was largely determined by a focus on people. Their blackness was certainly embedded in their everyday lives; yet, in their minds, their rural identity was prominent. Therefore, many of their choices were related to their rural identity. For example, when many of Hamilton's youth choose to stay home or return home shortly after leaving for college, it is not because they are lazy or corrupted by hip-hop, it is that they want to be near their home with their families.[3] Some of the behaviors that adults in the community lamented about the young people, they inadvertently fostered, just by imbuing their local lives with profound meaning.

The entire foray into the football drama of 2003–2004 and the metaphor of mess demonstrated how language and meaning are interlaced with inequality in everyday life in such a way that it makes them hard to be separated. Scholars of reproduction and resistance, such as Peter McLaren, have shown that schools perform the reproductive function of preparing working-class students for low-rung jobs, but not just through economics. Rather, "the dynamics of reproduction take place within a cultural terrain marked by contestation and struggle."[4] Certainly, struggle over "The Last Chance" ideology was one area of contestation. Additionally, the dialectic of misfortune and mess, expressed throughout the football drama during the 2003 and 2004 seasons, constituted another area of contestation. Using mess to deal with the misfortune-laced inequality helped to reproduce that same inequality.

Yet, the metaphor of mess was dynamic, generative, and creative. Using Victor Turner and Peter McLaren's understanding of how resistance takes places in liminal—temporarily unstructured or anti-structure—spaces, then, it becomes clear how something so destructive could at the same time be so generative. McLaren states it this way: "One of the consequences of Turner's doctrine of liminality can be neatly summarized in a contradiction: rituals can help dismember group cohesiveness or promote a creative unity."[5] Letice's evening phone-call ritual is just one example of the contradictory and creative power of mess.

Similarly, during the time that I was in Hamilton, the church structure, once vital to southern African American communities, seemed to have been diminishing in importance. Yet, when I approached the topic from a question of spirituality, I discovered that one young lady demonstrated creativity and resistance in very powerful ways. Once again, the point I wish to emphasize is that as researchers it is often the questions we ask that determine what we discover. I tried to ask a set of questions that would allow young people to rise above their oppression and their accommodation or resistance to that oppression. Kelly, for example, was a brilliant young writer, creative and bubbly, who was trying to distinguish herself from her mother, whom she admired except that her mother let her husband emotionally abuse her. James was a "laid-back guy" who also loved his family, especially his mom. But also he loved some hard, Down South music, even if "it does put the black woman down." Oh yes, and he loved *Saved by the Bell*, too. The socioeconomic hierarchy in America is real. It is impacting these young people's lives in tangible ways—what jobs they are likely to have, how much money will be in their bank accounts, and where they will live. But there is far more meaning to their lives that these unequal structures won't determine—the young people's relationships, how they see themselves, their relationship with God, as well as their humor and creativity.[6]

In the influential volume, *Identity and Agency in Cultural Worlds*, Dorothy Holland and her colleagues present a complex notion of "identity in practice."[7] Among the many nuances that they add to the concept of identity is a focus on the "figured worlds" of people: those areas that carry people's personal disposition, social identification, and personification. These factors call attention to people's "intimate terrain[s] as an outcome of living in, through, and around the forms practiced in social life."[8] This emphasis on the inner life is more pronounced in psychology, cultural studies, and philosophy through the subtexts of phenomenology and postmodernism. However, I agree with the authors that as scholars we must critically embrace the aspects of peoples' identities that are not just social, but inner and intimate, in anthropology, as well. Much of the scholarship that I appropriate throughout the rendering of this story highlights that same focus—John Jackson's reintroduction of "sincerity" to mainstream theorizing about blackness, Peter McLaren's focus on liminal spaces created through resistance to schooling rituals, and Victor Turner's foundational concept of social drama. My argument here is that the stakes are higher for African American youth who have been denied an inner, emotional, apolitical, meaningful aspect of their lives that does not center on hip-hop. This disservice is perpetuated by scholars who attempt to highlight the nearly insurmountable odds that many youth face. The answer is not to do less work about inequality, reproduction, and resistance; it is to do more work that investigates the grounded and figured worlds of African American youth.

Focusing on the subjective aspects of young people's identities leads to a light at the end of the tunnel. Turner and others have argued that aspects of the inner life, things that generate pleasure, become a "serious matter in innovative change."[9] After all, what is more motivating than experiences that personally stir us to love, hate, laugh, or cry. Indeed, Maira and Soep suggest that young people's *feeling* of disappointment at the lack of adequate vernaculars for dissent "unsettles the binaries of resistance and cooptation, and in a sense resonates with the disappointment of academics longing for theories to reinvigorate our own sense of political efficacy."[10] The key here is that disappointment is a powerful level of practiced identity, a figured world, an inner feeling that serves as a filter, a reaction to inequality, misfortune, and structural constraints, which can, itself, become generative. In the end, through all of the persistent inequality, hum-drum rote of everyday rituals, social dramas, and inner life, small changes in the social structure can be seen. In describing the outcomes of the fourth phase of social dramas, Turner puts it this way:

> Oppositions may be found to have become allegiances, and vice versa. Asymmetric relations may have become egalitarian ones . . . Closeness will have become distance and vice versa. Formerly integrated parts will have segmented; previously independent parts will have fused. Some parts will no longer belong to the field, others will have entered it. Institutionalized relationships will have become informal; social regularities will have become irregularities. New norms and rules may have been generated during attempts to redress conflict; old rules will have fallen into disrepute and have been abrogated.[11]

Indeed, many scholars who address the direst social conditions express a belief that hope should remain and that we have power to create change.[12]

During my same visit to Raleigh, I attended a Praise Night at a local black Christian Methodist Episcopal church. The event was held in honor of the pastor's anniversary. The participants' acts all were enjoyable. I, of course, enjoyed those presentations that included young people the most: a liturgical song/dance that was performed in sign language; a gospel miming act (these acts have become very popular); a duet of a very popular gospel song, sung that night by preteens; and my favorite—an original rap performed by Leviticus, a group of three young men who grew up in that church. They performed their own original piece with the hook, "Every single day, I get down on my knees and pray." Since I have been teaching at Morgan State University I have listened to a good deal of amateur rap. But to judge Leviticus's rap the way the young people in Hamilton would have judged it, I must say that the lyrics and the beat were "crunk." These young men were just that talented. Apparently, they have already performed at the Apollo Theatre, and I expect that soon they will be known on the gospel circuit. Leviticus highlights the interesting hybridities that define twenty-first-century identities. They were at once gospel and secular, local and translocal, rural and urban, black and colorless. Somehow the presentation all came together. This is the South of *Down Yonder*, the one that I was fortunate to know in Hamilton. And as I have tried to demonstrate, young people are engaged in border crossings and translocal identities that are far reaching. In *The Games Black Girls Play*, Kyra Gaunt discusses the impact of double-dutch and hand-clapping games on black popular music.[13] She shatters stereotypes about the flow of images and ideas. Like Leviticus, young Hamiltonians not only have pulled from diverse sources in the making of their identities, but before and beyond this book, they have also left traces of Hamilton all over the United States, as well.

This project began by highlighting Sabrina's concern about my representation of Hamilton. She wanted to make sure that people understood that Hamilton is not just "Down Yonder," that it is not defined solely by poverty, rurality, lack of education, and disconnectedness. I have tried to demonstrate that Hamilton is, if nothing else, connected.

When I asked Sabrina whether she thought small schools or larger schools were better, she explained her answer this way:

> I think for areas like this, a K–12 school is good for like anybody 'cause it gives you a feeling of **going from home to home.** Instead of calling it school it's more like a home because you learn but at the same time you're getting a family environment.

Home in Hamilton is migratory.[14] Of course, home starts with the family—the traditional connotation of home. However, a school that cultivates relationships, such as Jay Ellis, can become like a home. For many young people *down yonder*, home will remain in Hamilton. Because home is not necessarily fixed around space or place, but rather people, it will be interesting to see where Hamilton's youth find their homes in the future. Also intriguing is what will happen to Hamilton—the place and its institutions—if home is not found there but is found somewhere else.

Epilogue

Many events have transpired in Hamilton since I left in 2004. The central participants in *Raised Up Down Yonder* were between seventeen and eighteen years old at that time. Now, they are in their midtwenties and gradually entering the middle phase of their lives.[1] Some readers might be interested in what has happened to this dynamic cast of engaging characters, since seven years makes a world of difference in the lives of young adults. A number of Hamilton's youth have become parents, others have bought their first homes, and still others have pursued higher education or have begun their first careers. These young people are still resilient and nimble negotiators of a complex social structure. Scholars such as Henry Giroux have been vigilant in pointing out that youth in the United States are currently facing incredibly challenging circumstances. Giroux states:

> Youth have become the central site onto which class and racial anxieties
> are projected. Their very presence represents *both* the broken promises
> of capitalism in the age of deregulation and downsizing *and* a collective
> fear of the consequences wrought by systemic class inequalities and a
> culture of "infectious greed" that has created a generation of unskilled
> and displaced youth expelled from shrinking markets, blue collar jobs,
> and any viable hope for the future . . . If youth once symbolized the moral
> necessity to address a range of social and economic ills, they are now
> largely portrayed as the source of most of society's problems. The ongo-
> ing attacks on children's rights, the endless commercialization of youth,
> the downsizing of children's services, and the increasing incarceration
> of young people suggest more than confusion. In actuality, such policies
> suggest that, at best, adult society no longer cares about children and, at
> worse, views them with scorn and fear.[2]

As I mentioned in the body of *Raised Up Down Yonder*, rural environments actually mask some of this inequality, scorn, and fear. In rural communities, young people's lack of financial resources is often buffered by having safe and comfortable places to sleep, food to eat, and the generosity of neighbors and friends.

Despite a global economic meltdown, in which young African Americans ages eighteen to twenty-nine are unemployed at a rate of 22.3 percent,[3] the young people in Hamilton have crafted meaningful lives for themselves. They have maintained their humor and passion for life, and they still love home. Most young people have left Hamilton but have returned. They share that pattern of returning home with young people all over America who are pinched by the current economy and the rising cost of college education. They have been labeled "Generation Y," a group characterized by a contradictory desire for intimacy in a more interconnected but lonelier world.[4] This generation has become "friends" with the whole world through the use of social media Web sites such as Facebook, yet they are homebodies at heart. They move home out of economic necessity *and* a desire to remain within the fold of family. I should note that the increasing pattern of young people staying near home or moving back home after completing school reveals that rural youth, like those featured in this book, have been the cultural forerunners of their fellow millenials.

The following, then, is a brief update on Kelly, Darnel, Janelle, Missy, James, Sabrina, and Jay Ellis School, which was, in a sense, also a central character in *Down Yonder.*

Kelly

In 2004, Kelly told me that she loved to write. She has finally started to pursue writing again and sent me this very thoughtful "update" that I will present in her own words. (Now, you are published, Kelly!)

I graduated in May 2005 from high school and started classes at a university that same month, majoring in English with minor in Journalism. I had an epiphany that I wanted to become a hairstylist, so in August of 2006, I enrolled in trade school to become a certified cosmetologist. If I hadn't gone when I did, I wouldn't have met my two good friends there. After I graduated in December 2007, I moved to Florida. I really gained experience in being a cosmetologist there and what it was like to be a young adult with responsibility. But after two and a half years, I couldn't handle it financially, so I moved back home with my mom.

I continued doing hair, but that wasn't enough. I wanted my degree. I went to Georgia (ASU) in July 2011 . . . and came home December 2011. However, that one semester changed my life. They had the program that

I'd been searching for, but the tuition was too expensive. But I'm glad to have had the opportunity to go because my professor helped me obtain quite a few connections with people in the writing industry. Plus I met two great friends there as well. Also while I was there, I worked with a few amateur photographers as the models' hairstylist and was also a freelance graphic designer.

At one point in my life (last year) I began thinking negative. I felt lost in the world and felt like no one could understand or help me. I would look back and think about all the years I put myself last, helping others and not really taking care of me. But through prayer and mom's wisdom, I managed to get back up and keep striving for success.

The school that I "ran away" from is where I am again. Before I went back, I wondered "what is my purpose in this world?" I began to settle with the thought of becoming an elementary school teacher. But this past spring 2012, the creative writing program was created at my old school, and I truly rediscovered my purpose. I was so excited when I found out! Still am. I know I have so much creativity to share with the world, and I can't wait to do it.

So as of now, I'm a licensed cosmetologist. I'm a student at ULA, majoring in creative writing with a double major in theater and music. In my spare time, I'm an (aspiring) photographer and I also do freelance graphic design. I'm currently in the process of getting my own business started. Again, I feel I have so much to offer the world creatively.

My mom is still my hero. I currently live with her while I'm in school. We're a help to each other. She always said that if anything happens, I still have a room at home. But once I finish my degree and get on my feet, hopefully that bedroom will just be a trophy room.

Over the years, my relationship with my dad has been rocky. I talk to him every other day and visit him maybe once a month. I know I can't change past feelings, but I can certainly make the future ones better. My oldest half-sister took in my younger half-sister after she experienced diabetes at a young age. Really I don't talk to the two often, but when I do, there is a loving sisterly relationship. The "I love you's" or the "I miss you's" are said. And it is nice to have that sisterly bond when we visit one another.

It's amazing how years go by so quickly. I often look back on a lot of things and wish I could have done some things differently, but then again, if I had, I wouldn't have made an impact on the lives I've touched. I've made lifelong friends, lost friends, and continued to help others along the way. I have no regrets from mistakes I've made because they are lessons learned. I feel mistakes make me better as a person and it also helps me to help another to avoid certain mistakes by giving advice.

Like I always say, everyone has a story to tell, and my story is underway.

Darnel

After graduating from Jay Ellis School as captain of the football team, Darnel earned his associate's degree at Mississippi Delta Community College. He loved playing football there, but he also just enjoyed the experience of being away and learning new things. In fact, although he still listens to Lloyd Banks, his college friends turned him on to other musical genres, such as jazz and reggae that he now listens to more than rap.

Upon graduating from Mississippi Delta, Darnel moved back to the area and currently lives in Carlyle. He is the proud parent of a seven-year-old son, a four-year-old son, and a three-year-old daughter. He absolutely loves parenthood. He and his partner, the mother of his children, are thinking about getting married soon.

Presently, Darnel works in maintenance and grounds at the local hospital. He plans to go back to school for a semester-and-a-half welding program. He's contemplating a move to Texas, after finishing his welding program, just to try something new. As head of the catering staff at Jay Ellis, his mom still lovingly provides nourishment to the children of Jay Ellis.

Janelle

Janelle has been pursuing her bachelor's degree in Liberal Arts since she graduated from Jay Ellis. As of July 2012, she needs only twenty-eight credits to complete her degree. She also has a four-year-old daughter.

Missy

Unfortunately, I was unable to speak with Missy before completing this epilogue. But thanks to Facebook, one can find out a few things about folks just by being their "friends." I know that Missy moved away for some period of time. But she has moved back to Carlyle and works at Target. She looks just the same: confident, trendy, and fashionable. On her page, she also "likes" Joyce Meyer Ministries, a popular television ministry that centers on practical, faith-based, biblical life's teachings, especially focusing on women's issues such as self-esteem.

James

James is still a laid-back guy. After graduating from Jay Ellis, he finished welding school within a year, worked for a short while in construction, and has worked overnight as a mobile equipment operator at a cement factory in Carlyle since then. He says that he is happy at his job and does not foresee leaving it in the future. I enjoyed teasing him that he probably already makes more money than I do, which he was happy to confirm. Additionally, James just bought his first house with his soon-to-be fiancée, who is also from one of the nearby communities. He lives eight miles away from his parents.

James tells me that he really loves life and still enjoys the outdoors. Apparently, he turns the radio station if he hears that "crunk" music he used to enjoy. He says that "you do better when you get older." Now, ironically, he listens to Kanye West and other genres of music, such as R&B or gospel, more than rap. I tried not to poke too much fun at his musical 180-degree turn, but I couldn't resist. When I asked him how he used to view me back in those days—perhaps "the perky girl from the North?" I asked. He said that the students related to me better than anyone else at the school because I was only a few years older and could understand them.

After James's uncle kept hounding him about having left the church, James visited his uncle's church and has been going there ever since then (years).

Sabrina

In 2005, Sabrina graduated from high school as the class valedictorian and received a full scholarship to a nearby university. During her undergraduate years, she was as actively involved in campus activities as she was at Jay Ellis. She served on the student government association as a freshman senator, sophomore senator, business manager, and vice president. In addition, she was elected to the homecoming court in 2007 as a junior maid; she was a university ambassador throughout her matriculation, and she was inducted into several honor societies.

In the spring of 2009, she graduated magna cum laude with a BS in English Language Arts and started working at Carlyle Middle School as an eighth-grade teacher. In the fall of 2010, she received her MAT in English Language Arts and also started working as an adjunct English professor at a nearby university in 2011. Sabrina has her own apartment and a big, fancy, gas-guzzling SUV of some sort, that I enjoyed "janking" her about. She continues to watch Emeril cook on the Food Network, but now she actually cooks the food, too.

According to Sabrina, the Carlyle system still discriminates against low-income black students who are usually labeled as trouble. She said that "some days it really upsets her to see her black students mistreated"; however, she tries to be a role model for them and keep them on the right path. Sabrina also mentioned that although the student population is equal, in reference to race, the teacher ratio is not. She said that it is very hard for blacks to get hired in Carlyle city schools. At her school, the white/black teacher ratio is 5:1, and that pattern is typical.

Sabrina remains grateful for her experience at Jay Ellis. She knows that her time there allowed her to receive the instruction that she needed to go to college and succeed.

Jay Ellis

In 2010, Jay Ellis was awarded a federal School Improvement Grant (SIG), authorized under section 1003(g) of Title I of the Elementary and Secondary Education Act of 1965 (Title I or ESEA). According the United States Department of Education Web site:

> Since President Obama took office, Congress has appropriated more than $4 billion to help turn around the nation's lowest-performing schools. States were awarded nearly $3.5 billion in School Improvement Grant funds in 2010 to turn around their persistently lowest achieving schools. School districts then applied to the state for the funds this spring. When school districts applied, they were required to indicate that they would implement one of the following four models in their persistently lowest achieving schools:
>
> **Turnaround Model:** Replace the principal, screen existing school staff, and rehire no more than half the teachers; adopt a new governance structure; and improve the school through curriculum reform, professional development, extending learning time, and other strategies. **Restart Model:** Convert a school or close it and re-open it as a charter school or under an education management organization. **School Closure:** Close the school and send the students to higher-achieving schools in the district. **Transformation Model:** Replace the principal and improve the school through comprehensive curriculum reform, professional development, extending learning time, and other strategies.[5]

The Attala County Board of Education chose the "Transformation Model" and was awarded a four-million-dollar, three-year grant to "turn Jay Ellis School around." As was the case during my tenure in Hamilton, every story at Jay Ellis seems larger than life. This "good luck" grant and its implementation seem as if it has taken the form of another Turneresque social drama. Apparently, a compassionate employee of the Attala County Board of Education sought out this federal grant, and it was awarded to Jay Ellis because it was the "worst performing school" in the county. According to the Jay Ellis SIG application, the school enrollment had dropped from 250 to 203, and the graduation rate had fallen from 91 percent in 2007 to 71 percent in 2009. Additionally, the SIG application cited discipline problems, low parental involvement, and certain test results as indicators that Jay Ellis desperately needed this grant. Undergirding the SIG, which seems generous on its surface, is a high-stakes, winner/loser, all-or-nothing, success/failure ideology. The grant might become a death knell. It gives schools the opportunity to improve or face closure.

One of the original stipulations of the grant was that major administrative changes had to be made. Ms. Moore, the ineffective principal, was "relocated" to the Marengo County Board of Education as a truancy officer and has since moved on from the board altogether. There has been nearly a 100 percent turnover in the teaching staff; I can only identify one teacher who is still there from the time that I began this study, albeit in a different capacity. Thus far, the grant money primarily has been spent on massive technology upgrades and extensive professional development. The centerpiece of the new program has been to enhance technology-based education, and by all means the school has done that.

According to the technology plan on the Jay Ellis Web site, the students now have the use of at least one computer in each classroom, thirty-eight computers in two labs, and two computers in a media center. Students also have access to multimedia projectors, digital cameras, flip cameras, a class set of Ipod touches, as well as other technology inclusive of an Apple IMac, two class sets of Netbooks, eighty-six laptop computers for all students from grades seven through twelve. Additionally, all Jay Ellis classrooms have been designated as twenty-first-century technology classrooms. Each classroom has been equipped with an ELMO document camera, an Interwrite pad, a classroom response system, a multimedia projector, microphone, surround sound speakers, a VHS/DVD player, and a projection screen. Teachers have access to Geneva Logic's Vision class kit that allows teachers to monitor and instruct from the teacher's computer in both labs. By all means, this use of technology at Jay Ellis is revolutionary.

There are a number of other goals that the school has set, which will measure increased parental involvement at the school and improvement in student discipline, as well as increased performance on the third- through eighth-grade Alabama Reading and Math Test. Additionally, the technology plan is a professional development/enhanced pedagogy plan. The grant stipulates that teachers must effectively integrate technology into the classroom pedagogy; the largest sum of money in the grant allows teachers to receive ongoing training and provides money for substitute teachers when the regular teachers are being trained. Additionally, the county has hired a transformation specialist and an academic standards coach, who are responsible for overseeing the implementation of the grant. Finally, the school day has been extended from 7:30 a.m. to 3:30 p.m.

According to the current SIG report, Jay Ellis is achieving many of its benchmarks, but falling short on some others. I have made only one brief stop by the school since it has been awarded this generous grant, so I have not observed what is actually taking place in the school. However, I have talked with several community members who are invested in Jay Ellis's long-term success. I have received mixed reviews. On the positive side, I have been informed that the school is cleaner and that the faculty and administration are more cohesive. I was heartened when browsing the Jay Ellis Web site to see so many well-decorated, warm spaces, with an abundance of instructional resources and bright smiles from students and teachers. One particular series of photos posted on the Web site features Dr. Seuss-themed "Read Across America" day. On that day, the students ate green eggs and ham and wore Dr. Seuss hats.

On the negative side, I have been informed that the paperwork that comes along with the grant has frustrated the teachers. According to the 2012 SIG report, between the 2010–2011 school year and the 2011–2012 school year, five teachers transferred, retired, or resigned. One of the indicators that the school needed help was low teacher morale, which stemmed from the overburdened small staff, which I also examined in chapter 2 of this book. Contrary to what might have been expected, this SIG seems to have increased teacher burnout because of the extended days, continuous teacher training and assessment, a bevy of school assemblies, and parental outreach efforts that are listed in the SIG plan. One hundred percent of teachers are supposed to plan and implement programs every nine weeks to increase parental support. These programs are Family Day, Honors Day, PTO, Literacy Day, Christmas, Thanksgiving, Grandparents Day, Special Forces Day, Read Across America Day, and others. The bureaucratic paperwork found on the Web site for a school of two hundred students is dizzying. On the Web site one can download "The Technology Plan," "Continuous Improvement Plan (CIP)," "The Title I Plan," and six other documents that are "guiding" the school.

In keeping with the presentation of my subjective voice throughout *Raised Up Down Yonder*, I would say that I am cautiously optimistic. Where the No Child Left Behind Act has been roundly criticized for raising expectations without resources, the liberal awarding of these School Improvement Grants demonstrates that the Obama administration is willing to invest resources in schools. However, four matters still concern me. First, the manner in which the grants are awarded appropriates a narrow success/failure dichotomy. Jay Ellis was not a total "failure" and will not magically convert to being "successful" if it reaches the set benchmarks. Similarly, if Jay Ellis does not attain these benchmarks in three short years, it should not be labeled a failure because of many reasons for optimism that I present in this book.

Second, the school improvement plan, including Jay Ellis's own self-assessment, is well developed on many levels. The label of success or failure will not be based solely on high-stakes standardized tests, but rather on a number of other assessments, including teacher, student, and parent surveys, program implementation, attendance rates, graduation rates, and so forth. However, the transformation specialist and academic standards coach positions do not seem sufficient to offset the increased workload of an already overburdened staff. Further, the SIG report mentions this fact; there are still no teachers specifically hired to address curricula outside of the core courses, such as art or music teachers.

Third, if an inordinate amount of work is going to be required of administrators, teachers, students, and parents, it seems that a greater "buy-in" should have been established. Aside from the threat—"achieve these benchmarks or your school will close"—I have not read in any report or document what the long-term incentives for achievement are, beyond performance-based monetary incentives for the principal and students. In a recent local newspaper article, Superintendent Donaldson states that he hopes that Jay Ellis can become a model "transformation school" and increase its enrollment because of people's desire to "see why our kids are performing so well on tests." Again, framing the stakes so narrowly in terms of high-stakes test scores fails to inspire people's hearts and imaginations. One disturbing statistic found in the current Jay Ellis SIG report is that while 100 percent of students reported that one or more teachers encourage them to achieve more than they thought they ever could, 83 percent stated that they hate being in school. There were many other "positive indicators" cited by students, but if one "hates" to be in school, the positive effects are limited.

Finally, and this point directly relates to the previous one, the SIG application and report draws heavily upon the fact that Jay Ellis is rural and that the student body is 100 percent African American, but race and ethnicity are strangely absent from the grant's goals or plans. Anthropologists such as Mica Pollock have shown that deleting race words from the vocabulary of schools does not make them any less racial.[6] Instead, selectively deleting these words can frame race in very narrow and essentialist terms. Choosing a color-blind approach to improving Jay Ellis is a mistake. The proud and complex history of the school's African American community should be interwoven in any plans for its future. I would recommend pedagogical approaches to teaching Jay Ellis's students, such as those documented in Gloria Ladson-Billings's acclaimed book, *The Dreamkeepers: Successful Teachers of African American Children.*[7] In *The Dreamkeepers*, Ladson-Billings advocates cultural relevant teaching, "a pedagogy that empowers students intellectually, socially, emotionally, and politically by using cultural referents to impart knowledge, skills, and attitudes."[8] She argues that "when schools support [students'] culture as an integral part of the school experience, students can understand that academic excellence is not the sole province of white middle-class students."[9] Perhaps this kind of rhetoric is being espoused at the school or in faculty professional development seminars. However, the omission of African American culture from written documents makes a powerful statement.

In July 2013, the final evaluation of the School Improvement Grant's success will be published. If Jay Ellis has not met its benchmarks, even after the huge federal expenditure, the school may still be closed. Jay Ellis's students would have to choose between the Carlyle school system, and the nearest county school, which is twenty-eight miles away. But, if Jay Ellis does not meet these "benchmarks" and still remains open, that "exception" will seem to prove Superintendent Donaldson's point, discussed in chapter 4, that Jay Ellis "gets more than its fair share." That conclusion will further the stereotype that Jay Ellis is somehow a Last Chance School. Thus, the only "winning" solution seems to be for Jay Ellis to attain its benchmarks. The stakes certainly are high. I am praying for a positive next chapter to this story.

Appendix

Interview Schedule: Hamilton's Youth (two-hour interview)

Part I. Background Information and Family History

What is your name? (gender)

When were you born?

Where were you born? How old are you?

Who lives in your household?

How long have you lived there?

Do you have family members who don't live in your household? Who are they?

What are your parents' occupations?

How much money do you think they make per year?

How did your family wind up in Hamilton? Do you know how long your relatives have lived here?

What other families in Hamilton are you related to? Do you have cousins at school with you? Who?

Part II. School

Where do you go to school?

Do you like it?

Who are your favorite teachers?

What do you think about Jay Ellis? Is it a good school? Why?

Do you think people have a good opinion about Jay Ellis? Why?

How would you compare Jay Ellis to Carlyle High, Middle, or U.S. Jones?

What are some important issues at Jay Ellis?

Do you think uniforms are a good idea?

Do you think your parents are happy with your education?

Do you work hard in school?

What are your grades like?

What is your favorite class?

Do your teachers ever talk about movies, or music, or television in class?

What are you all supposed to be doing during your break time?

If you could change one thing about school what would it be?

Do you see yourself as the same or different from most of the kids at Jay Ellis? How about most of the kids at Carlyle?

Part III: Church and Recreation

What do you do with most of your free time?

About how often do you go to Carlyle? Tuscaloosa? Meridian? Birmingham? Montgomery? Other places?

Do you attend church? Where?

Would you describe yourself as very religious? Why?

Who else goes to church with you?

What is the purpose of going to church in your mind?

Part IV: Relationships and Aspiration

Who are the most important people in your life?

Do you have a boyfriend or girlfriend? Who? How long have you been together?

Tell me about your best friends.

Are you close to your family members?

What is one time that someone really hurt you or broke your trust?

What is the nicest thing someone has done for you?

Have many people in your family have gone to college? Do you want to go to college?

What do you think you will have to do to get there? Are you doing what's necessary?

Part V: Self-Perception

Describe yourself.

What are your favorite parts about yourself?

What are your least favorite parts?

How do you think other people see you?

Part VI: Popular Culture

How often do you go to the movies?

What is your favorite movie? Why?

What kind of music do you listen to? Favorite artists?

Do you have a CD player of your own? When do you listen to music?

Who buys the music for you?

Do your parents or guardians like the music you listen to? Do they approve of the music you listen to?

Do you have cable television? What stations?

How many hours of TV do you watch a day?

What stations and programs mostly?

What artist is most like you? What actor is most like you? What character is most like you?

Do you think the images you see of black people are positive?

Do you think artists, popular culture, etc., represent you? Black people in general?

Do you pay attention to politics?

Do you plan on voting in the next election?

Do you think you are part of the hip-hop generation? What does that term mean to you?

Do you think you are mostly the same as or mostly different from white kids your age? In what way?

Do you think you are mostly the same or mostly different from most black kids your age? Kids who grow up in the North? Big cities?

Do you agree with the war in Iraq? Do you know anyone who is or has been overseas in the war?

Describe a typical day in your life.

Part VII. Fill in the Blank

I am happiest when I _____.

I am grateful because _____.

When I wake up in the morning I feel_____.

When I go to sleep at night I feel _____.

In the future I want to _____.

The person who inspires me most is _____.

The biggest block to my future success will be _____.

If I could I would change _____.

In the future I want to live _____.

Notes

Acknowledgments

1. In actuality, one does not have to sacrifice storytelling in order to critique oppression. In fact Critical Race Theory explicitly embraces storytelling as one of its vital components. The other three vital components are acknowledging that racism is normal and not aberrant in our society, positing that liberalism should be replaced with efforts at sweeping change, and revealing that civil rights laws generally serve the interest of the powerful in order to pass (interest convergence). In presenting this brief vignette, I am simply emphasizing the importance of storytelling. For a readable and thorough introduction to Critical Race Theory, see Laurence Parker, Donna Deyhle, and Sofia A. Villenas, eds., *Race Is—Race Isn't: Critical Race Theory and Qualitative Studies in Education* (Boulder, CO: Westview Press, 1999).

Introduction

1. Most proper names, including the schools, the informants, and the towns about which I write, have been given pseudonyms. This common practice protects the identities of the people who have so selflessly given of their time.

Additionally, this book is written in past and present tense, for two reasons. First, anthropologists have recognized that the practice of writing in the ethnographic present hides the ever-changing nature of culture and assigns ethnographers an overly authoritative voice. Also, however, because it has been seven years since I left the field, it is quite clear in my case that many things have changed since my fieldwork, and writing about them in the present tense would be misleading. The fact that I am writing about youth only exacerbates the issue; the young people in this study are now adults, and the epilogue highlights the metamorphosis that they have undergone.

2. Throughout the book, I use the terms black and white to connote race as a social construction, rather than a biological reality. For this reason, I use lowercase letters for black and white, but capitalize African American, as it describes a particular cultural and ethnic identity. For a full exposition on the history of the concept of race, see Audrey Smedley, *Race in North America: Origin and Evolution of a World View* (Boulder, CO: Westview Press, 1993). See also Lee D. Baker, *From Savage to Negro: Anthropology and the Construction of Race, 1896–1954* (Berkeley and Los Angeles: University of California Press, 1998).

3. See chapter 6 for a larger discussion of moral panics.

4. There is a rich history of scholars who have examined the identity and decisions of African American adolescents within rural settings in the mid-twentieth century. See Allison Davis and John Dollard, *Children of Bondage: The Personality Development of Negro Youth in the Urban South*, 1st ed. (New York: Harper & Row, 1964); Edward Franklin Frazier, *Negro Youth at the Crossways: Their Personality Development in the Middle States* (Washington, DC: American Council on Education, 1940); and Charles Spurgeon Johnson, *Growing up in the Black Belt: Negro Youth in the Rural South* (Washington, DC: American Council on Education, 1941). However, much of the present work on rural settings has been on the economic conditions of the communities, racial inequality, rural urban migration, and urban rural return migration. See Emery N. Castle, *The Changing American Countryside: Rural People and Places*, *Rural America* (Lawrence: University Press of Kansas, 1995); Mark Alan Fossett and M. Therese Seibert, *Long Time Coming: Racial Inequality in the Nonmetropolitan South, 1940–1990*, Rural Studies Series of the Rural Sociological Society (Boulder, CO: Westview Press, 1997); Farah Jasmine Griffin, *"Who Set You Flowin'?": The African-American Migration Narrative*, Race and American Culture (New York: Oxford University Press, 1995); and Carol B. Stack, *Call to Home: African Americans Reclaim the Rural South* (New York: Basic Books, 1996). Frazier, in *Negro Youth at the Crossways*, identifies the following categories of analysis that are critical to understanding adolescent identity in the South: neighborhood structures and networks, churches, employment opportunities, social movements and ideologies, and schools.

5. George Lipsitz, Foreword, to *Youthscapes: The Popular, the National, the Global*, ed. Sunaina Maira and Elisabeth Soep (Philadelphia: University of Pennsylvania Press, 2005), x. Lipsitz is referring to the role of the mass media and public policy discourse in perpetuating the view of youth as social problems. I am extending his observation to include academic research on youth, as well.

The majority of the work on African American adolescents within the last thirty years has taken place in urban settings. These studies have often focused on social problems such as teenage pregnancy, academic disengagement, and social immobility. See, for example, Jay MacLeod, *Ain't No Makin' It: Leveled Aspirations in a Low-Income Neighborhood* (Boulder, CO: Westview Press, 1987); Shirley Brice Heath and Milbrey Wallin McLaughlin, eds., *Identity and Inner-City Youth: Beyond Ethnicity and Gender* (New York: Teachers College Press, 1993); Milbrey Wallin McLaughlin, Merita A. Irby, and Juliet Langman, eds., *Urban Sanctuaries: Neighborhood Organizations in the Lives and Futures of Inner-City Youth*, 1st ed. (San Francisco: Jossey-Bass Publishers, 1994); and Ronald L. Taylor, ed. *African-American Youth: Their Social and Economic Status in the United States* (Westport, CT: Praeger, 1995).

Many outstanding ethnographies have addressed African American adolescents and their often problematic position within American educational systems. See, for example, Shirley Brice Heath, *Ways with Words: Language, Life, and Work in Communities and Classrooms* (Cambridge: Cambridge University Press, 1983); Signithia Fordham, *Blacked Out: Dilemmas of Race, Identity, and Success at Capital High* (Chicago: University of Chicago Press, 1996); Ann Arnett Ferguson, *Bad Boys: Public Schools in the Making of Black Masculinity*, Law, Meaning, and Violence (Ann Arbor: University of Michigan Press, 2000); John U. Ogbu, *Black American Students in an Affluent Suburb: A Study of Academic Disengagement* (Mahwah, NJ: L. Erlbaum Associates, 2003); and Luke E. Lassiter, *The Other Side of Middletown: Exploring Muncie's African American Community* (Walnut Creek, CA: AltaMira Press, 2004). Despite how rich these school ethnographies are, usually the central themes have to do with education and achievement, and if questions like family dynamics or language are addressed, they are only done so in relation to those questions. Elsewhere in the book, I will engage with a few notable exceptions to that general observation, such as Mary Pattillo-McCoy, *Black Picket Fences: Privilege and Peril among the Black Middle Class* (Chicago: University of Chicago Press, 1999); Nikki Jones, *Between Good and Ghetto: African American Girls and Inner-City Violence*, The Rutgers Series in Childhood Studies (New Brunswick, NJ: Rutgers University Press, 2010); and Oneka LaBennett, *She's Mad Real: Popular Culture and West Indian Girls in Brooklyn* (New York: New York University Press, 2011). These recent ethnographies include thick descriptions and complex analyses that are not necessarily tied to achievement or to any particular social problem. Elizabeth M. Liew Siew Chin's *Purchasing Power: Black Kids and American Consumer Culture* (Minneapolis: University of Minnesota Press, 2001) also fits this description, except that she focuses on African American children as opposed to adolescents.

6. For a seminal text on everyday forms of resistance, see James Scott, *Weapons of the Weak: Everyday Forms of Peasant Resistance* (New Haven, CT: Yale University Press, 1985). I agree that forms of resistance, like the sort that Scott highlights among poor people in Latin America, constitute powerful displays of agency within limited, constraining structures. However, I also feel that it is vital that we call attention to the subjective areas of our lives that are meaningful irrespective of oppressive systems. Only in doing so can we truly grant our subjects agency and humanity.

7. See Cornel West, *Race Matters* (Boston: Beacon Press, 1993). Part of the dichotomous posture on the part of academics regarding behavior versus structure stems from the political context into which our research enters. Indeed, undergirding research agendas that focus on the "problems" of African American youth are foundational debates within sociology and anthropology on the relationship among poverty, kinship, and behavior. For example, the sociologist William Julius Wilson in his provocative study, *The Declining Significance of Race: Blacks and Changing American Institutions*, 2nd ed. (Chicago: University of Chicago Press, 1980), argues that the emergence of the modern industrial economy generated rapid political and economic

changes, which in turn enabled upward social mobility for blacks in the United States. See also William Junius Wilson, *The Truly Disadvantaged: The Inner City, the Underclass, and Public Policy* (Chicago: University of Chicago Press, 1987); and *When Work Disappears: The World of the New Urban Poor*, 1st ed. (New York: Knopf; Distributed by Random House, 1996). He posits that this upward mobility has created an increasing divide between the black middle class and what he coins "underclass," which undermines the chance for racial solidarity. He analyzes the social, economic, and political benefits of education, without denying the psychologically devastating impacts of racism across class. However, his work has been criticized for painting a shallow and bleak portrayal of the "depraved" underclass.

This is an example of one of the major fault lines regarding the "problematic" characterization of African Americans and, by extension, African American youth. Another of these foundational debates has centered on the supposed pathology of the black family. See Edward Franklin Frazier, *The Negro Family in the United States* (Chicago: University of Chicago Press, 1939), for an early argument against the depiction of the African American family as primitive. Frazier attributed the form of the black family to historical forces, including slavery, emancipation, and the development of the industrial working class. The African American family has continued to inspire rancorous debate both within and outside of the academy, highlighting researchers' hesitance to discuss behavior at all, or if so, only in vindicationist ways. For a discussion of the vindicationist tradition, see St. Clair Drake, "Further Reflections on Anthropology and the Black Experience," *Transforming Anthropology* 1, no. 2 (1990). Oscar Lewis's "culture of poverty thesis," found in *Five Families: Mexican Case Studies in the Culture of Poverty* (New York: Basic Books, 1959) and *La Vida: A Puerto Rican Family in the Culture of Poverty—San Juan and New York* (New York: Random House, 1966), and introduced to the general public by Daniel P. Moynihan in *The Negro Family: The Case for National Action* (Washington, DC: U.S. Government Printing Office, 1965), severely heightened the vitriol surrounding the black family, which has continued ever since. The point I wish to emphasize here is that these controversies color our portrayals of African American youth and influence what kinds of questions we ask. Laura Nader, in "Up the Anthropologist—Perspectives Gained from Studying Up," in *Reinventing Anthropology*, ed. Dell H. Hymes (New York: Pantheon, 1972), has suggested that "studying up" might be the only way to avoid depictions of the poor and powerless being preempted by the powerful toward destructive ends.

8. Throughout this ethnography, youth are presented as cognitively aware people. As such, their recollections of events and their own judgments are presented alongside my judgments and those of other adults in the community. My argument is that they neither have a greater connection to an essential youth perspective nor do they comprise a discrete category of people who present a skewed or underdeveloped adolescent perspective because they are primarily focused on resolving an identity

crisis; see Erik H. Erikson, *Identity, Youth, and Crisis*, 1st ed. (New York: W. W. Norton, 1968). Rather, as psychologist James E. Marcia, "Development and Validation of Ego-Identity Status," *Journal of Personality and Social Psychology* 3, no. 5 (1966), has suggested, I found that insomuch as young people are in the process of becoming and creating themselves, they are more similar than dissimilar to the adults in the community. In other words, the extent to which young people have access to privileged information is due to their participation in elements of the structure and culture, which, by definition, cater to them as the subjects. This argument is nearly as old as cultural anthropology, but bears emphasis because of a tendency of scholars to overcorrect, by privileging the "youth perspective," rather than to recognize that the youth perspective should be juxtaposed with all other standpoints. I conclude that Hamilton's adolescents live in very much the same overall social world as all other actors in the community.

9. John L. Jackson, *Real Black: Adventures in Racial Sincerity* (Chicago: University of Chicago Press, 2005).

10. Douglas E. Foley, *Learning Capitalist Culture: Deep in the Heart of Tejas*, 2nd ed., Contemporary Ethnography (Philadelphia: University of Pennsylvania Press, 2010).

11. I have been particularly influenced by MacLeod, *Ain't No Makin' It*. This ethnography describes youth culture and aspirations in an urban housing project, using social reproduction theory and analyzing the convergence of structure and culture. He explores adolescent identity formation without offering psychologically reductionist explanations for inequality or ignoring the ability of young people to participate in the consumption *and* creation of culture. Also, by following the "Hallway Hangers" and "Brothers" into adulthood, MacLeod gives a longitudinal portrayal of one group of youngsters, which is rare. Despite its many virtues, however, it still focuses on inequality, which limits the book's ability to "wrest meaning out of the flux of their lives," which, ironically, MacLeod advocates," 139. Another recent holistic portrayal of African American youth can be found in Pattillo-McCoy, *Black Picket Fences*. In it, Pattillo-McCoy emphasizes the complex negotiations of the black middle class, including the "economic, spatial, and cultural contexts that influence decision making, life transition, and outcomes"; ibid., 10. Her examination of adolescents includes a discussion of the consumption of popular culture by her informants, whom she classifies as consumed by it, thrilled by it, or marginal to it. Central to this ethnography is the close proximity of the middle-class and lower-class neighborhoods, and adolescents are portrayed as vulnerable to the underclass values that constantly threaten their development. In this manner, however, it reinforces the negative association between "underclass" or poor people, crime, and bleak futures. Once again, I hope to inject these rich ethnographies with a dose of the subjective.

12. Sherry B. Ortner, "Theory in Anthropology since the Sixties," *Comparative Studies in Society and History* 26 (1984).

13. See Talal Asad, "Anthropology and the Analysis of Ideology," *Man* 14, no. 4 (1979), for a critique of the total systems and structures of both Marxism and functionalism and an argument in favor of studying particular historical forces in more detail. See Deborah A. Thomas, *Exceptional Violence: Embodied Citizenship in Transnational Jamaica* (Durham, NC: Duke University Press, 2011), for a recent ethnography grounded in "history, political economy and practice," 5.

14. Foley, *Learning Capitalist Culture.*

15. Charles Tilly, *Identities, Boundaries, and Social Ties* (Boulder, CO: Paradigm Publishers, 2005), 5, described Weber's causal logic: cultural forms that generate new forms of consciousness, which then shape economic activity.

16. Many brilliant scholars have examined class reproduction in American education. I have listed just a few of the ones who have most influenced my thinking. See Michael W. Apple, *Ideology and Curriculum*, 3rd ed. (New York: Routledge Falmer, 2004); Henry A. Giroux, *The Giroux Reader*, ed. Christopher G. Robbins (Boulder, CO: Paradigm Publishers, 2006); *On Critical Pedagogy* (London: Continuum International Publishing Group, 2011), http://www.JHU.eblib.com/patron/FullRecord .aspx?p=762977; Peter McLaren, *Schooling as a Ritual Performance: Toward a Political Economy of Educational Symbols and Gestures*, 2nd ed. (London: Routledge, 1993); and *Life in Schools: An Introduction to Critical Pedagogy in the Foundations of Education*, 3rd ed. (New York: Longman, 1998). Critical pedagogy scholars not only examine the reproductive quality of schools, but also their unmet potential to be positive forces for social and political change. Other scholars of education and inequality are referenced in chapter 3.

17. Pierre Bourdieu, *Outline of a Theory of Practice* (Cambridge: Cambridge University Press, 1977); Richard K. Harker, "On Reproduction, Habitus and Education," *British Journal of Sociology of Education* 5, no. 2 (1984).

18. The term "adolescent," used intermittently throughout this project, conjures up psychosocial approaches to identity. Psychologists have emphasized the importance of discreet developmental stages in human life. See Bärbel Inhelder and Jean Piaget, *The Growth of Logical Thinking from Childhood to Adolescence: An Essay on the Construction of Formal Operational Structures* (New York: Basic Books, 1958); Erikson, *Identity, Youth, and Crisis*; and Peter Blos, *The Adolescent Passage: Developmental Issues* (New York: International Universities Press, 1979). Adolescence is defined as a stage marked by rapid biological and cognitive changes linking childhood and adulthood. When seen through this lens, identity is one of several psychosocial issues (for example, intimacy, autonomy, and sexuality) that are addressed throughout the life span. According to Erickson, the biological and cognitive changes that occur during

adolescence, as well as the particular demands of society, cause identity achieved versus identity diffusion (confusion or fragmentation) to be the primary focus. The challenge of adolescence according to Erikson is to resolve the identity crisis and emerge from it with a more coherent sense of self.

Perhaps most relevant to my anthropological query of identity is Erikson's thesis on the manner in which the identity crisis is resolved. Erikson posited that one's identity is comprised through interactions with other people; otherwise stated, that other individuals serve as a mirror reflection of who a person is and can be. Moreover, Erikson believed that society, more generally, helps shape the individual's sense of himself by offering a spectrum of potential choices. According to this paradigm, developing an integrated identity is both a mental and social process. Margaret Mead, *Coming of Age in Samoa: A Psychological Study of Primitive Youth for Western Civilisation* (New York: W. Morrow & Company, 1928); and *Growing up in New Guinea: A Comparative Study of Primitive Education* (New York: W. Morrow & Company, 1930), most famously introduced this argument into mainstream academia when she challenged G. Stanley Hall's assertion that adolescence was necessarily a period of "storm and stress." While aspects of her research in Samoa have been challenged over the years, her general thesis that culture and not biology largely shapes what we describe as adolescence has been seminal.

While Erik Erikson, *Identity and the Life Cycle: Selected Papers*, Psychological Issues (New York: International Universities Press, 1959), did pinpoint different stages in life in which one psychosocial crisis takes precedence over the others, he believed that the resolution of each crisis was to an extent lifelong. He wrote, "a sense of identity is never gained nor maintained once and for all," 118. Instead humans are engaged in a constant struggle to define who we are. Of course, the applicability of Erikson's theories to various societies varies; anthropologists as well as historians have been instrumental in making sure that theories of psychosocial development are used in relevant cultural contexts.

19. Fredrik Barth, *Ethnic Groups and Boundaries: The Social Organization of Culture Difference* Results of a Symposium Held at the University of Bergen, February 23–26, 1967, Scandinavian University Books (London: Universitetsforlaget; Allen & Unwin, 1969), 30.

20. Ibid., 30.

21. E. J. Hobsbawm and T. O. Ranger, *The Invention of Tradition*, Past and Present Publications (New York: Cambridge University Press, 1983).

22. Jonathan Friedman, "Myth, History and Political Identity," *Cultural Anthropology* 7, no. 2 (1992), 194.

23. Ibid.

24. See John L. Jackson, *Harlemworld: Doing Race and Class in Contemporary*

Black America (Chicago: University of Chicago Press, 2001), for an examination of the performative aspects of race and class identity among African Americans.

25. For a contemporary analysis of identity developed through relations created by boundaries, see Tilly, *Identities, Boundaries, and Social Ties*. He argues that "interpersonal transactions compound into identities, create and transform social boundaries, and accumulate into durable social ties," 7.

26. Literature about middle- and working-class rural African American youth identity is scant, having been overshadowed by the urban inner city and suburban youth. However, two widely read foundational texts on young middle-class African Americans and their psychological needs as they attempt to define their identity are William E. Cross, *Shades of Black: Diversity in African-American Identity* (Philadelphia: Temple University Press, 1991), and Beverly Daniel Tatum, *"Why Are All the Black Kids Sitting Together in the Cafeteria?" And Other Conversations About Race*, 1st ed. (New York: Basic Books, 1997). One theme that runs throughout these and other works is the difficulty of being culturally and economically distinct from both the black lower class and white middle class. Interestingly, W. E. B. Du Bois, *The Souls of Black Folk*, The Bedford Series in History and Culture (Boston: Bedford Books, 1997), and Davis and Dollard, *Children of Bondage*, documented similar psychological stresses of young African Americans attempting to grow up in the middle class a century, and a half century, ago, respectively.

27. I would disagree with any implication that because my subjects are black, the primary identity theorizing should center on racial identity. Not without controversy, Anthony Appiah and Amy Gutmann, *Color Conscious: The Political Morality of Race* (Princeton, NJ: Princeton University Press, 1996), similarly argue that "racial identity," while far superior to the concept of "race" or "African American culture," should not be treated as the dominant collective identity.

28. See chapter 6 for a greater engagement with literature on popular culture and identity.

29. These local disparities are linked to larger regional and national patterns. Decreases in racial inequality after the civil rights and voting rights legislation have slowed dramatically, especially in rural areas. See Fossett and Seibert, *Long Time Coming*. According to the U.S. Census broad population-level comparisons between whites and blacks in health, housing, education, employment, and income continue to reveal extensive inequality. The South, in general, is suffering due to the shrinking of the American manufacturing belt and competition from global markets. David L. Carlton and Peter A. Coclanis, *The South, the Nation, and the World: Perspectives on Southern Economic Development* (Charlottesville: University of Virginia Press, 2003).

30. See table in chapter 3 for a breakdown of employment in the greater Carlyle/Hamilton area.

31. Castle, *The Changing American Countryside*. Various scholars examine the dynamics of rural communities, which, while distinct in their local character, have been similarly impacted by global processes; in Kai A. Schafft and Alicia Youngblood Jackson, eds., *Rural Education for the Twenty-first Century: Identity, Place, and Community in a Globalizing World* (University Park: Pennsylvania State University Press, 2010).

32. LaBennett, *She's Mad Real*, 34, also acknowledges the dynamics of power and authority that come into play when researching youth.

Chapter 1

1. E. E. Evans-Pritchard, *Witchcraft, Oracles, and Magic among the Azande*, abridged with an introduction by Eva Gillies (Oxford: Clarendon Press, 1976), describes the significance of the Azande's use of witchcraft as the chief mode of explanation as thus:

> If a man is killed by a spear in war, or by a wild beast in hunting, of by the bite of a snake, or from sickness, witchcraft is the socially relevant cause, since it is the only one which allows intervention and determines social behavior . . . [Further], the attribution of misfortune to witchcraft does not exclude what we call its real causes but is superimposed on them and gives to social events their moral value. (25)

2. Janelle's story will be presented in depth in chapter 4.

3. This is a term that means "to joke," used daily in Hamilton.

4. The U.S. Census does not recognize Hamilton as a town or place. Therefore, I had to "build" the area that I call Hamilton based on my knowledge of the community geography and its members. I included the town center, the area people call Hamilton, as well as the neighborhoods and residences where Jay Ellis students live. Some of the students who go to Jay Ellis live in Carlyle, which I did not include because it is so populous. The "block groups" that I selected to represent Hamilton correspond fairly well to "reality." The only skew of the data may be that the census "block groups" include a few more miles south of the town center than is normally included. This will have increased the number of white residences and the median income of white families. However, because few if any black people reside in that area, the data on my community should be unaffected.

5. Unless specified otherwise, my data is on black people in Hamilton. The segregation of the community allows me to segregate my data easily. For example, I didn't learn of any black and white families living on the same side street or dirt road. Furthermore, at the "center" of black Hamilton where the three county roads meet, one would never see a white person out of his car unless something unusual was happening. The compound lifestyle and all the other features of kinship in this chapter refer to black families.

6. Carol B. Stack, *All Our Kin: Strategies for Survival in a Black Community*, 1st ed. (New York: Harper & Row, 1974), 28.

7. Chapters 2 through 4 will more fully explain the complex, interdependent nature of Hamilton families and Jay Ellis. While Jay Ellis can positively cement family relationships, the family can help foster mess in the school.

8. Their pantry supply comes from companies such as Nabisco who donate food that has almost reached its expiration date. It is no surprise that the waiting list for the pantry program is long.

9. See William W. Falk, *Rooted in Place: Family and Belonging in a Southern Black Community* (New Brunswick, NJ: Rutgers University Press, 2004).

10. See chapter 6 for more on adolescents' interpretations of popular culture.

11. The definition of "total income" according to the U.S. Census Bureau underscores the overall poverty of many of the families, since it includes "the sum of the amounts reported separately for wages, salary, commissions, bonuses, or tips; self-employment income from own nonfarm or farm businesses, including proprietorships and partnerships; interest, dividends, net rental income, royalty income, or income from estates and trusts; Social Security or Railroad Retirement income; Supplemental Security Income (SSI); any public assistance or welfare payments from the state or local welfare office; retirement, survivor, or disability pensions; and any other sources of income received regularly such as Veterans' (VA) payments, unemployment compensation, child support, or alimony."

12. Virginia Heyer Young, "Family and Childhood in a Southern Negro Community," *American Anthropologist* 72, no. 2 (1970): 272.

13. For a recent confirmation of this phenomenon in rural areas, more generally, see Anastasia Snyder, "Patterns of Family Formation and Dissolution in Rural America and Implications for Well-Being," in *Economic Restructuring and Family Well-Being in Rural America*, ed. Kristin E. Smith, Ann R. Tickamyer, and Rural Sociological Society (University Park: Pennsylvania State University Press, 2011).

14. According to the 2000 census 24 (9 percent) out of 274 children in households were classified as stepchildren. This data hides the extensive influence of divorce because these children were only designated as *step* in relationship to the householder who completed the interview. In other words, they might have been related by remarriage to someone in the house other than the interviewee. In addition, some students reported living in a household that included only members of their nuclear family, but stepsiblings from their parents' previous marriages, while not living in their household, were still part of their social worlds.

15. Sylvia Yanagisako, "Variations in American Kinship: Implications for Cultural Analysis," *American Ethnologist* 5 (1978).

16. Ibid., 20.

17. Stack, *All Our Kin*, 124.

Chapter 2

1. For an ethnographic examination of how schools engage in racializing practices, even while attempting to be colorblind, see Amanda E. Lewis, *Race in the Schoolyard: Negotiating the Color Line in Classrooms and Communities*, The Rutgers Series in Childhood Studies (New Brunswick, NJ: Rutgers University Press, 2003); and Mica Pollock, *Colormute: Race Talk Dilemmas in an American School* (Princeton, NJ: Princeton University Press, 2004).

2. James D. Anderson, *The Education of Blacks in the South, 1860–1935* (Chapel Hill: University of North Carolina Press, 1988), dispels the myth that the educational movement among rural, southern African Americans after the abolition of slavery was driven primarily by "Yankee benevolence" or "federal largesse." Instead, he argues that "the ex-slaves' educational movement was rooted deeply within their own communal values," 9. See also chapter 2 in David B. Tyack, *The One Best System: A History of American Urban Education* (Cambridge, MA: Harvard University Press, 1974), for a concise history of rural, African American education.

3. From http://www.rosenwaldschools.com/history.html. For more on the history of Rosenwald schools and their impact on African American education, see Edwin R. Embree and Julia Waxman, *Investment in People: The Story of the Julius Rosenwald Fund*, 1st ed. (New York: Harper, 1949); Anderson, *The Education of Blacks in the South, 1860–1935*; Adam Fairclough, *Teaching Equality: Black Schools in the Age of Jim Crow*, Mercer University Lamar Memorial Lectures (Athens: University of Georgia Press, 2001); and Mary S. Hoffschwelle, *The Rosenwald Schools of the American South: New Perspectives on the History of the South* (Gainesville: University Press of Florida, 2006).

4. See Michelle Jaffe-Walter, Reva Fine, Pedro Pedraza, Valerie Futch, and Brett Stoudt, "Swimming: On Oxygen, Resistance, and Possibility for Immigrant Youth under Siege," *Anthropology & Education Quarterly* 38, no. 1 (2007), for examples of three contemporary small schools that are effective in educating immigrant students in New York.

5. See Anderson, *The Education of Blacks in the South, 1860–1935*.

6. For an examination of the importance of the perceived differences between town and country in rural areas, see Barbara Ching and Gerald Creed, eds., *Knowing Your Place: Rural Identity and Cultural Hierarchy* (New York: Routledge, 1997). The authors argue that "the rural/urban distinction signifies far more powerfully than physical appearances suggest; inhabitants of areas where town and country seem nearly indistinguishable may nevertheless elaborate a difference through extensive cultural discourse," 2.

7. According to C. Vann Woodward, *Origins of the New South, 1877–1913*, A History of the South (Baton Rouge: Louisiana State University Press, 1951), 222, following reconstruction "for a long time to come, race consciousness would divide, more than class consciousness would unite, Southern labor."

Chapter 3

1. Marxist scholars Antonio Gramsci and Michel Foucault have been so influential in studies of race, ethnicity, and gender because their theories look not only at how inequality is produced by those in power, but also at how it is sustained and reproduced. They focus on the dialectical relationship of the powerful and powerless around systems of ideology. Gramsci posits that hegemony, the pervasive power of the ruling class, is sustained by the dialectic between consent and force. See Antonio Gramsci, *Selections from Prison Notebooks* (London: Lawrence & Wishart, 1971), 57–58. According to Gramsci, hegemony is so effective because of how rarely the ruling class has to use force to achieve consent. While the threat of force is ever present, the civil society and its ideologies actually do the work of upholding dominance. Moreover, the ruling class makes concessions demanded by the subaltern that may do nothing to disrupt the overall hegemony. In many ways, Foucault's concept of discourse can be seen as the space in which hegemony is maintained. In his volume on the history of sexuality, he demonstrates how the mechanisms that were initially set up to restrict the role of sex (in Victorian era society) wound up increasing its presence. See Michel Foucault, *The History of Sexuality*, trans. Robert Hurley, 1st American ed. (New York: Pantheon Books, 1978). In Foucault's terms, what is meant for "refusal, blockage, and invalidation" can actually lead to "incitement and intensification," 299. Recent anthropological studies drawing on these concepts have addressed the ideologies that underscore racism, ethnocentrism, and sexism. See Sylvia Junko Yanagisako and Carol Lowery Delaney, eds., *Naturalizing Power: Essays in Feminist Cultural Analysis* (New York: Routledge, 1995); Steven Gregory and Roger Sanjek, eds., *Race* (New Brunswick, NJ: Rutgers University Press, 1994); and George Lipsitz, *The Possessive Investment in Whiteness: How White People Profit from Identity Politics* (Philadelphia: Temple University Press, 1998).

2. For a foundational examination of pollution and purity as fundamental organizing principles in human life, see Mary Douglas, *Purity and Danger: An Analysis of Concepts of Pollution and Taboo* (New York: Praeger, 1966). She argues that things are labeled as polluted when they fall outside of a set of ordered relations or when they counter basic organizing principles of society. The zip codes and areas that are seen as contaminated usually contradict our notions of a free and democratic society and draw too much attention to the contradictions between lived reality and the "American Dream." This same argument could be made about schools like Jay Ellis that contradict our notions of post–*Brown v. Board of Education* progress.

3. One line from the series, in which a character refers to Baltimore as "Bodymore, Murderland," has been repeated to me more times than I care to remember.

4. Appropriating a Marxist framework for the analysis in this section does not mean that I maintain the base superstructure relationship is unidirectional in Hamilton. Indeed, I see them as dialectical.

5. See Ching and Creed, *Knowing Your Place*.

6. Peter L. Berger and Thomas Luckmann, *The Social Construction of Reality: A Treatise in the Sociology of Knowledge*, 1st ed. (Garden City, NY: Doubleday, 1966). For a full explication of the relationship between overt curriculum, hidden curriculum, and ideology as well as a good summary of literature on ideology from a pioneer in critical pedagogy, see Apple, *Ideology and Curriculum*.

7. Berger and Luckmann, *The Social Construction of Reality*, 3.

8. Ibid., 6.

9. Ibid., 173.

10. Ibid., 186.

11. Ibid., 1.

12. Karl Marx, in "The German Ideology," in *The Marx-Engels Reader*, ed. Karl Marx, Friedrich Engels, and Robert C. Tucker (New York: Norton, 1978), describes "the real premises from which abstraction can only be made in the imagination" as "the real individuals, their activity and the material conditions under which they live" (149).

13. For example, Fordham and Ogbu's widely debated thesis that an oppositional stance to academic achievement among African Americans stems from a reaction against "acting white" was entirely absent at Jay Ellis. See Signithia Fordham and John Ogbu, "Black Students' School Success: Coping with the Burden of 'Acting White,'" *Urban Review* 18, no. 3 (1986); Signithia Fordham, *Blacked Out: Dilemmas of Race, Identity, and Success at Capital High* (Chicago: University of Chicago Press, 1996); and Edmund T. Hamann, "Lessons from the Interpretation/Misinterpretation of John Ogbu's Scholarship," *Intercultural Education* 15 (2004).

14. For a volume whose many articles address the dynamics of school and community and the maintenance of inequality in diverse rural contexts, see Schafft and Jackson, *Rural Education for the Twenty-first Century*.

15. These spirit signs were a regular feature of football games in the county. At Jay Ellis, and I'm assuming at every school, they were large posters or paper banners painted before each game and intended to be impermanent. They were usually destroyed by the elements or just thrown away at the end of the games.

16. See George Lipsitz, "We Know What Time It Is: Race, Class, and Youth Culture in the Nineties," in *Microphone Fiends: Youth Music and Youth Culture*, ed. Andrew Ross and Tricia Rose (New York: Routledge, 1994). See also chapter 6 of this book for a further examination of these issues.

17. The kitchen and the gym are adjacent. However, students must walk through the gym doors to get to the kitchen. Then, after having gathered their food, students must walk back out of the lunch line area into the gym in order to enter the eating area. Because of the small size of the school, the gym is central to all of the school's activities. It is used for morning assemblies, daily recess, gym classes, sporting events,

special events and assemblies, commencements, after school practices, et cetera. Here and elsewhere I use the term fantasy, because images like the "kitchen in the gym" give the social construction of Jay Ellis's "Last Chance" identity an imaginative, illusory quality. In addition, I use the term "fantasy" to connote the fulfilling of certain psychological needs. While psychology is not the primary focus of this work, I would argue that individual and collective psychological needs, in addition to political economic factors, contribute to the persistence of the Jay Ellis caricature.

18. Berger and Luckmann, *The Social Construction of Reality*, 6.

19. See C. Vann Woodward, *Origins of the New South, 1877–1913*, A History of the South (Baton Rouge: Louisiana State University Press, 1951); *The Strange Career of Jim Crow*, Commemorative ed. (Oxford: Oxford University Press, 2002); Louis R. Harlan, *Separate and Unequal: Public School Campaigns and Racism in the Southern Seaboard States, 1901–1915*, Studies in American Negro Life (New York: Atheneum, 1968); and Anderson, *The Education of Blacks in the South, 1860–1935*.

20. For more on convict leasing, see Woodward, *Origins of the New South, 1877–1913*; For more on peonage, see Pete Daniel, *The Shadow of Slavery: Peonage in the South, 1901–1969* (Urbana: University of Illinois Press, 1972). For more on separate and blatantly unequal policies, see Anderson, *The Education of Blacks in the South, 1860–1935*.

21. For a historiography of race, racism, and antiracism scholarship, see Faye V. Harrison, "The Persistent Power of "Race" in the Cultural and Political Economy of Racism," *Annual Review of Anthropology* 24 (1995); and Leith Mullings, "Interrogating Racism: Toward an Antiracist Anthropology," *Annual Review of Anthropology* 34 (2005). In this book, I am answering Mullings's call to "resist using the passive exonerative voice and name racism and the forces that reproduce it" (685). I also examine racism using her definition: "a set of practices, structures, beliefs, and representations that transforms certain forms of perceived differences, generally regarded as indelible and unchangeable, into inequality," 684. See Gregory and Sanjek, *Race*, for a seminal collection of essays that examine race in its various social contexts. See Paul Gilroy, *"There Ain't No Black in the Union Jack": The Cultural Politics of Race and Nation* (London: Hutchinson, 1987), for a foundational treatment of race, nation, and class as interconnected and historically grounded.

22. Williams S. McFeely, "Afterword," in *The Strange Career of Jim Crow*, ed. C. Vann Woodward (Oxford: Oxford University Press, 2002).

23. Woodward, *The Strange Career of Jim Crow*, 8, quoting Professor Ulrich B. Phillips.

24. For examples of how race and class have consistently shaped education in the South, see R. Scott Baker, *Paradoxes of Desegregation: African American Struggles for Educational Equity in Charleston, South Carolina, 1926–1972* (Columbia: University of South Carolina Press, 2006); and Thomas E. Truitt, *Brick Walls: Reflections on Race*

in a Southern School District (Columbia: University of South Carolina Press, 2006). For a historical and political look at several key persons who shaped black education in the South and how their "work" was part of a larger ideology, see William H. Watkins, *The White Architects of Black Education: Ideology and Power in America, 1865–1954*, The Teaching for Social Justice Series (New York: Teachers College Press, 2001).

25. Data are from the 2000 U.S. Census Data Summary File Three. Chapter 2 includes a description of how the geographical area on which the information is based was created.

26. The Introduction to Jane Van Galen and George W. Noblit, eds., *Late to Class: Social Class and Schooling in the New Economy*, Suny Series, Power, Social Identity, and Education (Albany: State University of New York Press, 2007), makes a similar observation about rural areas masking the relative disadvantage of some groups.

27. 2000 U.S. Census, Summary File Three.

28. See Angela McMillan Howell, "Dynamic Youth and Static Religion: The Evolving Relationship between Church and Community in Rural Alabama," unpublished paper delivered at the Global American South Conference, University of North Carolina, Chapel Hill, March 2005.

29. See Harker, "On Reproduction, Habitus and Education."

30. See Robert M. Gibbs, "College Completion and Return Migration among Rural Youth," in *Rural Education and Training in the New Economy: The Myth of Rural Skills Gap*, ed. Robert M. Gibbs, Paul L. Swaim, and Ruy A. Teixeira (Ames: Iowa State University Press, 1998).

31. Complex and diverse motives have historically hedged blacks' occupational opportunities in the South. For example, according to Harlan in *Separate and Unequal*, "Massive financial discrimination against the already conveniently segregated Negro schools [during Jim Crow] apparently developed out of a conjunction of motives: increased white desire for education, white racial hostility, and efforts of tax-payers to limit taxation" (269).

32. This statement is based on the ethnographic and interview data that I collected as well as the 2000 U.S. Census household income data.

33. Paul E. Willis, *Learning to Labor: How Working Class Kids Get Working Class Jobs*, Morningside ed. (New York: Columbia University Press, 1981), examines the multivalent process by which working-class kids are directed to certain kinds of work in an industrial town in England. He especially focuses on the students' creation of a counter-school labor culture but maintains "that there is an objective basis for these subjective feelings and cultural processes" (3).

34. See chapter 6 for more on "crunk."

35. Anderson, *The Education of Blacks in the South, 1860–1935*, provides a thorough analysis of the ideological conflict about how blacks should be educated in the

South, vis-à-vis industrial occupations. Some philanthropists argued that industrial education would be most practical and therefore beneficial. For example, one Rosenwald report "recommended courses in 'washing and greasing'" to prepare Greenville, South Carolina's black high school population for jobs at automobile service stations (226). In 1931, Rosenwald ended its industrial campaign, partly because it discovered that "'Negro jobs' were mostly those left over after whites achieved full employment" (229).

36. As was alluded to in chapter 2, even prior to when the Carlyle school system was integrated, black city residents sometimes looked down upon the rural residents. However, I would argue that the intensified distance from and disdain toward Jay Ellis students that currently exists stems from the historical moment in which black students from Carlyle were forced to attend Carlyle High and were no longer permitted to attend Jay Ellis. Downgrading a place that they were blocked from attending might have been a coping mechanism or constituted "projection" for black Carlyle residents. Unfortunately, their inopportunity to attend Jay Ellis may not only have sparked feelings of resentment and competition, but it also simultaneously created the dramatic decrease in enrollment, which in turn led to many of Jay Ellis's very real issues. At the exact moment when more people would benefit from downgrading Jay Ellis, it was becoming in reality a "worse" school. Once again, this coalescence was not entirely accidental. Rather it was initiated, on purpose, by the white board of education in Carlyle, who wanted to retain the state dollars that accompanied those black bodies.

37. Lipsitz, *The Possessive Investment in Whiteness*, viii.

38. See Annette Lareau, *Unequal Childhoods: Class, Race, and Family Life* (Berkeley and Los Angeles: University of California Press, 2003), for an explication of how the way parents interact with institutions like schools relates to broader orientations to child-rearing. These orientations, she argues, are enacted as part of one's social class. She coins the term "concerted cultivation" to describe the manner in which middle-class parents raise their children. These child-rearing practices include, for example, valuing verbal negotiations inside and out of the house (as opposed to applying firm rules or corporal punishment). The "accomplishment of natural growth" model is the term she gives patterns of working-class parenting. One of the features of the natural growth style of parenting is viewing the school, its teachers, and administrators as experts whom they trust to do "their job" without undue interference from the nonexperts (parents and students). This pattern certainly characterizes the way parents often approached Jay Ellis. Tiffany was an exception in raising her children in the "concerted cultivation" style, which served her well in the Carlyle system.

39. See Jeannie Oakes, *Keeping Track: How Schools Structure Inequality* (New Haven, CT: Yale University Press, 1985), for a thorough analysis of racial and class dimensions of tracking in schools.

40. My analysis of students stems directly from the ethnographic data. However, the connection to "role play" is interesting. C. Vann Woodward, *American Counterpoint: Slavery and Racism in the North-South Dialogue*, 1st ed. (Boston: Little, Brown, 1971), for example, describes the "Old South" as a drama in which each of the major players enacted their roles. He said black slaves, especially, "sometimes put on rather magnificent performances" (40). Stereotype threat theory, first articulated by social psychologists Claude Steele and Joshua Aronson posits that one's behavior will conform to the stereotypes attributed to his or her self-identified social group. See Claude M. Steele and Joshua Aronson, "Stereotype Threat and the Intellectual Test Performance of African Americans," *Journal of Personality and Social Psychology* 69, no. 5 (1995). One might argue that stereotypes, like those about Hamilton and Carlyle's black youth, become self-fulfilling prophecies. These arguments, however, are best proved through controlled experiments, which fall outside of the scope of this research.

41. Robert C. Toll, *Blacking Up: The Minstrel Show in Nineteenth-Century America* (New York: Oxford University Press, 1974), is one of the first scholars to examine blackface minstrelsy who appropriately acknowledges its malignant nature, without losing the complexity of his analyses. Toll argues that the variegated portrayals of blacks fulfilled the diverse desires of the white audiences and the minstrels themselves. These desires always led to distortions, exaggerations, and misrepresentations of black dress, speech, and behavior; this is clearly manifest in the burnt-cork that was worn by the minstrels to represent black skin. More recently, W. T. Lhamon, *Raising Cain: Blackface Performance from Jim Crow to Hip-Hop* (Cambridge, MA: Harvard University Press, 1998), writes about the development and popularity of minstrelsy. By using concepts like "hybridity" and "cultural cycles," aimed at providing a complex interpretation of the exchange of cultural expressions, Lhamon portrays minstrelsy as a practice co-opted by those who wished to divide the proletariat. See Donald Bogle, *Toms, Coons, Mulattoes, Mammies, and Bucks: An Interpretive History of Blacks in American Films*, 3rd ed. (New York: Continuum, 1994), for a precise, in-depth description of the blackface archetypes. See the fourth chapter of Patricia Hill Collins, *Black Feminist Thought: Knowledge, Consciousness, and the Politics of Empowerment*, 2nd ed., Perspectives on Gender (New York: Routledge, 2000), for a thorough analysis of those images particularly directed at black women.

42. See Bogle, *Toms, Coons, Mulattoes, Mammies, and Bucks.*

43. Lipsitz, *The Possessive Investment in Whiteness*, vii.

Chapter 4

1. Paul Stoller, *The Taste of Ethnographic Things: The Senses in Anthropology*, University of Pennsylvania Press Contemporary Ethnography Series (Philadelphia: University of Pennsylvania Press, 1989), calls for the engagement of the senses in ethnography.

2. H. G. Bissinger, *Friday Night Lights: A Town, a Team, and a Dream* (Reading, MA: Addison-Wesley, 1990). See also Foley, *Learning Capitalist Culture.*

3. See Bourdieu, *Outline of a Theory of Practice*; Pierre Bourdieu and Jean Claude Passeron, *Reproduction in Education, Society and Culture*, trans. Richard Nice (London: Sage Publications, 1977).

4. For full-length ethnographies that appropriate cultural production theory, see Willis, *Learning to Labor*; MacLeod, *Ain't No Makin' It*; and Philippe I. Bourgois, *In Search of Respect: Selling Crack in El Barrio*, Structural Analysis in the Social Sciences (Cambridge: Cambridge University Press, 1995).

5. Bourgois, *In Search of Respect*, 9.

6. A local term used to refer to someone's rear-end. Also "duke" and "bedonkey donk" were used interchangeably.

7. "Mess": *The American Heritage Dictionary of the English Language*, 4th ed. New York: Houghton Mifflin Company, 2004. Dictionary.com; http://dictionary.reference.com/browse/mess (accessed Januay 12, 2007). "Messy": *The American Heritage Dictionary of the English Language*, 4th ed. Houghton Mifflin Company, 2004. Diction ary.com; http://dictionary.reference.com/browse/messy (accessed January 9, 2007). The online dictionary includes more exhaustive definitions, but these are the ones that are most relevant to Hamilton's metaphor.

8. According to linguist-turned-cultural-anthropologist Paul Stoller, "metaphors are literary tropes, devices, which by linking two semantic domains forge new meaning." Paul Stoller, "The Epistemology of Sorkotarey: Language, Metaphor and Healing among the Songhay," *Ethos* 8, no. 2 (1980): 118.

9. John R. Rickford and Russell J. Rickford, *Spoken Soul: The Story of Black English* (New York: Wiley, 2000). They borrow the term *Spoken Soul* from Claude Brown, *Manchild in the Promised Land* (New York: Macmillan, 1965).

10. Rickford and Rickford, *Spoken Soul*, 10.

11. Geneva Smitherman, *Black Talk: Words and Phrases from the Hood to the Amen Corner*, rev. ed. (Boston: Houghton Mifflin, 1994), 3. I use Smitherman's definition because of her dictionary's focus on enduring, cross-regional black expressions. However, at least one other full-length African American vernacular dictionary has been published: *Juba to Jive: The Dictionary of African-American Slang*, ed. Clarence Major (New York: Penguin Books, 1994). Rickford and Rickford, *Spoken Soul*, includes an exhaustive list of shorter informal glossaries in their chapter on "Vocabulary and Pronunciation," 93.

12. Smitherman, *Black Talk*, 159–60.

13. David Murray Schneider, *American Kinship: A Cultural Account*, Anthropology of Modern Societies Series (Englewood Cliffs, NJ: Prentice-Hall, 1968), 5. According to Schneider, "a unit in a particular culture is simply anything that is culturally defined and distinguished as an entity," 3.

14. Victor W. Turner, *Dramas, Fields, and Metaphors: Symbolic Action in Human Society: Symbol, Myth, and Ritual* (Ithaca, NY: Cornell University Press, 1974), 24–31.

15. Janelle and Keya did finally fight the next day in what was described to me as the fight of the year. In the post-fight narrative, it was reported that Ms. Scott, the math teacher, locked up her new computer and said, "y'all can fight, but you better not break by new computer." The fight was apparently several rounds, and the girls fought until they were tired and just held each other, panting with their shirts half off (a favorite detail of the boys). Some teachers eventually came in and "broke up the fight," which had basically ended on its own by that point.

16. Max Gluckman, "Analysis of a Social Situation in Modern Zululand," *Rhodes Livingston Institute Papers* 28 (1940), describes cross-cutting ties in a way that explains James's messy situation when he states:

> The shifting membership of groups in different situations is the functioning of the structure, for an individual's membership of a particular group in a particular situation is determined by the motives and values influencing him in that situation. Individuals can thus live coherent lives by situational selection from a medley of contradictory values, ill-assorted beliefs, interests and techniques. (29)

17. Schneider, *American Kinship*, 4.

18. "Misfortune." *WordNet* 2.1. Princeton University. Dictionary.com; http://dictionary.reference.com/browse/misfortune (accessed January 13, 2007).

19. For a call for more impassioned ethnographic material that confronts emotion head-on, see Andrew Beatty, "How Did It Feel for You? Emotion, Narrative, and the Limits of Ethnography," *American Anthropologist* 112, no. 3 (2010).

20. Turner's concept of social drama was born out of his fieldwork in southern Africa. Regarding how he developed his concept of social drama, he states: "I saw movement as much as structure, persistence as much as change, indeed persistence as a striking act of change. I saw people interacting, and, as day succeeded day, the consequences of their interactions. I then began to perceive a form in the process of social time. This form was essentially *dramatic*"; Turner, *Dramas, Fields, and Metaphors*, 32.

21. Ibid., 33.

22. Ibid., 36.

23. Ibid., 38–41.

24. The disappointment and frustration inspired me to become messy, too. As a result, I developed my own theories about how Remarcke got fired. In Alabama, football is everything, and the depth of the Alabama/Auburn rivalry cannot be overstated. I believe that Donaldson, an Auburn man, had always resented the attention that the University of Alabama star, Remarcke, attracted. Donaldson was also a basketball star,

and while Remarcke may have been a superior football coach, Coach Fireman was the superior basketball coach. Finally, once I saw Fireman come back and I witnessed his interactions with Ms. Moore, I realized that she never really loved Remarcke. I think she found his quiet confidence to be threatening. Remarcke also mentioned to me that he was suspicious about the money. In general, the political lines in the school were drawn around new guard/old guard loyalty. Remarcke was on the side of the old guard with Ms. Smith, the guidance counselor and Coach Brighton, who brought in Remarcke. Fireman's loyalties were to Principal Moore and he formed an alliance with the new guidance counselor who arrived at Jay Ellis in my second year.

25. Turner, *Dramas, Fields, and Metaphors*, 41.

26. Ibid., 41.

27. Bourgois, *In Search of Respect*, 8.

28. Scott, *Weapons of the Weak*, 282. Scott offers several relevant insights, one of which is that resistance is not necessarily directed at the immediate source of appropriation (35). When folks were declaring each other to be messy, then, it still may have constituted a form of resistance. Scott focuses on intentionality as the benchmark for whether resistance is present. But I agree with Peter McLaren, *Schooling as a Ritual Performance: Toward a Political Economy of Educational Symbols and Gestures*, 2nd ed. (New York: Routledge, 1993), that resistance is often embodied and therefore not always consciously rebellious.

29. Victor Turner, *Schism and Continuity in an African Society* (Manchester: Manchester University Press, 1957), 129; Carole E. Hill et al., "Anthropological Studies in the American South: Review and Directions," *Current Anthropology* 18, no. 2 (1977).

30. Patricia Turner, *I Heard It through the Grapevine: Rumor in African-American Culture* (Berkeley and Los Angeles: University of California Press, 1993), argues that the rumors and conspiracy theories that she documents among African Americans actually function as tools of resistance. She writes, "metaphors . . . collapse the threat to the group into a threat to an individual" (32).

31. See James W. Fernandez, "Patrolling the Border: Experiments in Poetics," *American Anthropologist* 98, no. 4 (1996).

32. Turner states that metaphors "may be misleading [because] even though they draw attention to some important properties of social existence, they may and do block our perception of others"; Turner, *Dramas, Fields, and Metaphors*, 25. See also George Lakoff and Mark Johnson, *Metaphors We Live By* (Chicago: University of Chicago Press, 1980).

Chapter 5

1. Kamari Maxine Clarke and Deborah A. Thomas, eds., *Globalization and Race: Transformations in the Cultural Production of Blackness* (Durham, NC: Duke University Press, 2006).

2. Gayatri Chakravorty Spivak, "Can the Subaltern Speak?" in *Marxism and the Interpretation of Culture*, ed. Cary Nelson and Lawrence Grossberg (Urbana: University of Illinois Press, 1988), has commented that Indian women have been the site of contestation over a number of issues, not the least of which are tradition versus modernity and British rule versus indigenous rule. Race, ethnicity, gender, and nationalism are all closely interwoven into Indian women's positionality. Spivak poignantly describes British intervention in the *sati* (self-immolation) debate as "White men saving brown women from brown men" (276). These things led Spivak to question whether the subaltern really can speak.

3. Paulo Freire, *Pedagogy of the Oppressed* (New York: Continuum, 2000).

4. Sherry B. Ortner, "Gender Hegemonies," *Cultural Critique* 14, The Construction of Gender and Modes of Social Division II, (Winter 1989–1990): 80.

5. LaBennett, *She's Mad Real*, 110. According to Foley, *Learning Capitalist Culture*, Dorothy Holland's charge to "study cultural identity production in a way that highlights agency and creative self-authoring within the constraints of . . . historical 'figured worlds'" is presently being fulfilled (200). The work to which he refers is Dorothy C. Holland, *Identity and Agency in Cultural Worlds* (Cambridge, MA: Harvard University Press, 1998).

6. See the Introduction to Sunaina Maira and Elisabeth Soep, eds., *Youthscapes: The Popular, the National, the Global* (Philadelphia: University of Pennsylvania Press, 2005).

7. I provide more detail about other definitions of resistance in the previous chapter.

8. See, for example, the oppositional style of the lads and their use of humor as a form of resistance in Willis, *Learning to Labor*; the classroom disruptions in the Catholic school in McLaren, *Schooling as a Ritual Performance*; the rebellious behavior, low academic achievement, and high dropout rate among the Hallway Hangers in MacLeod, *Ain't No Makin' It*; the under- and overachievement of students at Capital High in Washington, DC, presented in Fordham, *Blacked Out*; the "making out games" in classrooms in south Texas presented in Foley, *Learning Capitalist Culture*; and examples of young people commandeering space on subway cars in New York in LaBennett, *She's Mad Real*.

9. This view of adolescent "rebellion" is quite different from a psychological view of adolescence that would see such behaviors as onset by biological changes. Globalization is narrowing the distance between young people's everyday lives; thus, we must be vigilant not to confuse similar social locations with the primacy of biology over culture.

10. Jones, *Between Good and Ghetto*.

11. See, for example, Sofia A. Villenas, Donna Deyhle, and Laurence Parker, "Critical Race Theory and Praxis: Chicano(a)/Latino(a), and Navajo Struggles for Dignity,

Educational Equity, and Social Justice," in *Race Is—Race Isn't: Critical Race Theory and Qualitative Studies in Education*, ed. Laurence Parker, Donna Deyhle, and Sofia A. Villenas (Boulder, CO: Westview Press, 1999); Edmund T. Hamann, *The Educational Welcome of Latinos in the New South* (Westport, CT: Praeger, 2003); Fine et al., "Swimming"; and Foley, *Learning Capitalist Culture*.

12. See Howell, "Dynamic Youth and Static Religion."

13. The "Semi-Involuntary Thesis" of church participation in the rural South posits just that: that one of the most significant features of black churches in the South is the community context and moral pressure that make church participation almost mandatory. See Larry L. Hunt and Matthew O. Hunt, "Regional Patterns of African American Church Attendance: Revisiting the Semi-Involuntary Thesis," *Social Forces* 78, no. 2 (1999). According to social-psychological research, correlations among identity, religion, and adolescence might be framed in terms of risk factors, protective factors, and resiliency. A historical perspective often has yielded the conclusion that spirituality in the lives of African Americans has offset the intense psychological, emotional, and physical trauma that has been inflicted as part of U.S. slavery, its legacy, and the ongoing effects of racism. See Wendy L. Haight, *African American Children at Church* (Cambridge: Cambridge University Press, 2000). This perspective on the church is certainly what one might glean from the narratives of the elder members of the Hamilton community. When probed, they would note that in the years following slavery, "church-life"—that is, the church's rules, norms, characters, events, meals, competitions, education, etc.—were fused together with community involvement and, thus, the lives of young people. Participation in the church and its events was so integral to community life that saints and sinners could be found there together on Sunday. For an influential examination of the African American church, see Edward Franklin Frazier, *The Negro Church in America* (Liverpool: Liverpool University Press, 1964).

14. Anthropologists of education have broadened our perspective on education to include much more than schooling. See, for example, Bradley A. Levinson, Douglas E. Foley, and Dorothy C. Holland, eds., *The Cultural Production of the Educated Person: Critical Ethnographies of Schooling and Local Practice*, Suny Series, Power, Social Identity, and Education (Albany: State University of New York Press, 1996); and Hervé Varenne et al., *Successful Failure: The School America Builds* (Boulder, CO: Westview Press, 1998).

15. Stuart Hall and Tony Jefferson, eds., *Resistance through Rituals: Youth Subcultures in Post-War Britain* (London: Hutchinson, 1976).

16. See Marla F. Frederick, *Between Sundays: Black Women and Everyday Struggles of Faith* (Berkeley and Los Angeles: University of California Press, 2003), 213.

17. This examination is crucial in determining the role that students, who remain the focal point of this investigation, play in shaping their own school environment.

18. See Jones, *Between Good and Ghetto*, for an examination of the fluid identities of adolescent girls as they choose between "good" and "ghetto" behavioral options.

19. For a seminal analysis of black women's oppression and standards of beauty, see Collins, *Black Feminist Thought*.

20. Zora Neale Hurston, *Their Eyes Were Watching God* (Urbana: University of Illinois Press, 1991).

21. See Frederick, *Between Sundays*; and Cheryl Townsend Gilkes, *If It Wasn't for the Women: Black Women's Experience and Womanist Culture in Church and Community* (Maryknoll, NY: Orbis Books, 2001).

22. See Jackson, *Real Black*. Once again, Jackson's theoretical lens is relevant here. Perhaps this "real" spirituality can be seen as an ongoing, unpredictable "sincere" experience rather than as an authentic performance of a "black church" script. The former, which is more processual, alive, and engaged, may have satisfied Missy's hunger for spirituality.

23. See the introduction to Van Galen and Noblit, *Late to Class*.

24. Scott, *Weapons of the Weak*, 282.

Chapter 6

1. Stuart Hall, "Cultural Identity and Diaspora," *Framework* 36 (1989): 222.

2. Mary Douglas and Steven Ney, *Missing Persons: A Critique of the Social Sciences*, The Aaron Wildavsky Forum for Public Policy (Berkeley and Los Angeles: University of California Press, Russell Sage Foundation, 1998), argue that viewing human beings as rational and isolated entities with pronounced selves is a mistake made by social scientists who overemphasize the importance of objectivity. Martin Sokefeld, "Debating Self, Identity, and Culture in Anthropology," *Current Anthropology* 40, no. 4 (1999), however, views anthropologists' tendency to ascribe the people we study identities but no self (preferring the cultural, relational definition of identity) as a Western-centric bias that reinforces the dichotomy of self and other. Instead, he advocates a view of "self" as more or less human universal, which, at the very least, serves as a manager of an individual's identities (431). Anthony P. Cohen, *Self-Consciousness: An Alternative Anthropology of Identity* (New York: Routledge, 1994), has most thoroughly espoused that theoretical viewpoint.

3. See Jackson, *Harlemworld*, for a glimpse of African American performances and folk understandings of race and class.

4. According to Appiah and Gutmann, *Color Conscious*, "Collective identities . . . provide what we might call scripts: narratives that people can use in shaping their life plans and in telling their life stories" (97). Sokefeld, "Debating Self, Identity, and Culture in Anthropology," argues those aspects of an individual's identity that are affiliated with a group can place contradictory pressures on him or her. Moreover, these conflicting group identities often require the prioritization of one identity over

another. For example, in describing the hesitation of African American women to im-
merse themselves in the feminist movement and the tendency for them to be drawn
more to the struggle against racial oppression, Deborah K. King, "Multiple Jeopardy,
Multiple Consciousness: The Context of a Black Feminist Ideology," *Signs* 14, no. 1
(1988), calls attention to the formative nature of slavery, segregation, and discrimination and the impact that "the inerasable physical characteristics" of blackness have
had on the identity of African American women (53). She also points out that there
are "intraracial politics of gender and class" that "have made a strictly nationalistic
approach overly restrictive and incalculably detrimental to [their] prospects for full
liberation" (57). The third variable that King adds to the amalgamation of African
American women's identity is class. Together, King argues, these shared identities
(gender, race, and class) present a complex array of daily choices for these women.

5. Turner, *Dramas, Fields, and Metaphors*, states that "the social world is a world in
becoming not a world in being (except insofar as 'being' is a description of the static,
atemporal model men have in their heads), and for this reason studies of social structure *as such* are irrelevant" (24).

6. I am appropriating this term, which derives from a 2000 debate between then
presidential candidates George W. Bush and Al Gore. Bush accused Gore of using
"fuzzy math," but could not specify what that meant. Of course, he was lambasted in
the media for his perceived intellectual shortcomings. I use it here to provide an ap-
petizer to our discussion of popular culture and its creative capacity. I also find it to
be a particularly useful concept and hope that it remains in the lexicon.

7. For an examination of youth as a concept fraught with issues, see Henry A. Giroux, *Channel Surfing: Race Talk and the Destruction of Today's Youth* (New York: St.
Martin's Press, 1997). For an analysis of the sociopolitical issues underlying the creation of "youth culture" as a category, see Hall and Jefferson, eds., *Resistance through
Rituals*. Hall et al. advocate deconstructing the term "youth culture" in favor of a
more complex set of social categories. For example, working-class culture influences
its own youth subcultures to develop in particular ways, while middle-class culture
pushes its own youth subcultures in other directions. Also, not all youth participate in
distinctive subcultures that are set apart from adults. When one adds the complexity
of history and hegemony, nation-state and available forms of consumption, one can
see what terms like youth culture really "conflate."

The introduction to Maira and Soep, *Youthscapes*, calls for more varied explanations of youth culture(s), plural. It also enters into the politics of representation when
it states:

> Too often the field of youth culture studies itself is taken as the epistemological folk dev-
> il of academic knowledge production, the sensationalist sideshow that is simply an echo
> of the main act, or the site where extreme manifestations of widespread phenomena

are vividly described. Youth culture practices are not simply handy examples, suggestive cases to note in passing, or celebratory testaments to popular culture's possibilities. Youth is, after all, often the ideological battleground in contests of immigration and citizenship as well as the prime consumer target for the leisure industry. (xix)

8. See, for example, Tricia Rose, *Black Noise: Rap Music and Black Culture in Contemporary America*, Music Culture (Hanover, NH: Wesleyan University Press: Published by University Press of New England, 1994), which is the foundational text that examines the full artistic and political dimensions of rap music, lyrics, and culture. See also Neil Campbell, ed., *American Youth Cultures* (Edinburgh: Edinburgh University Press, 2004).

9. See K. Sue Jewell, *From Mammy to Miss America and Beyond: Cultural Images and the Shaping of U.S. Social Policy* (New York: Routledge, 1993), and Robin D. G. Kelley, *Yo' Mama's Disfunktional!: Fighting the Culture Wars in Urban America* (Boston: Beacon Press, 1997), for an examination of the complex interplay of pop-cultural images of African Americans, discrimination, social policy, and racial ideologies. Kelley explores the ongoing battle over the representation of "the black urban condition" in public policy, union halls, the workplace, and popular discourse. The book is premised on the idea that "culture and questions of identity have been at the heart of some of the most intense battles facing African Americans at the end of the century" (9). See also Bakari Kitwana, *The Hip-Hop Generation: Young Blacks and the Crisis in African American Culture*, 1st ed. (New York: Basic Civitas Books, 2002), and Molefi K. Asante, *It's Bigger Than Hip-Hop: The Rise of the Post-Hip-Hop Generation*, 1st ed. (New York: St. Martin's Press, 2008).

10. See, for example, the ethnographic work in Paul Hodkinson and Wolfgang Deicke, eds., *Youth Cultures: Scenes, Subcultures and Tribes*, Routledge Advances in Sociology (New York: Routledge, 2007).

11. See James Clifford, George E. Marcus, and School of American Research (Santa Fe, NM), eds., *Writing Culture: The Poetics and Politics of Ethnography* (Berkeley and Los Angeles: University of California Press, 1986).

12. See Cross, *Shades of Black*, for a foundational view of African American identity development from a psychological perspective. He argues that the development of ethnic identity of African Americans partially follows the process of general identity development, characterized by various periods of identification with mainstream culture and ethnic groups, and ideally a resolution somewhere in the middle. Cynthia García Coll et al., "An Integrative Model for the Study of Developmental Competencies in Minority Children," *Child Development* 67, no. 5 (1996), argue that it is more difficult for ethnic minorities in the United States than it is for the majority population to develop an integrated sense of identity.

13. The sample of adolescents that I interviewed was not representative. Therefore,

it should not be read that all adolescents in Hamilton have traveled widely. One of the weaknesses of my data is that the students I interviewed were a self-selected group, and I may have favored higher-achieving students. Still, the students I interviewed reflected the range of socioeconomic statuses in the community. Furthermore, what remains significant is the contrast between the ubiquitous belief that young people in Hamilton have not traveled and the fact that so many have, indeed, traveled outside of the state.

14. Du Bois, *The Souls of Black Folk*, famously penned that "the problem of the twentieth century is the problem of the color line." Early, pioneering ethnographers studied how the problem of the color line was negotiated and interpreted in the South in the mid-twentieth century. See John Dollard, *Caste and Class in a Southern Town* (New Haven, CT: Published for the Institute of Human Relations by Yale University Press, 1937); Hortense Powdermaker, *After Freedom: A Cultural Study in the Deep South* (New York: Viking Press, 1939); and Allison Davis et al., *Deep South: A Social Anthropological Study of Caste and Class* (Chicago: University of Chicago Press, 1941).

James's comments certainly allude to a certain black solidarity that was predominant in the twentieth century. However, scholars have struggled to reckon with what racial identity does and should mean in this new millennium. Some public voices from the right and left have tried to advocate a "color-blind" society, or at least challenge the salience of race as a philosophical or social category. See, for example, Paul Gilroy, *Against Race: Imagining Political Culture Beyond the Color Line* (Cambridge, MA: Belknap Press of Harvard University Press, 2000); and Appiah and Gutmann, *Color Conscious*. These ideas surfaced again with the election of President Barack Obama, whose ancestry is, itself, a challenge to twentieth-century notions of race.

Yet, many public intellectuals like Michael Eric Dyson, Cornel West, and Tavis Smiley have argued that race is still influential in everyday life, especially when one considers the disparities in health, employment, and other measures of society's "color-blindness." See, for example, Howard Winant, *New Politics of Race: Globalism, Difference, Justice* (Minneapolis: University of Minnesota Press, 2004); Manning Marable, Ian Steinberg, and Keesha Middlemass, eds., *Racializing Justice, Disenfranchising Lives: The Racism, Criminal Justice, and Law Reader*, 1st Palgrave Macmillan pbk. ed., Critical Black Studies Series (New York: Palgrave Macmillan, 2007); Tavis Smiley and Stephanie Robinson, *Accountable: Making America as Good as Its Promise* (New York: Atria, 2009); and Michelle Alexander, *The New Jim Crow: Mass Incarceration in the Age of Colorblindness* (New York: New Press, Distributed by Perseus Distribution, 2010).

Regarding racial identity and "feelings" of solidarity that may or may not be based on resistance to oppression, other scholars have argued that black identities, while not monolithic, are still vitally important to people's constructions of self. Many scholars draw heavily on Hall's explication of fluid and hybrid cultural and ethnic identities. See Stuart Hall et al., eds., *Stuart Hall: Critical Dialogues in Cultural Studies*, Comedia (London: Routledge, 1996); Stuart Hall, "New Ethnicities," in *Black British Cultural Studies: A Reader*, ed. Houston A. Baker, Manthia Diawara, and Ruth H. Lindeborg (Chicago: University of Chicago Press, 1996); and "What Is This 'Black' in Black Popular Culture?" *Social Justice* 20, no. 1/2 (1993): 51–52, and "Rethinking Race" (Spring/Summer 1993).

Mark Anthony Neal, *Soul Babies: Black Popular Culture and the Post-Soul Aesthetic* (New York: Routledge, 2002), argues that blackness is still a salient identity but that blackness has taken a postmodern turn; he argues this through an examination of popular culture. Touré, *Who's Afraid of Post-Blackness?: What It Means to Be Black Now* (New York: Free Press, 2011), recently argues for a more inclusive, less rigid blackness, while Jackson, *Real Black*, unearths "sincerity" as a conceptual tool that recognizes people as more than "simply racial objects (to be verified from without) but racial subjects with an interiority that is never completely and unquestionably clear" (18). Clarke and Thomas, eds., *Globalization and Race*, call for the continued study of blackness as relevant, but not monolithic. They argue "against a view of globalized blackness that assumes a homogenization of transnational black (American) identities" and instead advocate a view of blackness that is situated in local, historical contexts but can become rearticulated through "transnational interpretive communities" that provide elements of "similarity and contrast" (7).

15. At times I use "rural" and "southern" interchangeably. To me they are clearly distinct, which is why I originally separated the two categories when I asked the "mostly the same or mostly different" questions. However, after asking the question several times, and having some respondents tell me I was repeating myself, I realized that the adolescents saw rural and southern as so interconnected that they were almost synonymous. When I said "northern" they automatically assumed I meant big cities, and vice versa. Only when I pointed out that Birmingham and Atlanta were big cities in the South, did they entertain "repeating" themselves or revising their answers.

16. Falk, *Rooted in Place*, 188.

17. See C. J. Pascoe, *Dude, You're a Fag: Masculinity and Sexuality in High School* (Berkeley and Los Angeles: University of California Press, 2007) for a challenge to the way we erect boundaries like on-line and off-line when we write about youth. Her subjects integrated use of media and public space in everyday life.

18. For example, see Frazier, *The Negro Church in America*, and Vanessa Siddle Walker, *Their Highest Potential: An African American School Community in the Segregated South* (Chapel Hill: University of North Carolina Press, 1996).

19. See Aimee Cox, "The Blacklight Project and Public Scholarship: Young Black Women Perform against and through the Boundaries of Anthropology," *Transforming Anthropology* 17, no. 1 (2009), for a similar ethnographic story about reactions

to African American women wearing headscarves at a homeless shelter in Detroit. According to Cox, this headscarf-wearing transgressed the politics of respectability. For a larger discussion of respectability, see Victoria W. Wolcott, *Remaking Respectability: African American Women in Interwar Detroit*, Gender and American Culture (Chapel Hill: University of North Carolina Press, 2001).

20. Hall and Jefferson, *Resistance through Rituals*, 72. For the canonical introduction to moral panics, see Stanley Cohen, *Folk Devils and Moral Panics: The Creation of the Mods and Rockers* (New York: St. Martin's Press, 1980). For a collection on recent moral panics surrounding school shootings, the Internet, child pornography, child molesters, ADHD, undergraduate student ignorance, street children, and crime, see Charles Krinsky, ed., *Moral Panics over Contemporary Children and Youth* (Farnham, England and Burlington, VT: Ashgate, 2008).

21. This point of view has been substantiated most emphatically within academic discourse by the Frankfurt School of Critical Sociologists. Their research was born out of a desire to understand how Nazi Germany managed to inculcate the masses of poor Germans with an ideology that led to the decimation of Jewish people during the Holocaust. They "emphasized ideological control through an extensive, commercialized mass media that entertained and manipulated the masses." Foley, *Learning Capitalist Culture*, 182. The Birmingham Centre for Contemporary Cultural Studies, whose insights I rely upon heavily in this work, has demonstrated that whatever the influence of the media, people contest and reframe messages; they posit that media messages are not neatly or unproblematically absorbed.

22. See Tricia Rose, *The Hip-Hop Wars: What We Talk About When We Talk About Hip-Hop—and Why It Matters* (New York: BasicCivitas, 2008) for an explication of the top ten debates surrounding hip-hop music and culture as well as suggestions for how to move beyond these debates.

23. See T. Denean Sharpley-Whiting, *Pimps up, Ho's Down: Hip-Hop's Hold on Young Black Women* (New York: New York University Press, 2007), for an exploration of how black women have been impacted by hip-hop culture, including hip-hop's representation of black women. See Gwendolyn D. Pough, *Check It While I Wreck It: Black Womanhood, Hip-Hop Culture, and the Public Sphere* (Boston: Northeastern University Press, 2004), for an analysis of hip-hop as a space within the public sphere that has a history of female empowerment and a great deal of creative potential. She suggests that hip-hop is not reaching its potential, but that rather than discard it, we should use it to reach out to our youth. This focus on women's contributions to hip-hop (as opposed to my own focus on representation) probably led to the success of her discussions with her women's studies class featured in the seventh chapter of her book. See LaBennett, *She's Mad Real*, 131, for an ethnographic example of girls who enjoy "the bad girls of rap" as well as many other styles of expression.

24. See Joanne Hollows, *Feminism, Femininity and Popular Culture* (Manchester:

Manchester University Press; Distributed exclusively in the USA by St. Martin's Press, 2000), for a historical look at the development of feminism alongside popular culture. Hollows cautions feminists against seeing themselves as more enlightened than ordinary women. See Angela McRobbie, *Feminism and Youth Culture: From "Jackie" to "Just Seventeen"* (Boston: Unwin Hyman, 1991), for a reaction to the omission of girls from the foundational British subculture/resistance studies. She demonstrates that girls' resistance will look different from boys' because the two genders occupy different social spaces.

25. One indication that young people could decipher between entertainment and reality was that none of my interviewees cited obtaining any outrageous material possession or becoming pop-artists as future goals.

26. My data confirm Jackson's *Real Black* conclusions that the quest for the "real" in hip-hop is not as much based on some generic authenticity tests as one might think. Rather sincerity more often determines which artists are seen as real or not. "Sincerity . . . privileges the real as inside, ambiguous, and ultimately unverifiable" (196). This sincere version of "realness" allowed Hamilton's youth to enjoy many different artistic styles.

27. This pattern also led to a number of teen pregnancies.

28. See the anecdote in chapter 4 on the boys paying a dollar to see the girls fight, as well as the dream about all of the girls fighting.

See bell hooks, *Black Looks: Race and Representation* (Boston: South End Press, 1992), for a classic examination of black female commodification in the public sphere. See E. Frances White, *Dark Continent of Our Bodies: Black Feminism and the Politics of Respectability*, Mapping Racisms (Philadelphia: Temple University Press, 2001), for a historical perspective on the intersection of race and sex for black women and a call to expand beyond the politics of respectability. See Karen Brooks, "Nothing Sells Like Teen Spirit: The Commodification of Youth Culture," in *Youth Cultures: Texts, Images, and Identities*, ed. Kerry Mallan and Sharyn Pearce (Westport, CT: Praeger, 2003), for a broader examination of the commodification of youth culture by the media industrial complex.

29. http://www.urbandictionary.com/define.php?term=crunk.

30. See Ferguson, *Bad Boys*, for a discussion of the author's appreciation of hip-hop as the soundtrack to her own fieldwork.

31. Pascoe, *Dude, You're a Fag*, coins the term "compulsive heterosexuality" to describe the role that heterosexual gender practices play in defining her informants' male identity, which was itself defined by dominance. At Jay Ellis, sports dominance was more noticeable than was sexual dominance. But that could have been due to my social location and the politics of respectability, both of which have been discussed elsewhere in this book.

32. From http://www.musicremedy.com/l/Lil_Flip/videos/Game_Over-588.html.

33. See Hall, "What Is This "Black" in Black Popular Culture?" for a seminal statement on the contradictions inherent in black popular culture. He argues that these contradictions are an integral component of popular culture, as "popular culture" is at once deeply rooted in vernacular forms and intricately interwoven with the commodification process. He writes, "in black popular culture, strictly speaking, ethnographically speaking, there are no pure forms at all. Always these forms are the product of partial synchronization, of engagement across cultural boundaries, of the confluence of more than one cultural tradition, of the negotiations of dominant and subordinate positions, of the subterranean strategies of recoding and transcoding, of critical signification, of signifying. Always these forms are impure, to some degree hybridized from a vernacular base" (110). See Glyn Davis and Kay Dickinson, eds., *Teen TV: Genre, Consumption, Identity* (London: BFI Pub., 2004), for an examination of how teen culture and teen television reflect "industry-oriented values that express capitalism and consumerism" (96).

34. See Rupa Huq, "Resistance or Incorporation? Youth Policy Making and Hip-Hop Culture," in *Youth Cultures: Scenes, Subcultures and Tribes*, ed. Paul Hodkinson and Wolfgang Deicke (New York: Routledge, 2007), for an examination of the multiple and shifting uses of rap.

35. See Anoop Nayak and Mary Jane Kehily, eds., *Gender, Youth and Culture: Young Masculinities and Feminities* (New York: Palgrave Macmillan, 2008), for an analysis of "the production, consumption, regulation, and performance of gender" among youth (197). These scholars examine newly emergent masculinities and femininities— both how they are portrayed and lived. The new masculinity portrays men in crisis while the new femininity describes women's hyperfemininity, entitlement to sexual pleasure, and upward mobility.

36. Iain Chambers, "A Strategy for Living: Black Music and White Subcultures," in *Resistance through Rituals: Youth Subcultures in Post-War Britain*, ed. Stuart Hall and Tony Jefferson (London: Hutchinson, 1976), 161.

37. See McRobbie, *Feminism and Youth Culture*, for an ethnographic example of girls in England and the importance of female interpersonal relationships in their lives.

38. See JoEllen Fisherkeller, *Growing up with Television: Everyday Learning among Young Adolescents* (Philadelphia: Temple University Press, 2002), for a dynamic ethnographic exploration into the everyday lives of young people and their creation of television culture. She refutes a belief that young people are passive consumers. She also tamps down moral panics about children getting their main sources of identity from television when she states that despite the use of television to co-construct identity, "young people construct themselves as members of 'real life' social groups that are grounded by the positions of their actual (as opposed to virtual or mediated) lives" (125).

39. One reviewer of this manuscript cautioned me against making essentialist claims even as I attempt to debunk them. However, as stated in the introduction, the whole book is written in a subjective style that inserts my feelings alongside those of the youth, as they arose. I hope this decision prevents either my own voice or theirs from becoming too authoritative. Additionally, when I said I was "shocked" or "surprised" by something, it usually had to do less with essentializing the students and more with accessing knowledge about them that was theretofore hidden from me. These surprises manifested as our relationships became more intimate, in the same way that such surprises would surface in any developing relationship.

40. See Hall, "What Is This 'Black' in Black Popular Culture?" for a discussion of how performing one's own identity may negatively impact someone else's. He writes, "to put it crudely, certain ways in which black men continue to live out their counter-identities as black masculinities and replay those fantasies of black masculinities in the theaters of popular culture are, when viewed from along other axes of difference, the very masculine identities that are oppressive to women, that claim visibility for their hardness only at the expense of the vulnerability of black women and the feminization of gay black men" (112).

41. See Rose, *The Hip-Hop Wars*.

42. In the foreword to Maira and Soep, *Youthscapes*, George Lipsitz calls attention to the importance of rapper Nelly's success to his hometown of St. Louis. Lipsitz argues that in exporting his brand of "'Country Grammar' he validates local cultures of place, [and] enables young people who have been invisible in the media to see and hear their surroundings broadcast to a wider world" (xiii). This is the same process of validation that I see operating when young people in Hamilton get "crunk."

Conclusion

1. For a discussion of the racial and political dimensions of the attempted desegregation of HBCUs, see Edward Taylor, "The Desegregation of Higher Education," in *Race Is—Race Isn't: Critical Race Theory and Qualitative Studies in Education*, ed. Laurence Parker, Donna Deyhle, and Sofia A. Villenas (Boulder, CO: Westview Press, 1999).

2. Ching and Creed, *Knowing Your Place*, 27.

3. See Gibbs, "College Completion and Return Migration among Rural Youth."

4. Henry A. Giroux, Foreword to *Schooling as a Ritual Performance: Toward a Political Economy of Educational Symbols and Gestures*, ed. Peter Mclaren, 2nd ed. (New York: Routledge, 1993), xxv.

5. McLaren, *Schooling as a Ritual Performance*, 241.

6. See Lila Abu-Lughod, *Veiled Sentiments: Honor and Poetry in a Bedouin Society* (Berkeley and Los Angeles: University of California Press, 1986), for an ethnography that powerfully focuses on meaning, expression, and symbols, without ignoring

structures or inequality. There are obviously many outstanding ethnographies that likewise address meaning, but my argument is that more need to be conducted on African Americans, especially African American youth.

7. See Holland, *Identity and Agency in Cultural Worlds.* These practiced identities include four dimensions: "figured worlds, positionality, space of authoring, and making worlds."

8. Ibid., 8.

9. Turner, *Dramas, Fields, and Metaphors,* 16.

10. Maira and Soep, *Youthscapes,* xxi.

11. Turner, *Dramas, Fields, and Metaphors,* 42.

12. See Giroux, *On Critical Pedagogy;* McLaren, *Schooling as a Ritual Performance;* and Van Galen and Noblit, *Late to Class.*

13. Kyra Danielle Gaunt, *The Games Black Girls Play: Learning the Ropes from Double-Dutch to Hip-Hop* (New York: New York University Press, 2006).

14. For Sabrina, home has, quite literally, migrated. She lived in another rural community about fifteen minutes from Carlyle up until five years before my field research. Her dad had worked in Carlyle for several years, and when they moved there it became "home," as meaningful relationships could be found there. Furthermore, she had only been at Jay Ellis for a few years when I began my field research. As relationships grew out of that place, the school quickly became home to her. Most of the people at Jay Ellis and in my research actually were connected by networks of family and friends, rather than actually living in Hamilton. In this book, then, I have used Hamilton as the symbol of the group of people about whom I write. In different settings, Hamilton functions as a symbol of their identity. However, the young people in the study lived in about five different communities, including Hamilton. Many stayed a few nights with relatives in Hamilton and a few nights in Carlyle. In addition to being connected through networks of family and friends, they were all connected historically to Hamilton and Jay Ellis.

Epilogue

1. Perhaps the best longitudinal follow-up to an ethnography of youth is found in MacLeod, *Ain't No Makin' It.* In this outstanding ethnography, MacLeod's goal was to rework a theory of class reproduction to understand how race becomes a mediating factor in the reproductive process in the United States. As a result of this goal, the remaining three chapters in the 1995 edition of the book, in which he follows the Hallway Hangers and the Brothers into adulthood, are vital in proving MacLeod's argument about the ability of race to level attainment, in spite of high aspirations. There is no elaborate theorizing presented in this epilogue, because my goals are very different from MacLeod's.

2. Henry A. Giroux, "Class Casualties: Disappearing Youth in the Age of George

W. Bush," *Workplace: A Journal for Academic Labor* 6, no. 1 (February 2004), sections 1.12 and 2.6.

3. This data was reported from the United States Department of Labor: Bureau of Labor Statistics in July 2012, taken from Carlie Kollath, "Group: Unemployment Higher for Millennials," Northeast Mississippi News, djournal.com. For a larger discussion of unemployment trends, see "The African-American Labor Force in the Recovery," ed. U.S. Department of Labor (Washington, DC, February 12, 2012).

4. Stephen Marche, "Is Facebook Making Us Lonely?" *The Atlantic*, May 1, 2012.

5. "School Improvement Grants," U.S. Department of Education, http://data .ed.gov/grants/school-improvement-grants.

6. Pollock, *Colormute*.

7. Gloria Ladson-Billings, *The Dreamkeepers: Successful Teachers of African American Children*, 1st ed. (San Francisco: Jossey-Bass Publishers, 1994).

8. Ibid., 20.

9. Ibid., 12.

Bibliography

Abu-Lughod, Lila. *Veiled Sentiments: Honor and Poetry in a Bedouin Society.* Berkeley and Los Angeles: University of California Press, 1986.

"The African-American Labor Force in the Recovery." Edited by U.S. Department of Labor, 1–13. Washington, DC, February 12, 2012.

Alexander, Michelle. *The New Jim Crow: Mass Incarceration in the Age of Colorblindness.* New York: New Press, Distributed by Perseus Distribution, 2010.

Anderson, James D. *The Education of Blacks in the South, 1860–1935.* Chapel Hill: University of North Carolina Press, 1988.

Appiah, Anthony, and Amy Gutmann. *Color Conscious: The Political Morality of Race.* Princeton, NJ: Princeton University Press, 1996.

Apple, Michael W. *Ideology and Curriculum.* 3rd ed. New York: Routledge Falmer, 2004.

Aronowitz, Stanley. "Against Schooling: Education and Social Class." In *Workplace: A Journal for Academic Labor* 6, no. 1 (February 2004).

Asad, Talal. "Anthropology and the Analysis of Ideology." *Man* 14, no. 4 (1979): 607–27.

Asante, Molefi K. *It's Bigger Than Hip-Hop: The Rise of the Post-Hip-Hop Generation.* 1st ed. New York: St. Martin's Press, 2008.

Baker, Lee D. *From Savage to Negro: Anthropology and the Construction of Race, 1896–1954.* Berkeley and Los Angeles: University of California Press, 1998.

Baker, R. Scott. *Paradoxes of Desegregation: African American Struggles for Educational Equity in Charleston, South Carolina, 1926–1972.* Columbia: University of South Carolina Press, 2006.

Barth, Fredrik, ed. *Ethnic Groups and Boundaries. The Social Organization of Culture Difference.* London: Allen & Unwin, 1969.

Beatty, Andrew. "How Did It Feel for You? Emotion, Narrative, and the Limits of Ethnography." *American Anthropologist* 112, no. 3 (2010): 430–43.

Berger, Peter L., and Thomas Luckmann. *The Social Construction of Reality: A Treatise in the Sociology of Knowledge.* 1st ed. Garden City, NY: Doubleday, 1966.

Bissinger, H. G. *Friday Night Lights: A Town, a Team, and a Dream.* Reading, MA: Addison-Wesley, 1990.

Blos, Peter. *The Adolescent Passage: Developmental Issues*. New York: International Universities Press, 1979.

Bogle, Donald. *Toms, Coons, Mulattoes, Mammies, and Bucks: An Interpretive History of Blacks in American Films*. 3rd ed. New York: Continuum, 1994.

Bond, Horace Mann. *Negro Education in Alabama: A Study in Cotton and Steel*. New York: Atheneum, 1969.

Bourdieu, Pierre. *Outline of a Theory of Practice*. Cambridge: Cambridge University Press, 1977.

Bourdieu, Pierre, and Jean Claude Passeron. *Reproduction in Education, Society and Culture*. Translated by Richard Nice. London: Sage Publications, 1977.

Bourgois, Philippe I. *In Search of Respect: Selling Crack in El Barrio*. Structural Analysis in the Social Sciences. Cambridge: Cambridge University Press, 1995.

Brooks, Karen. "Nothing Sells Like Teen Spirit: The Commodification of Youth Culture." In *Youth Cultures: Texts, Images, and Identities*. Edited by Kerry Mallan and Sharyn Pearce. 1–16. Westport, CT: Praeger, 2003.

Brown, Claude. *Manchild in the Promised Land*. New York: Macmillan, 1965.

Campbell, Neil, ed. *American Youth Cultures*. Edinburgh: Edinburgh University Press, 2004.

Carlton, David L., and Peter A. Coclanis. *The South, the Nation, and the World: Perspectives on Southern Economic Development*. Charlottesville: University of Virginia Press, 2003.

Castle, Emery N. *The Changing American Countryside: Rural People and Places*. Rural America. Lawrence: University Press of Kansas, 1995.

Chambers, Iain. "A Strategy for Living: Black Music and White Subcultures." In *Resistance through Rituals: Youth Subcultures in Post-War Britain*. Edited by Stuart Hall and Tony Jefferson. 157–66. London: Hutchinson, 1976.

Chin, Elizabeth M. Liew Siew. *Purchasing Power: Black Kids and American Consumer Culture*. Minneapolis: University of Minnesota Press, 2001.

Ching, Barbara, and Gerald Creed, eds. *Knowing Your Place: Rural Identity and Cultural Hierarchy*. New York: Routledge, 1997.

Clarke, Kamari Maxine, and Deborah A. Thomas, eds. *Globalization and Race: Transformations in the Cultural Production of Blackness*. Durham, NC: Duke University Press, 2006.

Clifford, James, George E. Marcus, and School of American Research (Santa Fe, NM), eds. *Writing Culture: The Poetics and Politics of Ethnography*. Berkeley and Los Angeles: University of California Press, 1986.

Cohen, Anthony P. *Self-Consciousness: An Alternative Anthropology of Identity*. New York: Routledge, 1994.

Cohen, Stanley. *Folk Devils and Moral Panics: The Creation of the Mods and Rockers*. New York: St. Martin's Press, 1980.

Coll, Cynthia García, Gontran Lamberty, Renee Jenkins, Harriet Pipes McAdoo, Keith Crnic, Barbara Hanna Wasik, and Heidie Vázquez García. "An Integrative Model for the Study of Developmental Competencies in Minority Children." *Child Development* 67, no. 5 (1996): 1891–914.

Collins, Patricia Hill. *Black Feminist Thought: Knowledge, Consciousness, and the Politics of Empowerment.* Perspectives on Gender. 2nd ed. New York: Routledge, 2000.

Cox, Aimee. "The Blacklight Project and Public Scholarship: Young Black Women Perform against and through the Boundaries of Anthropology." *Transforming Anthropology* 17, no. 1 (2009): 51–64.

Cross, William E. *Shades of Black: Diversity in African-American Identity.* Philadelphia: Temple University Press, 1991.

Daniel, Pete. *The Shadow of Slavery: Peonage in the South, 1901–1969.* Urbana: University of Illinois Press, 1972.

Davis, Allison, and John Dollard. *Children of Bondage: The Personality Development of Negro Youth in the Urban South.* 1st ed. New York: Harper & Row, 1964.

Davis, Allison, Burleigh Bradford Gardner, Mary R. Gardner, and W. Lloyd Warner. *Deep South: A Social Anthropological Study of Caste and Class.* Chicago: University of Chicago Press, 1941.

Davis, Glyn, and Kay Dickinson, eds. *Teen TV: Genre, Consumption, Identity.* London: BFI Pub., 2004.

Dollard, John. *Caste and Class in a Southern Town.* New Haven, CT: Published for the Institute of Human Relations by Yale University Press, 1937.

Douglas, Mary, and Steven Ney. *Missing Persons: A Critique of the Social Sciences.* The Aaron Wildavsky Forum for Public Policy. Berkeley and Los Angeles: University of California Press. Russell Sage Foundation, 1998.

Douglas, Mary. *Purity and Danger: An Analysis of Concepts of Pollution and Taboo.* New York: Praeger, 1966.

Drake, St. Clair. "Further Reflections on Anthropology and the Black Experience." *Transforming Anthropology* 1, no. 2 (1990): 1–14.

Du Bois, W. E. B. *The Souls of Black Folk.* The Bedford Series in History and Culture. Boston: Bedford Books, 1997. 1903.

Embree, Edwin R., and Julia Waxman. *Investment in People: The Story of the Julius Rosenwald Fund.* 1st ed. New York: Harper, 1949.

Erikson, Erik H. *Identity and the Life Cycle: Selected Papers.* Psychological Issues. New York: International Universities Press, 1959.

———. *Identity, Youth, and Crisis.* 1st ed. New York: W. W. Norton, 1968.

Evans-Pritchard, E. E. *Witchcraft, Oracles, and Magic among the Azande.* Abridged with an introd. by Eva Gillies. Oxford: Clarendon Press, 1976. 1937.

Fairclough, Adam. *Teaching Equality: Black Schools in the Age of Jim Crow*. Mercer University Lamar Memorial Lectures. Athens: University of Georgia Press, 2001.

Falk, William W. *Rooted in Place: Family and Belonging in a Southern Black Community*. New Brunswick, NJ: Rutgers University Press, 2004.

Ferguson, Ann Arnett. *Bad Boys: Public Schools in the Making of Black Masculinity*. Law, Meaning, and Violence. Ann Arbor: University of Michigan Press, 2000.

Fernandez, James W. "Patrolling the Border: Experiments in Poetics." *American Anthropologist* 98, no. 4 (1996): 853–56.

Fine, Michelle, Reva Jaffe-Walter, Pedro Pedraza, Valerie Futch, and Brett Stoudt. "Swimming: On Oxygen, Resistance, and Possibility for Immigrant Youth under Siege." *Anthropology & Education Quarterly* 38, no. 1 (2007): 76–96.

Fisherkeller, JoEllen. *Growing up with Television: Everyday Learning among Young Adolescents*. Philadelphia: Temple University Press, 2002.

Foley, Douglas E. *Learning Capitalist Culture: Deep in the Heart of Tejas*. Contemporary Ethnography. 2nd ed. Philadelphia: University of Pennsylvania Press, 2010.

Fordham, Signithia. *Blacked Out: Dilemmas of Race, Identity, and Success at Capital High*. Chicago: University of Chicago Press, 1996.

Fordham, Signithia, and John Ogbu. "Black Students' School Success: Coping with the Burden of 'Acting White.'" *Urban Review* 18, no. 3 (1986): 176–206.

Fossett, Mark Alan, and M. Therese Seibert. *Long Time Coming: Racial Inequality in the Nonmetropolitan South, 1940–1990*. Rural Studies Series of the Rural Sociological Society. Boulder, CO: Westview Press, 1997.

Foucault, Michel. *The History of Sexuality*. Translated by Robert Hurley. 1st American ed. New York: Pantheon Books, 1978.

Frazier, Edward Franklin. *The Negro Church in America*. Liverpool: Liverpool University Press, 1964.

———. *The Negro Family in the United States*. Chicago: University of Chicago Press, 1939.

———. *Negro Youth at the Crossways: Their Personality Development in the Middle States*. Washington, DC: American Council on Education, 1940.

Frederick, Marla F. *Between Sundays: Black Women and Everyday Struggles of Faith*. Berkeley and Los Angeles: University of California Press, 2003.

Freire, Paulo. *Pedagogy of the Oppressed*. 183 p. New York: Continuum, 2000.

Friedman, Jonathan. "Myth, History and Political Identity." *Cultural Anthropology* 7, no. 2 (1992): 194–210.

Gates, Henry Lewis. *The Signifying Monkey: A Theory of Afro-American Literary Criticism*. New York: Oxford University Press, 1988.

Gaunt, Kyra Danielle. *The Games Black Girls Play: Learning the Ropes from Double-Dutch to Hip-Hop*. New York: New York University Press, 2006.

Gibbs, Robert M. "College Completion and Return Migration among Rural Youth."

In *Rural Education and Training in the New Economy: The Myth of Rural Skills Gap.* Edited by Robert M. Gibbs, Paul L. Swaim, and Ruy A. Teixeira. 61–80. Ames: Iowa State University Press, 1998.

Gilkes, Cheryl Townsend. *If It Wasn't for the Women: Black Women's Experience and Womanist Culture in Church and Community.* Maryknoll, NY: Orbis Books, 2001.

Gilroy, Paul. *Against Race: Imagining Political Culture Beyond the Color Line.* Cambridge, MA: Belknap Press of Harvard University Press, 2000.

———. *"There Ain't No Black in the Union Jack": The Cultural Politics of Race and Nation.* London: Hutchinson, 1987.

Giroux, Henry A. *Channel Surfing: Race Talk and the Destruction of Today's Youth.* New York: St. Martin's Press, 1997.

———. "Class Casualties: Disappearing Youth in the Age of George W. Bush." *Workplace: A Journal for Academic Labor* 6, no. 1 (February 2004).

———. Foreword. In *Schooling as a Ritual Performance: Toward a Political Economy of Educational Symbols and Gestures.* Edited by Peter McLaren. 2nd ed. New York: Routledge, 1993. 1986.

———. *The Giroux Reader.* Edited by Christopher G. Robbins. Boulder, CO: Paradigm Publishers, 2006.

———. *On Critical Pedagogy.* London: Continuum International Publishing Group, 2011.

Gluckman, Max. "Analysis of a Social Situation in Modern Zululand." *Rhodes Livingston Institute Papers* 28 (1940).

Gramsci, Antonio. *Selections from Prison Notebooks.* London: Lawrence & Wishart, 1971.

Gregory, Steven, and Roger Sanjek, eds. *Race.* New Brunswick, NJ: Rutgers University Press, 1994.

Griffin, Farah Jasmine. *"Who Set You Flowin'?": The African-American Migration Narrative.* Race and American Culture. New York: Oxford University Press, 1995.

Haight, Wendy L. *African American Children at Church.* Cambridge: Cambridge University Press, 2000.

Hall, Stuart. "Cultural Identity and Diaspora." *Framework* 36 (1989): 222–37.

———. "New Ethnicities." In *Black British Cultural Studies: A Reader.* Edited by Houston A. Baker, Manthia Diawara, and Ruth H. Lindeborg. Black Literature and Culture, 163–72. Chicago: University of Chicago Press, 1996.

———. "What Is This 'Black' in Black Popular Culture?" *Social Justice* 20, no. 1/2 (1993): 51–52, and "Rethinking Race" (Spring/Summer 1993): 104–14.

Hall, Stuart, and Tony Jefferson, eds. *Resistance through Rituals: Youth Subcultures in Post-War Britain.* London: Hutchinson, 1976.

Hall, Stuart, David Morley, Kuan-Hsing Chen, and Horace Howard Furness Memorial Fund, eds. *Stuart Hall: Critical Dialogues in Cultural Studies*, Comedia. New York: Routledge, 1996.

Hamann, Edmund T. *The Educational Welcome of Latinos in the New South*. Westport, CT: Praeger, 2003.

———. "Lessons from the Interpretation/Misinterpretation of John Ogbu's Scholarship." *Intercultural Education* 15 (2004): 399–412.

Harker, Richard K. "On Reproduction, Habitus and Education." *British Journal of Sociology of Education* 5, no. 2 (1984): 117–27.

Harlan, Louis R. *Separate and Unequal: Public School Campaigns and Racism in the Southern Seaboard States, 1901–1915*. Studies in American Negro Life. New York: Atheneum, 1968.

Harrison, Faye V. "The Persistent Power of "Race" in the Cultural and Political Economy of Racism." *Annual Review of Anthropology* 24 (1995): 47–74.

Heath, Shirley Brice. *Ways with Words: Language, Life, and Work in Communities and Classrooms*. Cambridge: Cambridge University Press, 1983.

Heath, Shirley Brice, and Milbrey Wallin McLaughlin, eds. *Identity and Inner-City Youth: Beyond Ethnicity and Gender*. New York: Teachers College Press, 1993.

Hill, Carole E., Wilfrid C. Bailey, Alvin L. Bertrand, Bruce Alden Cox, Satadal Dasgupta, Martin W. Horeis, James William Jordan, eds. "Anthropological Studies in the American South: Review and Directions." *Current Anthropology* 18, no. 2 (1977): 309–26.

Hobsbawm, E. J., and T. O. Ranger. *The Invention of Tradition*. Past and Present Publications. Cambridge: Cambridge University Press, 1983.

Hodkinson, Paul, and Wolfgang Deicke, eds. *Youth Cultures: Scenes, Subcultures and Tribes*. Routledge Advances in Sociology, vol. 26. New York: Routledge, 2007.

Hoffschwelle, Mary S. *The Rosenwald Schools of the American South*. New Perspectives on the History of the South. Gainesville: University Press of Florida, 2006.

Holland, Dorothy C., William Lachicotte Jr., Debra Skinner, and Carole Cain. *Identity and Agency in Cultural Worlds*. Cambridge, MA: Harvard University Press, 1998.

Hollows, Joanne. *Feminism, Femininity and Popular Culture*. Manchester: Manchester University Press; Distributed exclusively in the USA by St. Martin's Press, 2000.

hooks, bell. *Black Looks: Race and Representation*. Boston: South End Press, 1992.

Howell, Angela McMillan. "Dynamic Youth and Static Religion: The Evolving Relationship between Church and Community in Rural Alabama." Unpublished paper presented at *Global American South Conference*. University of North Carolina, Chapel Hill, March 2005.

Hunt, Larry L., and Matthew O. Hunt. "Regional Patterns of African American Church Attendance: Revisiting the Semi-Involuntary Thesis." *Social Forces* 78, no. 2 (1999): 779–91.

Huq, Rupa. "Resistance or Incorporation? Youth Policy Making and Hip-Hop Culture." In *Youth Cultures: Scenes, Subcultures and Tribes.* Edited by Paul Hodkinson and Wolfgang Deicke. 79–92. New York: Routledge, 2007.

Hurston, Zora Neale. *Their Eyes Were Watching God.* Urbana: University of Illinois Press, 1991. 1937.

Inhelder, Bärbel, and Jean Piaget. *The Growth of Logical Thinking from Childhood to Adolescence: An Essay on the Construction of Formal Operational Structures.* New York: Basic Books, 1958.

Jackson, John L. *Harlemworld: Doing Race and Class in Contemporary Black America.* Chicago: University of Chicago Press, 2001.

———. *Real Black: Adventures in Racial Sincerity.* Chicago: University of Chicago Press, 2005.

Jewell, K. Sue. *From Mammy to Miss America and Beyond: Cultural Images and the Shaping of U.S. Social Policy.* New York: Routledge, 1993.

Johnson, Charles Spurgeon. *Growing up in the Black Belt: Negro Youth in the Rural South.* Washington, DC: American Council on Education, 1941.

Jones, Nikki. *Between Good and Ghetto: African American Girls and Inner-City Violence.* The Rutgers Series in Childhood Studies. New Brunswick, NJ: Rutgers University Press, 2010.

Kelley, Robin D. G. *Yo' Mama's Disfunktional!: Fighting the Culture Wars in Urban America.* Boston: Beacon Press, 1997.

King, Deborah K. "Multiple Jeopardy, Multiple Consciousness: The Context of a Black Feminist Ideology." *Signs* 14, no. 1 (1988): 42–72.

Kitwana, Bakari. *The Hip Hop Generation: Young Blacks and the Crisis in African American Culture.* 1st ed. New York: Basic Civitas Books, 2002.

Kollath, Carlie. "Group: Unemployment Higher for Millennials." Northeast Mississippi News, djournal.com.

Krinsky, Charles, ed. *Moral Panics over Contemporary Children and Youth.* Farnham, England: Ashgate, 2008.

LaBennett, Oneka. *She's Mad Real: Popular Culture and West Indian Girls in Brooklyn.* New York: New York University Press, 2011.

Ladson-Billings, Gloria. *The Dreamkeepers: Successful Teachers of African American Children.* 1st ed. San Francisco: Jossey-Bass Publishers, 1994.

Lakoff, George, and Mark Johnson. *Metaphors We Live By.* Chicago: University of Chicago Press, 1980.

Lareau, Annette. *Unequal Childhoods: Class, Race, and Family Life.* Berkeley and Los Angeles: University of California Press, 2003.

Lassiter, Luke E. *The Other Side of Middletown: Exploring Muncie's African American Community.* Walnut Creek, CA: AltaMira Press, 2004.

Levinson, Bradley A., Douglas E. Foley, and Dorothy C. Holland, eds. *The Cultural*

Production of the Educated Person: Critical Ethnographies of Schooling and Local Practice. Suny Series, Power, Social Identity, and Education. Albany: State University of New York Press, 1996.

Lewis, Amanda E. *Race in the Schoolyard: Negotiating the Color Line in Classrooms and Communities*. The Rutgers Series in Childhood Studies. New Brunswick, NJ: Rutgers University Press, 2003.

Lewis, Oscar. *Five Families: Mexican Case Studies in the Culture of Poverty*. New York: Basic Books, 1959.

———. *La Vida: A Puerto Rican Family in the Culture of Poverty—San Juan and New York*. New York: Random House, 1966.

Lhamon, W. T. *Raising Cain: Blackface Performance from Jim Crow to Hip-Hop*. Cambridge, MA: Harvard University Press, 1998.

Lipsitz, George. Foreword. *Youthscapes: The Popular, the National, the Global*. Edited by Sunaina Maira and Elisabeth Soep. Philadelphia: University of Pennsylvania Press, 2005.

———. *The Possessive Investment in Whiteness: How White People Profit from Identity Politics*. Philadelphia: Temple University Press, 1998.

———. "We Know What Time It Is: Race, Class, and Youth Culture in the Nineties." In *Microphone Fiends: Youth Music & Youth Culture*. Edited by Andrew Ross and Tricia Rose. 17–28. New York: Routledge, 1994.

MacLeod, Jay. *Ain't No Makin' It: Leveled Aspirations in a Low-Income Neighborhood*. Boulder, CO: Westview Press, 1987.

Maira, Sunaina, and Elisabeth Soep, eds. *Youthscapes: The Popular, the National, the Global*. Philadelphia: University of Pennsylvania Press, 2005.

Marable, Manning, Ian Steinberg, and Keesha Middlemass, eds. *Racializing Justice, Disenfranchising Lives: The Racism, Criminal Justice, and Law Reader*. 1st Palgrave Macmillan pbk. ed., Critical Black Studies Series. New York: Palgrave Macmillan, 2007.

Marche, Stephen. "Is Facebook Making Us Lonely?" *The Atlantic*, May 1, 2012.

Marcia, James E. "Development and Validation of Ego-Identity Status." *Journal of Personality and Social Psychology* 3, no. 5 (1966): 551–58.

Marx, Karl. "The German Ideology." In *The Marx-Engels Reader*, edited by Karl Marx, Friedrich Engels and Robert C. Tucker. 146–200. New York: Norton, 1978.

McFeely, Williams S. Afterword. In *The Strange Career of Jim Crow*, edited by C. Vann Woodward. 221–32. Oxford: Oxford University Press, 2002.

McLaren, Peter. *Life in Schools: An Introduction to Critical Pedagogy in the Foundations of Education*. 3rd ed. New York: Longman, 1998.

———. *Schooling as a Ritual Performance: Toward a Political Economy of Educational Symbols and Gestures*. 2nd ed. New York: Routledge, 1993. 1986.

McLaughlin, Milbrey Wallin, Merita A. Irby, and Juliet Langman, eds. *Urban Sanctu-*

aries: Neighborhood Organizations in the Lives and Futures of Inner-City Youth. 1st ed. San Francisco: Jossey-Bass Publishers, 1994.

McRobbie, Angela. *Feminism and Youth Culture: From "Jackie" to "Just Seventeen."* Boston: Unwin Hyman, 1991.

Mead, Margaret. *Coming of Age in Samoa: A Psychological Study of Primitive Youth for Western Civilisation.* New York: W. Morrow & Company, 1928.

———. *Growing up in New Guinea: A Comparative Study of Primitive Education.* New York: W. Morrow & Company, 1930.

Moynihan, Daniel P. "The Negro Family: The Case for National Action." Washington, DC: U.S. Government Printing Office, 1965.

Mullings, Leith. "Interrogating Racism: Toward an Antiracist Anthropology." *Annual Review of Anthropology* 34 (2005): 667–93.

Nader, Laura. "Up the Anthropologist—Perspectives Gained from Studying Up." In *Reinventing Anthropology.* Edited by Dell H. Hymes. New York: Pantheon, 1972.

Nayak, Anoop, and Mary Jane Kehily, eds. *Gender, Youth and Culture: Young Masculinities and Feminities.* New York: Palgrave Macmillan, 2008.

Neal, Mark Anthony. *Soul Babies: Black Poplular Culture and the Post-Soul Aesthetic.* New York: Routledge, 2002.

Oakes, Jeannie. *Keeping Track: How Schools Structure Inequality.* New Haven, CT: Yale University Press, 1985.

Ogbu, John U. *Black American Students in an Affluent Suburb: A Study of Academic Disengagement.* Mahwah, NJ: L. Erlbaum Associates, 2003.

Ortner, Sherry B. "Gender Hegemonies." *Cultural Critique* 14, The Construction of Gender and Modes of Social Division II (Winter 1989–1990): 35–80.

———. "Theory in Anthropology since the Sixties." *Comparative Studies in Society and History* 26 (1984): 126–66.

Parker, Laurence, Donna Deyhle, and Sofia A. Villenas, eds. *Race Is—Race Isn't: Critical Race Theory and Qualitative Studies in Education.* Boulder, CO: Westview Press, 1999.

Pascoe, C. J. *Dude, You're a Fag: Masculinity and Sexuality in High School.* Berkeley and Los Angeles: University of California Press, 2007.

Pattillo-McCoy, Mary. *Black Picket Fences: Privilege and Peril among the Black Middle Class.* Chicago: University of Chicago Press, 1999.

Pollock, Mica. *Colormute: Race Talk Dilemmas in an American School.* Princeton, NJ: Princeton University Press, 2004.

Pough, Gwendolyn D. *Check It While I Wreck It: Black Womanhood, Hip-Hop Culture, and the Public Sphere.* Boston: Northeastern University Press, 2004.

Powdermaker, Hortense. *After Freedom: A Cultural Study in the Deep South.* New York: Viking Press, 1939.

Rickford, John R., and Russell J. Rickford. *Spoken Soul: The Story of Black English.* New York: Wiley, 2000.

Rose, Tricia. *Black Noise: Rap Music and Black Culture in Contemporary America.* Music Culture. Hanover, NH: Wesleyan University Press: Published by University Press of New England, 1994.

———. *The Hip-Hop Wars: What We Talk About When We Talk About Hip-Hop—and Why It Matters.* New York: Basic Civitas, 2008.

Schafft, Kai A., and Alicia Youngblood Jackson, eds. *Rural Education for the Twenty-first Century: Identity, Place, and Community in a Globalizing World.* University Park: Pennsylvania State University Press, 2010.

Schneider, David Murray. *American Kinship: A Cultural Account.* Anthropology of Modern Societies Series. Englewood Cliffs, NJ: Prentice-Hall, 1968.

"School Improvement Grants." U.S. Department of Education, http://data.ed.gov/grants/school-improvement-grants.

Scott, James. *Weapons of the Weak: Everyday Forms of Peasant Resistance.* New Haven, CT: Yale University Press, 1985.

Sharpley-Whiting, T. Denean. *Pimps up, Ho's Down: Hip-Hop's Hold on Young Black Women.* New York: New York University Press, 2007.

Siddle Walker, Vanessa. *Their Highest Potential: An African American School Community in the Segregated South.* Chapel Hill: University of North Carolina Press, 1996.

Smedley, Audrey. *Race in North America: Origin and Evolution of a World View.* Boulder, CO: Westview Press, 1993.

Smiley, Tavis, and Stephanie Robinson. *Accountable: Making America as Good as Its Promise.* New York: Atria, 2009.

Smitherman, Geneva. *Black Talk: Words and Phrases from the Hood to the Amen Corner.* Rev. ed. Boston: Houghton Mifflin, 1994.

Snyder, Anastasia. "Patterns of Family Formation and Dissolution in Rural America and Implications for Well-Being." In *Economic Restructuring and Family Well-Being in Rural America.* Edited by Kristin E. Smith, Ann R. Tickamyer, and Rural Sociological Society. 124–35. University Park: Pennsylvania State University Press, 2011.

Sokefeld, Martin. "Debating Self, Identity, and Culture in Anthropology." *Current Anthropology* 40, no. 4 (1999): 417–47.

Spivak, Gayatri Chakravorty. "Can the Subaltern Speak?" In *Marxism and the Interpretation of Culture.* Edited by Cary Nelson and Lawrence Grossberg. x, 738 p. Urbana: University of Illinois Press, 1988.

Stack, Carol B. *All Our Kin: Strategies for Survival in a Black Community.* 1st ed. New York: Harper & Row, 1974.

———. *Call to Home: African Americans Reclaim the Rural South*. New York: Basic Books, 1996.

Steele, Claude M., and Joshua Aronson. "Stereotype Threat and the Intellectual Test Performance of African Americans." *Journal of Personality and Social Psychology* 69, no. 5 (1995): 797–811.

Stoller, Paul. "The Epistemology of Sorkotarey: Language, Metaphor and Healing among the Songhay." *Ethos* 8, no. 2 (1980): 117–31.

———. *The Taste of Ethnographic Things: The Senses in Anthropology*. University of Pennsylvania Press Contemporary Ethnography Series. Philadelphia: University of Pennsylvania Press, 1989.

Tatum, Beverly Daniel. *"Why Are All the Black Kids Sitting Together in the Cafeteria?" and Other Conversations about Race*. 1st ed. New York: Basic Books, 1997.

Taylor, Edward. "The Desegregation of Higher Education." In *Race Is—Race Isn't: Critical Race Theory and Qualitative Studies in Education*. Edited by Laurence Parker, Donna Deyhle, and Sofia A. Villenas. 181–204. Boulder, CO: Westview Press, 1999.

Taylor, Ronald L., ed. *African-American Youth: Their Social and Economic Status in the United States*. Westport, CT: Praeger, 1995.

Thomas, Deborah A. *Exceptional Violence: Embodied Citizenship in Transnational Jamaica*. Durham, NC: Duke University Press, 2011.

Tilly, Charles. *Identities, Boundaries, and Social Ties*. Boulder, CO: Paradigm Publishers, 2005.

Toll, Robert C. *Blacking Up: The Minstrel Show in Nineteenth-Century America*. New York: Oxford University Press, 1974.

Touré. *Who's Afraid of Post-Blackness?: What It Means to Be Black Now*. New York: Free Press, 2011.

Truitt, Thomas E. *Brick Walls: Reflections on Race in a Southern School District*. Columbia: University of South Carolina Press, 2006.

Turner, Patricia. *I Heard It through the Grapevine: Rumor in African-American Culture*. Berkeley and Los Angeles: University of California Press, 1993.

Turner, Victor. *Schism and Continuity in an African Society*. Manchester: Manchester University Press, 1957.

———. *Dramas, Fields, and Metaphors: Symbolic Action in Human Society*. Symbol, Myth, and Ritual. Ithaca, NY: Cornell University Press, 1974.

Tyack, David B. *The One Best System: A History of American Urban Education*. Cambridge, MA: Harvard University Press, 1974.

Van Galen, Jane, and George W. Noblit, eds. *Late to Class: Social Class and Schooling in the New Economy*. Suny Series, Power, Social Identity, and Education. Albany: State University of New York Press, 2007.

Varenne, Hervé, Ray McDermott, Shelley V. Goldman, Merry Naddeo, and Rosemarie Rizzo-Tolk. *Successful Failure: The School America Builds*. Boulder, CO: Westview Press, 1998.

Villenas, Sofia A., Donna Deyhle, and Laurence Parker. "Critical Race Theory and Praxis: Chicano(a)/Latino(a), and Navajo Struggles for Dignity, Educational Equity, and Social Justice." In *Race Is—Race Isn't: Critical Race Theory and Qualitative Studies in Education*. Edited by Laurence Parker, Donna Deyhle, and Sofia A. Villenas. 31–52. Boulder, CO: Westview Press, 1999.

Watkins, William H. *The White Architects of Black Education: Ideology and Power in America, 1865–1954*. The Teaching for Social Justice Series. New York: Teachers College Press, 2001.

West, Cornel. *Race Matters*. Boston: Beacon Press, 1993.

White, E. Frances. *Dark Continent of Our Bodies: Black Feminism and the Politics of Respectability*. Mapping Racisms. Philadelphia: Temple University Press, 2001.

Willis, Paul E. *Learning to Labor: How Working-Class Kids Get Working-Class Jobs*. Morningside ed. New York: Columbia University Press, 1981. 1977.

Wilson, William J. *The Declining Significance of Race: Blacks and Changing American Institutions*. 2nd ed. Chicago: University of Chicago Press, 1980.

———. *The Truly Disadvantaged: The Inner City, the Underclass, and Public Policy*. Chicago: University of Chicago Press, 1987.

———. *When Work Disappears: The World of the New Urban Poor*. 1st ed. New York: Knopf, Distributed by Random House, 1996.

Winant, Howard. *New Politics of Race: Globalism, Difference, Justice*. Minneapolis: University of Minnesota Press, 2004.

Wolcott, Victoria W. *Remaking Respectability: African American Women in Interwar Detroit*. Gender and American Culture. Chapel Hill: University of North Carolina Press, 2001.

Woodward, C. Vann. *American Counterpoint: Slavery and Racism in the North-South Dialogue*. 1st ed. Boston: Little, Brown, 1971.

———. *Origins of the New South, 1877–1913*. A History of the South. Baton Rouge: Louisiana State University Press, 1951.

———. *The Strange Career of Jim Crow*. Commemorative ed. Oxford: Oxford University Press, 2002.

Yanagisako, Sylvia. "Variations in American Kinship: Implications for Cultural Analysis." *American Ethnologist* 5 (1978): 15–29.

Yanagisako, Sylvia Junko, and Carol Lowery Delaney, eds. *Naturalizing Power: Essays in Feminist Cultural Analysis*. New York: Routledge, 1995.

Young, Virginia Heyer. "Family and Childhood in a Southern Negro Community." *American Anthropologist* 72, no. 2 (1970): 269–88.

Index

CPSIA information can be obtained at www.ICGtesting.com
Printed in the USA
BVOW02s1601040815

411668BV00001B/6/P